To Mom and Dad

No one else has loved me or
will love me as much as you do.

Thank you.

THE GUERRILLA FEMINIST

A SEARCH FOR BELONGING ONLINE & OFFLINE

This first edition published by *Iskra Books* © 2025

10 9 8 7 6 5 4 3 2 1

ISKRA BOOKS
US | England | Ireland
ISKRABOOKS.ORG

ISKRA BOOKS is a nonprofit, independent, scholarly publisher—publishing original works of revolutionary theory, history, education, narrative, and art, as well as edited collections, new translations, and critical republications of older works.

979-8-3305-9519-8 (*Softcover*)
979-8-3305-9532-7 (*Jacketed Hardcover*)

British Library Cataloguing in Publication Data
A catalogue record for this book is available from the British Library

Library of Congress Cataloging-in-Publication Data
A catalog record for this book is available from the Library of Congress

Cover Art, Interior Art by JENNA BLAZEVICH
Book Design and Typsesetting by BEN STAHNKE

THE GUERRILLA FEMINIST

A SEARCH FOR BELONGING ONLINE & OFFLINE

LACHRISTA GRECO

iskra books
olympia | london | dublin

Contents

INTRODUCTION   **1**

1. THE ONLINE PLAYGROUND I DIDN'T KNOW I NEEDED   **5**

2. DISABILITY AND DESIRE   **33**

3. THE HERPES OF IT ALL: A BODY HAUNTED BY MEN   **51**

4. THE GAMIFICATION OF LOVE & SEX   **69**

5. TRAUMA STORYTELLING AS CURRENCY & COMMODITY   **89**

6. HYPERVIGILANCE IS A PORTAL   **111**

7. HOW DO I LOOK?   **123**

8. THE MILLENNIAL MOTHERHOOD QUESTION   **139**

9. FRIENDSHIP IN THE TIME OF COVID & GENOCIDE   **159**

10. GET OFF THE INTERNET   **179**

ACKNOWLEDGEMENTS   **200**

BIBLIOGRAPHY   **202**

Introduction

I HAVE NEVER CRAVED DANGER, because I have lived too many lives of it. I've witnessed and experienced violence online and offline and been told repeatedly, "It's not a big deal." I'm chronically hypervigilant from various traumas, and the internet does not assuage this. Being online is messy, beautiful, and loud with too many heartbeats. It won't get us free, but it's a helpful tool for many of us to continue to exist in a world that doesn't care if we live or die.

Social justice issues have received much more visibility through the use of social media platforms like Twitter, Facebook, Instagram, Tumblr, Pinterest, Snapchat, and TikTok. For me, digital activism means using social media as a tool of respair. I learned of this 14th century word from a 2017 article in *The Economist*. "Respair" means the "return of hope after a period of despair."[1] Perhaps the 90s and early aughts weren't exactly a period of *despair*, but it may have felt like it to Millennials in various marginalized communities. If it didn't feel like despair to us then, it certainly does now as we try to navigate and survive a global pandemic, multiple genocides, and increased fascism. In the early aughts, we wanted more ways to collaborate and more efficient ways to discuss global injustices so we could do something about them. The immediacy of digital activism allows for instantaneous communication, visibility, and resistance. It allows for our voices to be heard—on our terms. Social media platforms—never static entities—continue to reinvent themselves in (often) not great ways. Thus, this book only captures what was happening at the time of my writing (between 2015 and 2024).

I have found belonging in online spaces more than I've found

---

1   Johnson, "Why Words Die," *The Economist*, March 4, 2017, http://www.economist.com/books-and-arts/2017/03/04/why-words-die.

it offline. This grew exponentially when I created the *Guerrilla Feminism* Facebook page in 2011 and its Instagram account in 2013. I'm an elder millennial who had a childhood without the internet. I was a teenager when I first got it. During my time online, I have witnessed courageous vulnerability in private Facebook groups for survivors of sexual violence. I have taken advice from people on Herpblr, the online hashtag associated with Tumblr's herpes-positive community. I've swam through the Sensory Processing Disorder Reddit board, seeing myself in each post. I, too, have been rejected for who and what I am. I, too, wanted to create something where people felt like they belonged—even if just for a moment while they browsed my posts on social media.

These essays are about my history and present on social media and the broader internet, as I search incessantly for belonging. The first essay discusses my childhood, upbringing, and background of *Guerrilla Feminism*. The second is about how I've navigated my disabilities amidst feelings of unworthiness. The third focuses on herpes and finding belonging with other herpes-positive folks. The fourth is about my trash bag-size dating trauma. The fifth discusses the act of trauma storytelling online for clout and the concerns I have with seeing and participating in this. The sixth speaks to hypervigilance and what this can mean for our movements. The seventh focuses on beauty filters, AI, and aging. The eighth is about my ambivalence around motherhood/parenting. The ninth is about friendship during a global pandemic and multiple genocides. The final essay discusses my current fears about using social media for activism and asking where we go from here. All of these essays have an ongoing thread of searching for, finding, and losing community in online spaces and off.

This is a love letter to all of us who have found (and still find) belonging in online spaces. For those of us who cozied up to medical Reddit threads that made us breathe a sigh of relief, felt believed when we joined a private Facebook group about feminism that acted as a digital consciousness-raising group, and settled into the unsettling stories of #MeToo on Instagram and Twitter because we saw ourselves in them. We are here online and off. We can find these spaces online and off. We belong to ourselves and each other. All I've ever wanted in my life were friends, co-conspirators, love. I have this in some ways, and in others I'm still searching, longing. I think of the internet as my online playground. It can be messy, loud, and crowded. It can also feel like a peaceful cottage in the woods, depending on the spaces (and people) you find. I write about and hold both/and all of this.

As a human with multiple marginalized identities, I have struggled to find and feel belonging because of disabilities, illnesses, trauma, and online abuse. This is a book about a life of ambivalence, hypervigilance and a never ending search for belonging and love. I hope you'll find a sense of community in these pages.

Chapter One

THE ONLINE PLAYGROUND I DIDN'T KNOW I NEEDED

I am what I am and you can't take it away with all the words and sneers at your command.

—CHERRÍE L. MORAGA

"2-4-6-8, HOW DO YOU KNOW YOUR KID IS STRAIGHT?!" I chanted as the other kids followed me. I was in preschool and had attended my first Gay Pride March with my mom and her new partner the day prior. The parade was like a playground: loud, crowded, and exciting with adults and children everywhere. Children climbing on their parents, adults climbing on structures to see better. People chanting urgently through megaphones. I didn't quite understand it, but I liked it. This parade was my first experience with activism. It propelled me into a life-long passion for social justice. Activism is storytelling and storytelling is activism. I wanted to hear others' stories. I wanted to have experiences and stories of my own. This is a story of my search for belonging online and offline.

I came of age in the '90s and early aughts. I'm an "elder" millennial who had a life before the internet. My upbringing is varied, but follows a consistent path of abandonment, disappointment, struggle, and a deep desire to fit in. I have two vivid memories from before I was five. The first, me running downstairs on Christmas Eve, stopping to look in the living room to see if Santa had come. I saw a dark figure who stopped and stared at me. I ran to my parents' bedroom and exclaimed, "Santa's here! Santa's here!" Who knows what or who

I actually saw, but my brain has sunk its teeth into that memory. The second memory I had before five was my parents sitting my older brother and I down at the kitchen table telling us they were getting a divorce. I was four and my small little life was upended as I knew it. My parents' eyes were watery and translucent. I knew this news was bad. My sweet 8-year-old brother sitting next to me said, "It's okay. We'll be okay." I didn't know what "divorce" was, but in my four-year-old binary thinking I understood it was not good. I got up from my chair and ran to the door that opened to the garage and shouted, "Nobody is leaving!" Then, I ran to the front door, attempting to block it with my small body, and exclaimed even louder, "Nobody is leaving!" Like a scene out of a movie, I slowly slid my body down against the door and weeped. The memory ends after that.

Because both of my parents were counselors, they loved a group, and promptly had my brother and I go to the "Children of Divorce" group at our elementary school. We would mostly eat pizza and get talked at by adults. One day the group facilitator brought a cop in to speak to us about the danger of drugs. The cop had a shadow box that contained examples of about ten different drugs. I was only in first grade and didn't understand any of it, but I liked the "drug box." It was colorful, ornate. Someone spent time on that box. In my mostly white, upper-class suburban school, the assumption was that if a kid's parents divorce when they're young, they're bound to start doing drugs in the elementary school playground. I didn't get anything out of the group. At the very least, I was with other kids who also seemed to come from the "wrong side of the tracks." My dad's house was on the "poor" side of the literal train tracks in town, and just on the other side were the big houses—where we lived pre-divorce. My initial understanding of class was that the kids who lived in houses with an upstairs were wealthy. Because most of the kids who went to my school lived in big houses, I was often ashamed to have any of them over to mine. This was my initial understanding of class consciousness. I no longer lived in a house with an upstairs. A new life was beginning for me—against my wishes.

At a doctor's appointment when I was six, my mom said there was a gun in the house. It's a common question that doctors ask for safety reasons: "Is there a gun in the home?" I felt embarrassed and startled by my mom's answer. I felt unsafe. My mom began dating a woman far too soon after the divorce. I was six, so the fact that this person was a woman wasn't the issue. Kids don't care about that. Keri was the first "Gold Star" butch lesbian cop I had ever met. The cop part was the main issue for me—even as a child. During one of the first nights Keri slept over, there was a thunderstorm. It woke me up and scared me. I ran to my mom's bedroom seeking comfort. I ran right into Keri who had blocked the doorway to my mom's room. I said "Mom!" and tried to look through the small opening of her bedroom door, but she didn't seem to stir. Keri responded: "She's sleeping." "Oh, ok..." my small voice trailed off. I ran to my brother's room and peered in. He was asleep. I ran back to my room to grab my tiny lambskin rug and laid it down next to my brother's bed. I spent the night sleeping there, listening to the enormous storm. He didn't know I was there, but his presence comforted me. My mom was always out of reach when Keri was around. I felt neglected and emotionally abandoned.

Keri and my mom bought a house together in a suburb of Madison. We lived there along with Keri's two children from a previous relationship. Jack, a year younger than my brother, was Keri's oldest son. My brother and Jack got along great and would spend hours playing video games together in the basement. Matt was Keri's youngest son. He was a few years younger than me. Matt and I had vastly different interests and rarely played together. I was the only girl and no longer the youngest. It was isolating and I didn't know my place. I spent a lot of time in my bedroom dancing to my Paula Abdul - "Forever Your Girl" 1988 cassette tape. My room acted as a tiny sliver of solace. When we moved in, there was a small placard on the door to my room that read, "Laundry Room," in a floral cursive font. The placard never came off. I liked my room, but was scared of it, and of the haunted house I was living in. The house felt too big and like it could harm me. I would often try to sleep on the floor in my brother's room on a small mattress we had for guests. He hated this, but would often acquiesce.

The house was big, old, and far away from my school. It was foreboding and vacant. It was an uninviting house. I was certain ghosts lived there. There was no air conditioning and summers felt oppressive. I spent summers sleeping with a single sheet and a box fan in my window. Living with Keri began to feel oppressive, too. I noticed the verbal and emotional abuse almost immediately. I never liked her, but after witnessing how Keri treated my mom, my hatred for her grew ten sizes. She would also make fun of my dad in front of me. She would belittle him just like she would belittle my mom and I. My brother and I went back and forth between that house and our dad's house in another suburb of Madison. I began to see my dad as my savior. Each time he picked up my brother and I, I felt safe again, like I could breathe again. His house also had air conditioning, which was a bonus.

Though I felt safe at my dad's house, I couldn't be a kid there. I was now in a mother/wife role for the two men in my family. As a child, I felt like I needed to take care of my dad, needed to make sure he was okay. Similarly, I felt like I needed to make sure my brother was all right. My brother was eight-years-old when the divorce happened and it seemed to completely shut him down. He became more introverted and quiet. The divorce and my mom's sexual orientation capsized my dad's life. I felt bad for him—even if he was also to blame for their marriage ending. At the time, I mostly saw it as my mom's fault. She was the one who left. I didn't know about the intricacies of their relationship and marriage until much later. My parents co-parented beautifully—another thing Keri didn't like. I hated school. I hated home. I didn't feel safe anywhere.

When I was in fourth grade, Keri told me the local newspaper was doing a story about her. A converted Buddhist and alcoholic in recovery, she brought meditation practice to the police force in Madison, and this was considered a big deal. She wanted to mention my mom as her partner in the news article. Even my mom was uncomfortable with it, because my mom was (and still is) a very private person. I told Keri I didn't like the idea.

"Why don't you want me to mention your mom in the article?"

"...because I don't want to be made fun of at school."

"Well, if you're made fun of, those kids don't sound like friends."

"I know, but..."

At the age of nine I couldn't articulate that I was fearful about my own survival in a homophobic school. This was the early 90s and kids began saying, "That's so gay." In the same year, I overheard a kid say "gay people go to hell." I wasn't raised religious, but it struck terror in me for my mom. I knew right then and there that I didn't want these kids to know anything more about my life than was necessary. I didn't want to be punished for my mom's personal life. Keri eventually accepted what my mom and I had wanted. My mom was not mentioned in the news article. I had a small private win. I knew Keri hated me for this. I was glad.

When I was a pre-teen and teenager, I wondered if I was homophobic. I started to have OCD related to my sexual orientation. I had intrusive thoughts about being gay that felt distressing. Had Keri been a kind, nurturing, non-abusive person, maybe this wouldn't have happened. My dislike of Keri contributed to my own internalized homophobia. Perhaps I would have explored my bisexuality earlier if I hadn't met her. I never felt safe with her. For a long time, I felt scared anytime I was in the presence of a butch lesbian. I felt guilty about this, but it made sense. Keri was my first abuser. I never felt safe in that house.

Having lived with Keri was the biggest secret I carried. I didn't tell anyone until I was eighteen. I was terrified of what people would think. I wasn't ashamed of my mom. I was ashamed of Keri and her verbal and emotional abuse. This was my introduction to butch/femme dynamics and I didn't like it. I didn't have the language or understanding for it. Keri would constantly criticize my mom, even as my mom was the main person caring for Keri's two children in the home. She would blame my mom for any little thing she could. Keri would make fun of us, yell at my mom for no reason, and act jealous of my mom's friendship with my dad. I would try to stand up for my mom and would get shut down or humiliated in return. Keri could be threatening without saying anything. She was intimidating and knew it. Her cop training, coupled with her personality, made for an organized chaos. I was ashamed to have lived in an abusive home where I felt unsafe and unable to change my circumstances. Though things were not great at my dad's house, there wasn't abuse, just parentification.[1] I would take that over Keri any day.

---

1   AUTHOR'S NOTE: When a child is forced to take on an adult role within their family.

My mom eventually left Keri when I was twelve. I wasn't sure what ended things, but my mom seemed to have had enough. I didn't question it because it's what I wanted since they started dating. My mom couldn't afford to rent an apartment so we lived in a hermitage for a few months on the grounds of a monastery outside of town. The hermitage, tucked away amongst hundreds of trees, scared me. It was dark and buggy. Unlike the house with Keri, this place was small, desolate, and quiet. There were two bedrooms, a small kitchen, a bathroom, and a large living room, all complete with furniture from the 1970s. My mom and I shared a bedroom that had two, twin-size beds. My brother got the other bedroom to himself. I liked being away from Keri. I liked singing and dancing in the spacious living room to my "Annie" - original Broadway cast recording cd. I felt unsettled, though. My environment kept changing. My dad's house was my stability.

My memory is fragmented from that time, because I tried so hard to forget it, to bury it, to kill it. It took me several years to even talk about it in therapy. Keri has since died after having succumbed to major injuries that stemmed from a bicycle accident. When I heard of her passing, I immediately cried. I was relieved. She had haunted me while she was alive—even long after her and my mom broke up. For a while after the breakup, Keri would send me money on my birthday. I didn't like this. I didn't want anything from her. Later, she found my *Guerrilla Feminism* Facebook page, and commented: "Wow, who would have thought that *this* is what you'd be up to!" It seemed like she didn't think I would be a feminist because of my childhood dislike of her. Knowing what I know about her, she also probably wanted me to credit her for any feminist awakening I had. The truth is, in that big old haunted house I lived in, I was deterred from embracing feminism *because* of her. She had the infamous Rosie the Riveter "We Can Do It" poster framed on a wall near the kitchen. I hated that poster for years because I associated it with Keri.

After she died, all of the narratives of her being "THE BEST PERSON EVER" began pouring in. To those of us she abused, this felt like more abuse. Because Keri had done some volunteering with the local domestic abuse shelter, they had memorialized her on the homepage of their website. It greatly affected my mom to see it. My mom contacted them to say Keri was an abuser, and that maybe it wasn't the best to put an enormous picture of her on their homepage. Their response was: "Well, she's dead so we can't get her side of the story." I guarantee they would not have said this had Keri been a man.

People are not all bad or all good (except maybe a small few). Binaries are pointless. Keri did do some good things in her life. However, we shouldn't be giving abusers "saint" status or memorialize them on agency websites. I'm glad she's gone, and I don't feel bad saying that. I'm glad she is out of my life. Living ghosts are worse than dead ones, and a cop is still a cop.

While my mom and Keri were together, I was diagnosed with two learning disabilities: Dyscalculia[2] and Language Processing Disorder.[3] Needless to say, I was going through some things. I was harboring the secret of my mom's bisexuality. I was harboring my own secret of being learning disabled. These were heavy secrets for a child to hold. I was intimate with the feeling that I didn't belong anywhere. By the age of eight, I had tried too hard to fit in at school and at home when living with Keri and her kids. I was already tired, jaded. At school, I tried to dress "preppy" to fit in, but it didn't help and I hated the clothes anyways. I tried to hide my neurodivergence, but masking this led to burnout and sobbing tantrums. Part of me didn't want to belong if it meant losing even an ounce more of myself. I knew I was an odd kid. I wrote to my favorite author at the time, Kevin Henkes, and he wrote back—a high I savored for the entire week. I liked myself, but I didn't like that my peers didn't like me.

I didn't really have friends and wanted them desperately. When I was seven, I asked my parents if I could start dance classes. It was ex-

---

2   "[A] specific learning disability with an impairment in mathematics, which can affect calculations, problem solving, or both. It impacts all sorts of numerical tasks and it is inborn, meaning you are born with it…the DSM-5 mentions difficulties with number sense, memorization of basic math facts, and accurate and fluent calculation. An estimated 4-7% of students have dyscalculia."

LDRFA, "What Is Language Processing Disorder?," LD Resources Foundation, Inc., March 18, 2023, https://www.ldrfa.org/what-is-language-processing-disorder/.

3   "[A] type of learning disability that affects an individual's ability to understand, express, and process language… People with LPD have difficulty in understanding and using spoken and written language, which can make communication and learning challenging." Ibid.

pensive, but they both chipped in to pay for it. I loved moving my body in ballet, jazz, modern, and tap. As we did barre work *en pointe*, I would watch snowflakes fall outside. It all felt romantic. I found friendship. I found an appreciation for my body and what it could do. I belonged in that space to an extent, but I never felt good enough or thin enough or petite enough. During one class, before I was about to move across the floor doing a waltz, three girls from a neighboring suburb began staring at my back and snickering. When I turned around, they asked accusingly: "What *is* that?" It was the pot-hole scar that's the size of a nickel from getting a precancerous mole removed when I was four. I missed my cue to cross the floor with the group I was in and scurried off.

At the age of fourteen, like any teenager, I spent a lot of time in my room. I was precocious and curious and tried cybersex with strange men in online chatrooms. I didn't do this out of my own plea-sure-seeking, unfortunately. It was more out of curiosity than anything else. They would type erotic things to me and I would barely type back. I learned quickly that sex was something *done to* women. I also spent my evenings reading online message boards on my red iMac that I named Rockstar Ruby. Initially, these message boards were devoted to bands I loved at the time: The Smashing Pumpkins and Weezer (my brother's influence clearly seeped in). I read as strangers on the inter-net debated what Rivers Cuomo was sorry for in the song, "Butterfly," or more broadly, what did Billy Corgan mean in any of his songs? My brother was the one who introduced me to Riot Grrrl bands like Bikini Kill and Sleater-Kinney. Their music blew my mind. I felt I had found my kin. I felt some semblance of belonging.

During this time, I had my first boyfriend. It was the summer before I started high school. Lucas was a skater boy with dyed blue hair. He initially liked my friend, but she wanted nothing to do with him. I was the next best option. It was a short-lived summer romance bookended with the music of Pavement's *Slanted & Enchanted* album. Listening to "Summer Babe—Winter Version" takes me right back to warm, blue-tinted nights making out on his parent's front lawn and showing him my new striped bra. He was my first kiss. It was the most attention any boy had ever shown me. I felt addicted to this atten-tion. I wanted visibility and love but I often lost myself when I had it. Lucas broke up with me before the school year started. I was hurt, but not heartbroken. It would be over a decade before I would know real, gut-wrenching, dangerous heartbreak—that losing-yourself type of love and loss.

When I was little, I used to pray for a group of friends. I typically had one or two close friends, but I was dreaming up a foursome. Finally, in 7th grade, my dreams came true. I met Misti first. We were in the same choir class together. I was a heavy listener of Veruca Salt at the time and Misti looked like Nina Gordon. She was funny and smart. We would sing the harmonies to That Dog songs; her soprano matching my alto effortlessly. She introduced me to her friends, Sadie and Nyla. They all went to middle school together. I loved these girls so much. We would hang out most weekends. We watched the movie "Fear," starring Mark Wahlberg and Reese Witherspoon, where Wahlberg's character quickly becomes abusive and possessive of Witherspoon. My friends and I would talk about how fucked up the movie was, even if, privately, the film had excited me. I often daydreamed about men being possessive of me. I thought that was love. I wanted that kind of attention, or so I thought. Though I didn't speak this to them, it was clear that we were all wanting of something. My friends and I talked about our periods, sex, boys, and sexism. I had finally found my people.

When highschool began, we still had each other. We then incorporated another friend into our group, Ella. She was shy, kind, and gorgeous with long black hair. Ella was also in Special Ed like me, so she and I had a specific, top-secret bond. We never talked about Special Ed in front of the rest of our friends, but knowing we were both learning disabled was comforting. By sophomore year, Nyla had gone her own way as did Ella. Misti, Sadie and I were still together. In gym class one day, I was talking to a girl named Gemma. I always liked Gemma. She was loud in the ways I wanted to be, made me laugh, and we would commiserate about how awful running was. Gemma had just told me that her best friend of several years had abruptly stopped talking to her. I felt such immense compassion for her. I told her she should hang out with my friends and I.

Our friend group had morphed and evolved. We were a fearsome foursome. When Misti, Sadie, and I started a band called, The Aviators,

Gemma acted as our manager. We had a listening party where we invited other people from school to hear us play in Sadie's parent's basement. We bought a pack of white men's tank tops and wrote the letter "A" with black Sharpie on the front of each one. Our opening consisted of Sadie, the drummer, using the drum kick repeatedly, accompanied by the Misti's, the bassist's three-chords, and my vocals. The song started out slowly, and gradually sped up. It was the most fun I ever had at that point. We went to the movies. We walked around at night unafraid because we were together. My prayers had been answered. I began confiding more in each person, and they were confiding in me. We mostly hung out all together, but also still had our one-on-one time with each other. Sadie and I had started talking about how Misti would randomly shut down during band practice. We would be playing and Misti would suddenly stop and go sit down. I was not the best in these situations. I got upset. I would ask Misti what's wrong, but she would go mute. Sadie would try talking to her and Misti still wouldn't say anything. We would sit in silence until eventually Misti's dad came to pick her up. Looking back, I'm still not sure what these "episodes" were, but I have more compassion now. At one point, I talked to Gemma about this. She agreed it was odd behavior. I mentioned it was hard for me to not know what was going on with Misti. I was worried about her, but perhaps the way I showed it was judgmental and catty.

After my winter break as a sophomore, I had what I like to call my first breakdown. Misti, Sadie, and Gemma ostracized me from our group and proceeded to bully me. The entire thing came out of nowhere and completely changed my life's trajectory. This was the catalyst for my being medicated and in therapy. I woke up one Sunday morning and checked my Hotmail account on my mom's shitty Dell computer. I noticed I had received four emails: one from each friend telling me how terrible I was and one final email signed by all of them. The email from all of them started with, "Hello Mary Sunshine, how's the queen of the bitches been doing?" I laughed thinking it was a joke. It was not.

They had apparently bonded over their growing hatred of me at a party the night before—a party I opted out of attending. They were upset that I "talked shit" about each of them to the other. The "talking shit" was me confiding in them about Misti shut-downs, and other miniscule things that they also agreed with. My charge was that I "talk-ed shit," but they were talking shit about me. It didn't make sense. In the main email from all of them, they admitted: "We all know we've said shit about each other, but when it comes down to it, you're the one that can't get over it." The email ended with: "Sit and think for a moment Lachrista, think about every bad thing you have ever said about us, can you even remember half of it?" Yes, I could remember the things I've said about each of them. None of it was particularly bad. It was small, insignificant shit. The things that slightly grate, until they release from the chest, and then they're gone. They had each told me various things about the other, in confidence, and I never shared any of this information. I thought what I had done was similar—because it was, but they changed the rules. I wrote in my diary at the time, "I could have shared something that could have been super damaging to Sadie (something that Gemma had said about her)." I still never brought it up. Sometimes I wish I would have.

The emails reeked of an intruder. I knew Gemma was the mastermind behind it, which hurt, since I was so welcoming to her after her bestie left her. I felt like I was having a midlife crisis at age 16. They asked me to not sit with them at lunch anymore, so I was ostracized from my regular table, which seemed weirder for the other people there, who began asking why I wasn't sitting there anymore. Like a good little rule follower, I made up some lie, since my ex-friends, now-bullies wrote in the email: "We're not going to talk about you to other people, let's hope you're big enough to do the same." They knew me all too well. They knew I would want to look "mature," so they asked for my silence, and I gave it willingly. I used to wonder, would this have happened if I had just gone to that damn party?

I started eating lunch in the girls' gym locker room, which was anxiety-producing. I was constantly worried a teacher would see me in there and yell at me. Or worse, I was worried that one of the popular girls would walk in, see me eating my peanut butter sandwich, and go tell everyone. I didn't like eating lunch there—the stench of puberty, body odor, and my food didn't mix well. I had my first experience with depression during this time, and my ever-present anxiety increased. I became slightly agoraphobic. I felt like I would pass out anytime I walked through the doors of my high school. I also got physically ill, dealt with disordered eating, and was out of school for four months. When I came back to school, much to my surprise, people had noticed my absence. I came back as a numb version of my previous self. I eventually got up the courage to speak to Sadie, my ex-friend I had felt the closest to. I apologized for having hurt her in any way, and said I would like to be friends. She talked it over with Gemma and Misti, and they all decided I could be "let" back in. They said they missed me. I was invited over to Gemma's one day, and I felt hesitant about going. The whole time I was there, I felt uncomfortable. What they did to me completely changed me. They had not changed in any way, and I could no longer trust them. The three of them had a bond that I could never be a part of, and their bond originated from their mutual hatred of me. I stopped talking to them.

Thankfully, I had friends from other spaces, namely dance class, but I was mostly alone during this time. This was one of my first periods of "*wintering*," as Katherine May calls it in her book of the same name, "a fallow period in life when you're cut off from the world, feeling rejected, sidelined, blocked from progress, or cast into the role of an outsider."[4] When I wasn't asleep from the too-high-dose-for-me Zoloft, I was mostly online during this time—looking for my community; looking to belong to something, somewhere.

In the spring of 2004, I was a senior in highschool. After school one day, I did what I usually did: connect to the internet. The dial-up always felt excruciatingly long. Once connected, I looked up a website I had read about in an issue of *Bust Magazine*. The site was called *Feministing*. It was co-founded by sisters, Jessica and Vanessa Valenti. I identified with them immediately through their writing and later due to their Italian-American ancestry. At the time, I didn't identify as a feminist. I had been raised by one, but I also grew up watching (and hating) the character Jessie Spano of "Saved By The Bell." She had big curly hair, was loud and brash, and called every man a "chauvinist pig." I hated her because I *was* her (I did call my gym teacher a "misogynist" once). I, of course, didn't know she was a character created by men at the time. This was my lone representation of feminism in pop culture and it made me uncomfortable.

____

4   Katherine May, *Wintering: The Power of Rest and Retreat in Difficult Times* (Waterville, UK: Thorndike Press, 2021), 10.

I looked through the website, and it inspired and provoked me. I kept scrolling. This wasn't doom-scrolling, this was bliss-scrolling. By the end, I decided that, yes, I was a feminist afterall. I was hooked. I was ready to fight against all of the injustices I read about: sexism, misogyny, racism, and more. I specifically read posts about abortion news throughout the United States. I read about Sexual Assault Awareness Month. I read women's stories about sexism and discrimination. This was my initial foray into cyberfeminism,[5] and I really needed it. I was still reeling from my friend breakup and bullying. I felt I finally had an avenue out of this heavy grief.

To my surprise (and probably to some teachers' surprise, too), I got into college. I received a fine arts grant for poetry and majored in Creative Writing and minored in Women's Studies. Through this education, I gained knowledge that allowed me to contextualize my feminism and activism on a deeper level. I finally had language to confirm things I had known and felt about society for years. I started the first feminist club at my college and attended my first Take Back The Night[6] march the same year. My activism was turned on and all the way up. I was ready and willing to fight. I also started volunteering at the local Rape Crisis Center, and heard many stories of victimization, resistance, and survivorship. Because of these stories, I developed an even stronger desire to be an advocate, an educator, and an activist. The stories of others enabled me to act.

While studying in Rome, I created a project titled, "Visual Silencing: Italian Women's Identities and Visual Culture." Through this project, I looked at Italian advertisements replete with sexism, but in a different way than the Americanized version I had been used to. I interviewed Italian women of various ages asking about their experiences with sexism, misogyny, and feminism. One notably said, "We're living in 1950s America here." They felt their country was behind the times. I felt like mine was. This project furthered my hunger for activism, and was an important step in claiming my Italian American iden-

---

5   "Cyberfeminism," *Wikipedia*, September 11, 2024, https://en.wikipedia.org/wiki/Cyberfeminism.

6   AUTHOR'S NOTE: Take Back the Night is an international event and non-profit organization with the mission of ending sexual violence in all forms. https://takebackthenight.org/

tity. I began studying my working-class ancestors from Calabria and Sicily for how they *activated* their activism. Jennifer Guglielmo, writer, historian and associate professor at Smith College, writes about Italian immigrant women saying, "...they generally did not seek inclusion or authority within the modern nation-state."[7] She continues, "...they turned most often to strategies of mutual aid, collective direct action, and to the multiethnic, radical subculture that took shape within their urban working-class communities." I was proud to be of this ilk. I was proud to be of a people who belonged as much to themselves as each other.

By the time I graduated from college, I was firmly rooted in my identification of "Feminist." This identity was as important to me as breathing. My feminist identity had brought me a long-yearned for sense of belonging—at least for a little while.

I created *Guerrilla Feminism* in May 2011. I was 24 years old, and newly graduated from a Master's program in Women's & Gender Studies. The words "problematic" and "contentious" took up space in my vocabulary. I used each in nearly every sentence I spoke or wrote. I felt smart and like no one could tell I had learning disabilities or had been in Special Ed. I accepted the only job I was offered at the time: a literacy specialist for AmeriCorps. My placement was at a local nonprofit that acted as a day program and a tutoring space for disabled adults. At the interview, my supervisor asked: "So, you have your Master's in Women's & Gender Studies. Are you a feminist?" I said "Yes," and then qualified it with "But, I mean, I'm not all that radical or anything." My supervisor replied, "Oh ok, good, I was a little worried." We both chuckled and I felt like a fraud. I needed the job, even though it meant being on food stamps since it barely paid.

I ended up loving the work I did at the agency, and I enjoyed the clientele, but my supervisor was verbally abusive. At one point, she came into my tiny, windowless office, slammed the door, and stood over my desk yelling at me because I had printed out the monthly newsletter that announced her resignation "too early." I cried every

---

7   Jennifer Guglielmo, *Living the Revolution: Italian Women's Resistance and Radicalism in New York City, 1880-1945* (Chapel Hill, NC: University of North Carolina Press, 2012), 4.

day at that job. I needed to do something else, but the AmeriCorps position was a one-year commitment. I was deeply unhappy. I needed community. I desired kinship just like I had all those years ago.

While in my AmeriCorps position, I started collaging again—one of few art forms that felt accessible to me as someone who absolutely cannot draw or paint. After I was bullied and sick, collaging became a part of my therapy. It didn't have to be perfect or look like anything specific. I liked that. Then, I began printing and laminating images and phrases. The first phrase I printed was: "Rape is Rape." I remember seeing this phrase on the cover of the 2011 spring issue of *Ms. Magazine*. The image is simple visually and in its wording: a red background with the double use of the word "RAPE" capitalized in black with "is" in white lowercase centered on top—overlapping both instances of "RAPE." Simple, with a big message. Rape IS rape. All rape is rape. This was saying no instance of rape was "worse" than another. At this point, I was coming to terms with having been raped at the age of eighteen. Little did I know that I would be raped again in 2013, 2015, and 2016. I would continuously relearn that *rape is rape*; that partner rape isn't "less serious" than stranger rape; that being inebriated doesn't mean I "asked for it." One way that I attempted to heal from my own rapes was to situate it into the broader context of rape culture. This made me feel less isolated; less alone; less powerless. My feminism pulled me up and through.

I papered the city of Chicago with my arsenal of feminist phrases and images. My friend Audrey and I would place the phrases on buses, trains, newspaper stands, dingy bar bathrooms, and anywhere else we could imagine. The idea was to spark awareness and interest in feminism and rape culture. Sometimes I would wait for people to interact (or not interact) with an image. Many would take the image with them—almost like picking up a lucky penny. I saw what I was doing as a "surprise attack" on the patriarchy, or greater kyriarchy,[8] that was

---

8   AUTHOR'S NOTE: Term coined by feminist theologian, Elisabeth Schüssler Fiorenza, that analyzes "interactions of gender, race, class, and imperial stratifications, as well as research into their discursive inscriptions and ideological reproductions. Moreover, it highlights that people inhabit several shifting structural positions of race, sex, gender, class, and ethnicity at one and the same time." https://ebookcentral.proquest.com/lib/wisc/detail.action?docID=3118320.

always trying to hold back marginalized people. Even if the people interacting with the messages weren't thinking all that deeply about them, at least I made them *feel* something in that moment. At least I confronted them with important issues.

Initially, my goal was to facilitate feminist street activism in other locations around the world. In order to do this, I knew I needed to utilize social media to get the word out. I had a private Facebook account since my college days. I remember when my college finally got access. This was back when Facebook was classist and exclusionary and only allowed people with ".edu" email addresses to sign up. I was familiar with Facebook, but not as intimately as I would eventually become. In May 2011, I created a Facebook page titled, *Guerrilla Feminism*. Because there are so many different types of feminism (and some types I would argue are not actually feminist at all (i.e. *Trans Exclusive Radical Feminism* and *White Feminism*), I needed to be intentional about wording and definition. I felt that until feminists adopted an aggressive stance on the subjects of feminism and rape culture, we could not hope to end oppression. The name was also to pay homage to the feminist art group, Guerrilla Girls[9]. I began posting images of feminist flyering and graffiti on the Facebook page as motivation for others. Within months, the page erupted with likes and follows. This was back when "Feminist" was still a dirty word in mainstream culture, before Beyoncé had the word illuminated on stage behind her in 2014.

In my decade-plus time participating in digital feminist activism on social media, I have been called-out, ostracized, and told to "take accountability" more times than I can remember. I took accountability for various missteps in front of hundreds of thousands of people. Some instances of criticism were valid and happened early on in my learning process of social justice and social media etiquette. Some of this criticism was completely made up. I was a hardcore bitch most of this time. I was angry about a lot of things with no where to put it.

Shortly after its creation, the page evolved to sharing news, articles, essays, images, video, and more. I decided I couldn't do this alone—

---

9   AUTHOR'S NOTE: "The Guerrilla Girls are anonymous artist activists who use disruptive headlines, outrageous visuals and killer statistics to expose gender and ethnic bias and corruption in art, film, politics and pop culture." https://www.guerrillagirls.com/

not at this scale—so I asked my grad school colleague and friend, Cortney, to help with posting and comment moderation. Eventually, after "meeting" people on the Facebook page, more people joined in as volunteers to post and moderate. After a few years of having the Facebook page, and adding on several volunteers, we created our initial tenets of *Guerrilla Feminist* (GF). They were:

1.   Anti-Ableism: against the discrimination or prejudice of disabled people

2.   Anti-Imperialism: against the power of any State or Country over another

3.   Anti-Kyriarchy: against the social system or set of connecting social systems built around domination, oppression, and submission (Elisabeth Schüssler Fiorenza)

4.   Decolonization: working to undo the effects of colonialism

5.   Interlocking Oppressions: experiencing oppressions simultaneously (Patricia Hill Collins)

6.   Intersectionality: a lens to see where power dynamics collide and combine, specific to Black women's experiences (Kimberlé Williams Crenshaw)

7.   Pro-Sex Work/ers: support the decriminalization of sex work and support sex workers

8.   Trans inclusive: feminism should be trans inclusive and supportive of trans folks

9.   Prison Abolition: challenging the belief that caging and controlling people makes us safe (Critical Resistance)

10. Trauma-Informed: nuanced understanding of the personal, collective, and generational impact of trauma on the mind, body, and spirit (The Breathe Network)

These tenets came from having read important works by Black, Brown, Indigenous People of Color. I also incorporated Carla Lonzi's idea of *autocoscienza* from Italian feminism. This was similar to US feminists in the 70s' "consciousness-raising" groups, but I appreciated that the Italian term emphasizes the importance of things that the US term does not. Paloa Bono and Sandra Kemp write of this distinction:

Unlike the English phrase 'consciousness-raising', the term *autocoscienza* stresses the self-determined and self-directed quality of the process of achieving a new consciousness/awareness. It is a process of the discovery and (re-) construction of the self, both the self of the individual woman and a collective sense of self: the search for the subject-woman.[10]

Also, I was not interested in equality, but rather *equity* and *liberation*. I wasn't interested in being *equal* to men. I wanted to be liberated from them, from patriarchy, from kyriarchy. I wasn't concerned with *Guerrilla Feminism* being palatable to men or white people. I didn't need it to be nor did I want it to be. This further defined what feminism meant to me, and what *Guerrilla Feminism* was to be. After followers of GF would read the tenets and begin to interact on the page, the group and I were often classified as "Academic Feminism." Part of this was because other volunteers and myself expected a certain level of knowledge from followers who commented on posts. We consistently said, "This isn't a Feminism 101 space," which, looking back, is very pretentious and shitty, but we didn't have the time (or ability) to educate these people. GF also went along with the motto, "It's not my job to educate you." It wasn't until I got my second Master's Degree, this time in Library and Information Science, that I realized how ableist and detrimental this motto is. While, yes, Google is free, people don't necessarily know what search terms to use or what they are actually looking for. At the very least, I/we could have directed people by giving search words. Eventually this changed, but not until much later.

The idea that I was an "Academic Feminist" irked me, and it never felt right that GF was referred to as such either. This was because of my own turbulent experiences as a student. I knew that traditional education did not mean a person knew more or better than someone else. I knew that neurotypical folks were not "smarter" than me—even if teachers had told me they were long ago. I still get offended when people call me an "academic," because I often do not feel like I belong in that world. People would sometimes comment on the GF Facebook page, "Not all of us have educational backgrounds in this stuff." Even though I have two Master's Degrees, my feminism has been less informed by scholarly work. Reading theory is good and important, but it can be incredibly inaccessible—especially to those of us with cognitive or learning disabilities. I utilize some classically academic theories and texts in my GF work, but most everything I learned about feminism (and everything I continue to learn) was/is from feminists

---

10   Paola Bono and Sandra Kemp, *Italian Feminist Thought: A Reader* (Oxford: Basil Blackwell, 1991), 9.

online. In *Hood Feminism* by Mikki Kendall, she writes: "[Feminism] isn't a matter of saying the right words at the right time. Feminism is the work that you do, and the people you do it for who matter more than anything else."[11] *Guerrilla Feminism* was never about "right words." It was never about academia. It was about connection and belonging.

Many people have written about *Guerrilla Feminism* over the years, and perhaps it's better to show how they define GF. Dr. Penny Griffin, Senior Lecturer in Politics and International Relations in the School of Social Sciences at UNSW Sydney wrote of GF in her 2015 book saying:

> Guerrilla Feminism emerged as an anti-sexism stickering and graffiti campaign that developed into a Facebook group... and which also exhibits something of a punk 'hooligan' approach to social activism. The group debates sexism, advertising, pornography and women's bodies openly and, often, stridently. Guerrilla Feminist work is often witty, inspired and subversive, perhaps with a lighter touch than its cultural antecedents, such as Riot Grrrl... Guerrilla Feminists are no less serious, however, in their campaigning against sexism.[12]

This is an intriguing way to describe *Guerrilla Feminism* and Guerrilla Feminists. I'm not sure anyone else has said GF had a "lighter touch." Often, GF (and by extension, myself) was accused of being "too" angry, "too" brash. This was primarily because we moderated comments—every single comment. Myself and eventually others would spend hours moderating comments and blocking people. Sometimes hundreds of people would be blocked each day. Comment moderation was intensely important to myself and the GF team. Most Facebook and Instagram pages were not doing this at the time. We became known for our take-no-shit attitude. I heard from various GF commenters that they left other pages, because the admins were not aggressive when it came to moderating. As feminists, we're told, "Don't read the comments!" Generally, this is a good rule of thumb. These comments can enact harm to yourself and others, but when at-

---

11   Mikki Kendall, *Hood Feminism: Notes From the Women That a Movement Forgot* (New York, NY: Penguin Books, 2021), xiii.

12   Penny Griffin, "In Popular Form (Feminism and Antifeminism in Popular Culture)," *Popular Culture, Political Economy and the Death of Feminism: Why Women Are in Refrigerators and Other Stories (Popular Culture and World Politics)*, 1st ed. (London, UK: Routledge, 2015), 119–75, 169.

tempting to create a safer community space for marginalized folks online, moderating comments needs to be a priority. If myself or another GF team member didn't moderate a comment or missed a particularly nasty comment, we would hear about it. In many ways, it became clear that our "audience" was in charge—not us.

After the Facebook page found its footing, I looked elsewhere to gain more traction and get more people involved. In 2013, I created the Instagram account, which has amassed more followers than the initial Facebook page. During this time, I was an impromptu crisis counselor for those who direct messaged me about their various traumas. I tried to write back to everyone. I tried to be there. It began to take a toll, though. For a while, *Guerrilla Feminism* had branches all over the world, from Italy to Iran. It was exciting to receive messages and emails from people who asked if they could create a GF branch for their country or state. I never told anyone no.

Suddenly, I was thrust into a leadership role managing 50 volunteers and overseeing their pages while having a full-time 9-5 job. I had a "core" team of people I knew IRL (in real life or offline) and people I only knew from the internet. Our small team was majority women of color. It was important to me that there was consistency in what was posted on all branch pages (in terms of our ideals). I didn't want anything transphobic posted. Nothing whorephobic. People needed to be on the same page about this. I'm sure this came off as controlling. I'm sure I was controlling at times. GF was my baby and I wanted nothing but the best for my baby.

During this time, I was consistently told by followers and people on my team: "Whether you like it or not, you are held to a higher standard because you created *Guerrilla Feminism*." This felt immensely unfair and, with it, came a pressure I knew I couldn't handle. People put me on a pedestal and I never asked for this. If they wanted to hold me to a "higher standard," then that was their choice. I knew they would become disappointed when I would inevitably fall from the pedestal they created and put me on. Burn your idols, especially if I'm your idol.

In 2015, *Guerrilla Feminism* was briefly a nonprofit. Mostly because a white guy who inherited a bunch of money decided he wanted to give 10K to GF. Making it a nonprofit was a lot of work and I was doing most of it. I also had a full-time job. Eventually, there was a kerfuffle. We had a board of directors (four of us to be exact), and the Secretary (a Black woman), another GF volunteer (a white woman), and myself (white woman) were discussing ways to fundraise for the organization. The three of us met virtually with a white man who the GF volunteer knew personally. He was overpromising that if we put on a gender studies conference, we could make some money from it. I knew this was 1) complete bullshit (putting on a conference will expend more money than it will bring in—especially for baby orgs), and 2) it was not worth what this man was asking of us.

The meeting was tense, and it became more so when he said it wasn't a "good look" that one of the few trans women of color volunteers was "so" open about her suicidal ideation on the GF Facebook page (SIDE NOTE: this person has since died by suicide, R.I.P. XK). I lost my cool at this moment. I started crying. I abruptly left the meeting. I shut off my laptop. I was angry. Was this the best way to handle it? No, probably not. But how dare this white man tell me that a trans woman of color on my team shouldn't talk about her suicidal ideation because it might make people uncomfortable! I came back to the meeting, and said: "No, we're not doing this. I'm not comfortable with this." I was shocked and surprised that the GF Secretary and the GF volunteer saw no issue with what this man was saying. Later, I received an email from the GF Secretary saying she was resigning. She accused me of turning down "a huge amount of money" (there was never any money) for my own self-interest. She then spent the next few years consistently spreading lies, rumors, and general vitriol about me. She claimed I never paid her for the writing she did for the long-dead GF website (I did pay her--I have PayPal receipts). I have even posted screenshots of these payments, however, it has her government name on them (which I blotted out), so no one believed me. She also allotted an entire podcast episode to how terrible I was, and compared me to Rachel Dolezal, which, frankly, I'm still confused by since I never once pretended to be someone or something I wasn't. Perhaps most egregious, she outed me as a former sex worker—something I'm not ashamed of, but something I wasn't very open about at the time for various reasons. These two women created a smear campaign so severe that I contemplated suicide. I still struggle with paranoia and PTSD from this experience. Onlookers impulsively trusted GF's former Secretary, and I know a big part of that was because of race. I'm a white woman and she's a Black woman. People supported the other GF volunteer (who was white) because she aligned herself with the Black woman.

Before this, I, too, recklessly believed anything a more marginalized person said in the social justice realm of the internet. It's generally a good rule of thumb, especially for people of color, to not trust white people. There is a tremendous amount of pain and trauma around the many, many, many lies that white people--specifically white women—have told and continue to tell. I have never (and would never) fault a Black person or person of color for not believing white people, and I would never tell them what to do or what not to do. I do, however, have concerns around the idea that we should just "believe" the most marginalized person in any given situation. This is an ongoing issue in social justice spaces, specifically. As Kai Cheng Thom writes:

> I find that social justice or leftist communities also tend to misapply social analysis to individual situations of abuse, suggesting that individuals who belong to oppressed or marginalized groups can never abuse individuals who belong to privileged groups (that is, that women can never abuse men, radicalized people can never abuse white people, and so on). But neither of the above ideas is true. Survivors of abuse in one relationship can, in fact, be abusive in other relationships. And it's easier for privileged individuals to abuse others because of the extra power social privilege gives them, but anyone is capable of abusing alone given the right (or rather, wrong) circumstances.[13]

I don't necessarily think my experience constitutes abuse, but the point still stands when in conflict with others.

I have been lambasted for blocking women of color from my page (even when I didn't know their race). I have been called out for acting "defensive" when my literal character was under attack. I am considered completely undeserving of anything good because I have a big following on Instagram (even though I built that account up). I have learned so much from Black and brown women who have often been at the helm of social justice movements. I am forever indebted to these women.

---

13   Kai Cheng Thom, "What to Do When You Have Been Abusive," *Truthout*, January 26, 2020, https://truthout.org/articles/what-to-do-when-you-have-been-abusive/.

What I experienced completely changed how I think and feel about call-outs. It's unfortunate that, until it happened to me, I, too, relished in that attack dog digital activist life. I spent a lot of time yelling at people online, engaging in cross-platform harassment, and using my large following to humiliate and shame others. At the time, I remember thinking: "I'm not like them. I'm better than them." But that's not true. And that's what most white people won't admit. Many white people act like this online as a way to distract from themselves and their own failings. If you're constantly pointing the finger at others, then no one will look at you (including yourself). Harassing someone online and saying it's a "call-out," honestly does a disservice to call-outs, and of course, to the humanization of all of us. *Guerrilla Feminism*, and by extension me, was shitty in a lot of ways. We were elitist. We were always saying, "We don't do Feminism 101 here." We thought we were better than every other feminist page out there. People's egos, including my own, often got in the way of anything substantive we were trying to do.

When I devoured Kathleen Hanna's memoir and read what she had to say about the Riot Grrrl movement, I felt such kinship. I'm not saying that GF was ever as big as Riot Grrrl, but we had the same problems. In the book, Hanna talks about retreating from the movement and one woman in particular who kept harassing her about how problematic [Hanna] was. I knew GF was bigger than me, but it was also something I created, something I poured my blood, sweat and tears into. Eventually, I shut it down and I asked all the pages to shut down or change their name. Was that fair to them? Maybe not. But by that time, I just wanted to hide from the world and didn't want my name attached to anything other people were doing. I also didn't want people who were committed to hating me and misunderstanding me to take something I had started. As a neurodivergent person, I'm always terrified of being misunderstood. I'm always worried that I'm not articulating myself how I mean to.

I am not the same person I was ten years ago and thank god. I have learned, grown, read a lot, done a lot of therapy, and I continue to do all of these things. People who know me (like, really fucking know me) see that I'm always working on myself. I will never be able to convince people to see my side of things. Even if what a small sect of people said about me was true, I could do all the penance in the world and they would not be happy until I'm dead (or, at the very least, not online). Knowing this doesn't feel great, but I continue to do my "mediocre" writing (which, by the way, feels like breathing to me so I'll never stop), and I continue to share about Palestine and various atrocities, and I continue to post silly little memes.

Carceral feminism will not free us. There is room for all of us.

Over time, I've used GF as a space for feminist news/views, activism, education, and personal musings. The two main things that have differentiated GF from other feminisms is: 1) the lens with which I created it, and 2) my specific attention to uplift and amplify certain issues that haven't consistently (if at all) been covered in "mainstream" or liberal feminism. These issues include: sexual health (specifically normalizing contracting STIs), race and racism, ableism, LGBTQIA+ right to live and thrive, Universal Basic Income (UBI), Marxism, prison abolition, decriminalization of sex work (and the distinction between sex work and human trafficking), mutual aid, and more. I separated myself early on from liberal feminism—not because I didn't care about the issues those feminists spoke on—but rather their analysis and activism often began and ended with white cis women. Though all issues are important and matter (and that we can care about more than one thing at a time), focusing all our energy on something like shaving or not shaving our body hair might not be the best use of our collective time. Intuitively, I knew liberal feminism was problematic, but I couldn't articulate why until I studied more works by Black, Indigenous, and other feminists/Womanists. That's the thing: if you only read things by white women, you quickly become a White Feminist™, and your activism erodes.

Eventually, it became easier for me to continue *Guerrilla Feminism* by myself. I always felt bad that I couldn't pay people to help. I couldn't pay myself either. But if it was just me doing it (and not getting paid), that seemed better than having unpaid volunteers. Since 2016, GF has been a solitary project. There's a common misconception that if a person has a lot of followers on Instagram, they get paid. This isn't true. Having a following has definitely brought me opportunities I wouldn't have had, but it does not automatically equal money.

As the common call-and-response protest chant goes: "Whose

streets? Our streets!" and with GF I wasn't taking back the streets like I had initially intended; I was taking back the internet. Whose internet? Our internet. Digital activism was born from 90s kids on message boards searching for places to fit in and voice our opinions. Though we didn't have hashtags back then, we passed along messages via the World Wide Web. How else could we all have heard the same rumor about Marilyn Manson removing a rib so he could give himself a blow job? When I speak of "Digital Activism," I'm referring to a type of activism that uses social media and other online spaces to collectivize, organize, and resist. This includes the branch of "Hashtag Activism" (i.e. #BlackLivesMatter, #MeToo #WhyIStayed).

As someone with a language processing disorder, translating my thoughts verbally has never come easily—even though I'm a very verbal person. Using social media has allowed for my expression to flow. When I hear people say that digital activism doesn't do anything or that it's "easy" or not "real" activism, I know that they're excluding countless people. Not only is this way of thinking incredibly ableist (for others like me who struggle with language or other disabilities), it's also just generally unhelpful in collective and organizing work. There are many benefits and challenges to digital activism. The benefits include: global reach (potentially reach far more people online than in person), accessibility (not everyone is able to attend a protest or march for various reasons—housebound, lack of childcare, etc), convenience, inclusivity, safety, and open-access resources are plentiful. The challenges that exist are: moderating comments, criticism that digital activism is not "legitimate" activism, Western-centric (internet is slower or unreliable in some places and is less accessible and expensive), trolls, performative posting/reposting, and safety. Notice I wrote "safety" as both a benefit and a challenge since, for marginalized people, no space on or offline is truly ever safe. Another challenge is that platforms like Facebook, Instagram, and Twitter will often ban activists/organizers on purpose, which then stymies communication amongst us. This can slow down progress. All in all, I find the pros to outweigh the cons, since digital activism (and digital platforms) can efficiently and simultaneously collect, catalog, and archive stories.

In *How To Do Nothing*, Jenny Odell asks: "What does it mean to construct digital worlds while the actual world is crumbling before our eyes?"[14] Though I consider both digital and non-digital spaces to be *actual* worlds, I appreciate Odell's question. Digital spaces (and digital activism) have given me hope in very painful times, but I can't ignore or deny how it has maimed my mental health. It often triggers my PTSD and increases my anxiety. If you're a marginalized person, sharing your opinions online often puts you in harm's way. It has put me on Reddit threads which allowed trolls to send me death and rape threats. It has led to seriously scary situations online and offline. In the decade-long (and then some) that I have built this following on social media using digital activism, I often have to ask the difficult question of: "Is it worth it?" I don't always have a hard-and-fast answer. The effects to my mental health are compounded by the fact that, initially with GF, I always read the comments. There is a sort of unwritten internet rule that says: "Never read the comments." However, if you're trying to create or maintain some elements of a "safe space" online, you *have* to read the comments. I didn't take into account how brutal this was for me (and others). The more marginalized identities a person has, the more potential to come into contact with brutal, heinous language that can injure deeply. Myself and other white volunteers would often attend to comments that were racist so the women of color on our team didn't need to see them. It seemed like a decent process, but reading random comments on the internet means you can't ever be sure what people will write. You create, or fortify, your hypervigilance. This becomes exhausting over time and isn't sustainable. Social media is fragmented, and we continue to be fragmented by it.

Working to enact change within digital activism can often feel like an uphill battle. It can be difficult to collectivize with those you've never met in person.[15] The majority of people who volunteered with GF were people I had never met offline. Some lived in different countries. I loved the idea of organizing and working with feminists from all over the world, but in practice, it was often tenuous—either because of scheduling meetings across several different time zones or because of not being able to come to a common ground. Even if we would

---

14   Jenny Odell, *How to Do Nothing: Resisting the Attention Economy* (New York, NY: Melville House, 2021), xiv.

15   AUTHOR'S NOTE: I refrain from using "IRL" (in real life) since the internet IS real life.

chat via video, there was still something missing—or so I felt. In many ways, there is amazing technological accessibility in online organizing, and in others, the accessibility didn't always feel accessible to the ways I worked, learned, and processed. I was not always a good leader during this time either. I was reactionary and controlling. It was hard for me to let people in, and to let people proceed with something I created. I was consumed with worry over being misunderstood. Much of this fear stemmed from my feelings and struggles with my language processing disorder as well as my anxiety disorder.

Nowadays, I post less about all the bad things that are happening in the world, because, quite frankly, I don't have the emotional bandwidth. The current landscape of digital activism is as diverse in its tactics as its people. The main difference is that the preferred platform has changed. Many younger people, primarily Gen Z, are using Tik-Tok instead of Instagram, Facebook, or Twitter to discuss and shed light on various social justice issues. Blogs and websites like *Feministing* are long gone. People want bite-sized infographics that they can like, share, and save. With GF, there is no longer a website or long-form reads. Today, GF is a one-person endeavor (mostly on Instagram) where I post about what is happening in the U.S. and beyond. My goal is, and has always been, to bring factual information to the people. There are call-to-action items, images of self-care, cultural critiques, memes, and more.

Guerrilla Feminism was a movement, but it started as my story. It started as the online playground I never knew I needed. A playground where I felt like I belonged.

Chapter Two

DISABILITY AND DESIRE

We're gone in a blizzard of seconds. Love the body human while we're here. Give thanks or go home a waste of spark.

—MARTY MCCONNELL

MY PERIOD CAME IN FOURTH GRADE. I was at home and saw a small patch of bright blood in my underwear. I ran to my mom and she told me this was a special moment. Puberty invaded me too soon. I was ten and still playing with Barbies sometimes. My breasts became grenades waiting to be set off. I got a set of curves that I didn't know what to do with and hated because they didn't fit the ballerina aesthetic I was trying hard to embody. Was it the Italian in me that grew curves? Or was it the American in me—from growing up on a steady diet of McDonald's and Lunchables? My body embarrassed me. My brain embarrassed me. By this point, I had been in Special Ed for a few years. I knew the drill. The difference now, though, was I had started maturing. My body was changing. My brain was changing. I still had to go to Special Ed. All we did was eat pizza—lots and lots of pizza.

My parents advocated for me to get tested in third grade. My mom, in particular, noticed I was struggling in school, and she was worried about my increasingly low self-esteem. She saw that I kept getting quieter and more subdued. My dad worked for the state's Department of Vocational Rehabilitation, so he had knowledge around disabilities and advocacy. It's a privilege to have parents advocate for you, and for them to have the time, energy, and resources to do so. Being white from a white family most certainly helped me get testing and resources as well.

My memory of the testing still lives in my body. I was in a small, windowless room at my school with a garish overhead light, and an authoritative figure. I knew something was "wrong" with me, because that's how the entire experience was presented. I remember feeling immense pressure to give the right or correct answer. It's human nature to want to please people, especially as a small child. The testing process felt like I was being interrogated; it felt carceral. I watch a lot of "Dateline," and learning disability testing looks similar to the experience of lie detector testing. I was trying so hard to physically shrink myself, but I couldn't, because I was one of only two people in the room. I felt like I was being found out—and not on my terms. All I wanted to do was hide. All I wanted to do was get out of that room and run for my life.

I have glimpses of embarrassing levels of confidence in first and second grade, before the diagnoses. In second grade, I called the most popular boy in my grade, and asked him out on my dad's landline. Noah was already dating one of the most popular girls, Sofia. My friend Riley, who I met in preschool and now went to a different elementary school than I, dared me to do this. My small voice beamed, "Is Noah there?" A timid "...hello?" responded back. "Hey, it's Lachrista. Do you want to go out?" My entire body lit with heat awaiting his answer. Noah replied, "um... no." I hung up—embarrassed and afraid.

The following day, a Saturday afternoon, Riley and I walked down to the school playground. Within five minutes of being there, three boys rode up to us on their bikes. I recognized them all: Ryan, Justin, and Noah. They started circling Riley and I. Noah began interrogating me: "Why did you call me? Why did you ask me out?" I felt dizzy from the questioning and the circle they kept riding around in. Noah was no longer timid like he had been on the phone. I shrugged and said, "I don't know. Sorry." The truth was, I didn't know. I didn't know what dating was. I didn't know how or why I had the audacity to call the most popular boy in my grade. It seemed harmless, but it wasn't—not for Noah. His reaction taught me the social order of things. I had already known the difference between the popular kids and the rest of us. He solidified it for me. I was not allowed to go outside of my social class. Measly little me wearing my stir-up pants and oversized sweaters asking out the most popular boy in my grade was an embarrassment to him. It was an embarrassment to *all* the popular kids. It was a transgression. I felt bad for causing him such anguish. I said sorry and meant it. How dare I do such a thing? What did I think would happen? I just wanted to date, which at the time, meant sitting next to the person at lunch and hanging out with them at recess. I learned I was an embarrassment. I learned the popular kids saw me as a threat to their image and the micro society of second grade.

As the year progressed, my brash confidence began to fade. I started to feel unsure of myself at school. My first grade report card notes, "Lachrista seems uncertain of herself and needs to listen better." I really liked my second grade teacher and that made the school year easier for me, but this teacher didn't understand me or what I needed. After listening to her directions for an assignment, I still had difficulty understanding it. What would have been helpful was having the directions written down. I didn't feel like I could ask for that. Sometimes I would gather the courage to ask the teacher to repeat the directions. I would then be told, "You need to listen better." I *was* listening, but my brain was not processing what I was hearing, and I wasn't able to keep the verbal direction in my brain long enough to comprehend it. It really did seem to go in one ear and out the other. No amount of attentiveness would help keep it in my brain. Eventually, whenever I asked a question or advocated for myself, I was shut down. I stopped talking in class. I tried to be compliant, but even this didn't help me become a desirable student.

The diagnosis of two learning disabilities was absolutely horrifying to my third-grade-curly-haired self. I wish I would have had these words of writer and activist Leah Lakshmi Piepzna-Samarasinha: "I often correct people when they ask me 'when I was diagnosed with autism,' to let them know that I use the phrase *when I came home/when I figured it out*, instead."[1] This language would have been immensely helpful to me at the time. It was truly a coming home, and I'm fortunate I got to *come home* to my learning disabilities at such a young age.

I knew the learning disabilities that I *came home to* was something negative from the way it was presented to me. I was sat down by my parents. I wondered, "Are they getting another divorce somehow?"

---

1   Leah Lakshmi Piepzna-Samarasinha, *The Future is Disabled: Prophecies, Love Notes, and Mourning Songs* (Vancouver, CA: Arsenal Pulp Press, 2022), 25.

I don't remember the exact words they used, and I know they were loving about how they said it, but the seriousness of it all made me uneasy. I'm certain that they didn't say "disabled" or "disability." I was often described as "special" by loved ones, because they didn't know any better, and because this was typical of the language used in the early 90s. The word felt demeaning. It *is* demeaning. At the same time, I couldn't think of myself as disabled. I didn't want to. I couldn't wrap my head around that identity. I leaned into nothingness.

I now had an IEP (Individualized Education Plan). An IEP is poorly named, because it's only "individualized" as much as a system will allow it to be. In the U.S., there is a strong, one-size-fits-all mentality in all things, but especially in education. Some teachers resent IEPs and having to abide by them. Some feel that accommodations make things "easy" for students. That's kind of the point, since those of us with disabilities have to work much harder than non-disabled people. However, an accommodation only gets us to an *almost* level playing field with others.

Teachers in the U.S. are not provided with enough training, support, time, or money to do their job. This adds to disabled students not receiving great, or even adequate, education. In most cases, it's up to the teacher to take the initiative to learn about disabled students and how best to teach us. Between active shooter drills, managing large classrooms, and lesson planning, a teacher would need to educate themselves about disabled students in their free time. I can understand the resentment that teachers might have, but I can't understand the cruelty. I could always tell when a teacher was less than enthusiastic that they had a student in their classroom with an IEP. I remember eye-rolls, dismissiveness, and cold body language. Many times I had the realization that adults wanted me to be everything that I wasn't.

At the beginning of each school year, I would panic about each of my teachers receiving my IEP. It felt like I had "LD" stamped on my forehead. I worried about this as a child as well as an adult who later received disability accommodations in college and grad school. I was concerned about what teachers thought about me before I even met them. As a child, this felt especially powerless. I was scared of their own biases. I knew I needed to work harder to prove to myself and my teachers that I was smart, and not a bother.

Special Ed class was fun for a while. I left my "regular" classes early to go hang out with the other disabled kids. It was the one place I could be myself, because there were no popular kids around to intimidate me. We would also get snacks all the time. It was similar to being in kindergarten and having a milk break—except, we had pizza breaks. The infantilization ran deep. No one knows what to do with a person when they're learning disabled, so they put us with kids who are kinda-sorta like each other in one large room, and let us sit and think about why we're there. It all ends up feeling like "The Room for the Unwanted." I felt bad. I felt dangerous. I felt like I was being punished. This is where "bad" kids go—and not even the "cool" smoker bad kids. Looking back, it was ridiculous, but it was also a place where us weirdos celebrated each other and felt free. Similar to the first rule of the book and film, "Fight Club,"[2] us disabled students never talked about being in Special Ed *outside* of Special Ed. Some of us would barely acknowledge each other in the hallways. Sometimes we nodded at each other, but more often than not, we just kept looking straight ahead. We all guarded our collective secret. At least I ate well during my time in Special Ed.

I generally liked my Special Ed teachers. They all seemed to know a bit more about disabilities than the other teachers at school. However, I did have one Special Ed teacher who gaslit me into thinking I was born in a different year than I actually was. I was in her office—more of a cubicle with a sliding door—and she asked:

"Are you *sure* you were born in '85? I think you were born in '86."

"...No, I'm pretty sure it was '85... I think."

She continued to argue with me about this. But I *knew* that I knew my birthdate. Yet, I doubted myself because this adult with power questioned me. After my disability diagnosis, I stopped believing anything I knew about myself or the world. I started assuming that adults knew me better than I knew myself. I started assuming anybody knew me better than myself.

---

2   "The first rule of fight club is you don't talk about fight club." Chuck Palahniuk, *Fight Club* (London: Vintage Books, 2007).

My elementary school didn't practice inclusion[3], so I would leave in the middle of "regular" classes with the Special Ed kids to go to our Special Ed class. It killed the small amount of self-esteem I had left. Leaving my "regular" class to go to Special Ed was always humiliating. I would have to get up in the middle of class and walk out the door. This always caused a disruption for my peers and for the teachers. I remember thinking, "There has to be a better way to do this." One time in fifth grade, my teacher—who had a mean, old face and was obsessed with pigs—abruptly stopped teaching. She looked at me and the other girl who was leaving and asked angrily, "Where do you two think you're going?" I froze and thought, "Like you don't know." This was just a way for my teacher to feel in control and to embarrass us in front of everyone. This is what many of us disabled kids had to face. Because the other student who was leaving with me was quieter, I spoke up and said, "We have to go to Ms. Conaway." I remember pleading with my teacher through my eyes not to make me say "SPECIAL ED" in front of the entire class. I started to feel hot all over as I looked around at twenty-five of my peers who sat and looked back at me. The teacher thought for a moment, and finally responded: "Oh, that's right. OK." Permission was granted. I wanted to dissolve.

It's hard for me to recall teachers who treated me like a human being, because there weren't many that did. Typically, the teachers who showed me any kindness were the English and Art teachers. Nearly every science and math teacher I had seemed to hate me, and I hated them back. It makes sense. Those were my two most difficult subjects because typically there are "right" and "wrong" answers or "right" and "wrong" ways of doing things. I never worked well in those conditions. I still don't. The science and math teachers were the ones who felt that I didn't try hard enough. The truth is, I tried exceptionally hard at both of those subjects. I had so many math tutors that I don't even remember their names. Having a tutor was a privilege, even if I hated it. My older brother was tasked with tutoring me at one point—something we both despised. Unlike me, he excelled in math, science, art, English—basically all subjects. I excelled in reading and writing,

---

3   AUTHOR'S NOTE: Inclusion, which is more typical today, doesn't force students out of their traditional classes to go elsewhere. They are typically able to stay in the same classroom as their non-disabled peers.

but I was so unsure of myself. I never believed I was good at anything. I remember seeing one of the popular girls reading a book one day in class. She had to form the words with her mouth as she read. I found it intriguing. I didn't need to read like that, but I started doing so because she did.

What I disliked most about being tutored was how intimate it felt. The one-on-one was too much for me. The tutor would ask me to solve a word problem, and I could feel them staring at me as I worked. In those moments, I couldn't think. My brain felt like goop. I started to mask this by contorting my face into inquisitive looks. I got really good at looking like I was thinking hard about something. I would furrow my brows, gaze in the distance, purse my lips together. I would either guess the answer or say "I don't know" and shrug my shoulders. In those moments, there was nothing going on in my brain except high anxiety. Pretending to think became familiar and comfortable. My parents also had me go to Sylvan Learning Center after school for one day a week. Again, this was a privilege in some ways, but my experience was harmful. SLC boasts itself as "personalized" and "individualized" learning for kids. When I attended SLC, the instructors would reward students with a toy of our choosing if we got correct answers. Even at the time, I knew this was only going to make me feel worse, because again, it assumed *I* was the problem; it assumed *I* wasn't applying myself. If you're a person with dyscalculia, no amount of bribing with a cute pink piggy bank is going to help. I wondered, what do I get if I get it wrong, because I will definitely be doing that.

I soon realized that trying hard took too much out of me and it was pointless since it didn't result in good grades or kindness from teachers. I eventually stopped trying so hard and just did what I needed to do to get by. Teachers hated that, but they didn't give me another way. I had teachers who called me "stupid" and said I would "always be different from other kids." I had one teacher in sixth grade who asked me, "Does the word 'test' scare you?" It became abundantly clear to me then that most of the adults around me didn't know what the fuck they were talking about. Yet, I still trusted them more than I trusted myself. I was considered their "problem child," because they had to work harder to figure out how to teach me. Most teachers didn't have the time or the funds to do anything other than one-size-fits-all teaching.

I was an undesirable student. I was an undesirable person.

Freshman year of high school, I was sitting in biology class when the boy next to me abruptly said: "I didn't know you had a disability." I was startled. "What? How do you know?" I asked nervously. He replied, "Oh, I heard the teacher giving you special instructions for the test." I slumped in my chair further. The boy then told me dismissively, "You don't look like you have a disability." At the time, I wasn't able to articulate to him that not all disabilities are visible. Immediately, I felt lesser. Unwanted.

People with nonvisible[4] illnesses and disabilities often have difficulty in school and in the workplace. In a National Public Radio feature about nonvisible disabilities, reporter Naomi Gingold says, "When a disability isn't immediately obvious, others—at work, school or even at home—sometimes doubt it exists and accuse those who suffer from invisible conditions of simply angling for special treatment." Because of my nonvisible disabilities, I live in a state of hybridity. People will not know about my disabilities, for the most part, unless I tell them. I straddle these two worlds of disabled and nondisabled. In her book, *The Rejected Body: Feminist Philosophical Reflections on Disability*, Susan Wendell writes of this phenomenon:

> ...I live between the world of the disabled and the world of the non-disabled. I am often very aware of my differences from healthy, non-disabled people, and I often feel a great need to have my differences acknowledged when they are ignored... I am very aware of how my social, economic, and personal resources, and the fact that I can 'pass' as non-disabled among strangers, allow me to live a highly assimilated life among the non-disabled; I have more choices in this respect than many other people with disabilities.[5]

Often I have felt not disabled enough for the disabled community, and not neurotypical enough for the abled community. Far too often, I have questioned where I fit in these worlds. It's hard to find belonging in the hybridity.

---

4   AUTHOR'S NOTE: I use "nonvisible" instead of "invisible," since the latter can feel delegitimizing

5   Susan Wendell, *The Rejected Body: Feminist Philosophical Reflections on Disability* (Hoboken, NJ: Taylor and Francis, 2013), 76.

In grade school, I was always embarrassed when I had to leave my "regular" class to go to Special Ed class, or whenever I received accommodations. This embarrassment was heightened once I hit puberty. My body developed, and I tried not to notice. I had been estranged from my body since my parent's divorce. It didn't help that I only saw my body as a site of pain due to near chronic urinary tract infections as a young child. So I broke up with this body of mine. I decided to live in my head. I ruminated and became increasingly internal. I had to start wearing a bra, which I hated. I felt more perceivable, if only because none of my friends at the time were wearing bras. Mostly it was fine, except for one day in gym class. Our class was instructed to run from one end of the gym to the other. I hated gym class, but was a rule follower and perpetually terrified of getting in trouble. A majority of this was because, as a Special Ed student, I wore a big target on my back and teachers judged me more harshly than my non-disabled peers. I started running with the rest of the class until I heard boys chanting in unison: "Lachrista's wearing a bra, Lachrista's wearing a bra" followed by maniacal laughter. I was wearing a slightly-too-big-for-me tank top and they saw my bra under my armpits. I felt ashamed. Immediately tears swelled, but I bit my lip to keep them from spilling out. I kept running as instructed. I was forced to perceive my body because others perceived it. I resented that.

A year or two later when more girls were wearing bras, I would overhear boys talk about how "hot" it was to see a girl's bra straps. I was privy to a lot of conversations like these, because I was, plainly, not seen—especially by boys. I was always in the background. I remember wondering, "Why was it embarrassing when I wore a bra? Why was it not considered 'hot' when I did it?" The only reason that came to me was that it was because I was unwanted. I was not the right kind of girl. Even the girls didn't like me. I badly wanted to be one of the popular girls, but they wouldn't have me. I wanted to be their friend. I wanted to know what they talked about, so I started retrieving their notes to each other from the recyclable bin. The notes were boring, and didn't give me any insight into who they were, but I felt I owned something of them. They never noticed me. I was not seen or thought of, and I badly wanted to be seen and thought of. I was an embarrassment to my peers and to myself. I was undesirable.

When I got to middle school, Special Ed was even worse. There was less for us to do, barely any pizza, and I was becoming a dreaded teenager, so I had crushes that were never reciprocated. Boys were mostly uninterested in me, which seemed to make me more interested in them. Leaving in the middle of class during this time was agonizing. My sexuality was budding, and I remember telling myself: "No boy is ever going to want me, because I'm disabled." Even back then, I felt that having learning disabilities would stop anyone from sexually desiring me. Disabled people are often thought of as non-sexual beings. People with visible disabilities deal with this on a profound level. In her essay "Nobody Catcalls The Woman In The Wheelchair," Kayla Whaley notes, "People register 'disabled' before they register 'woman' and the former always overrides the latter, because in our ableist society a disabled body is necessarily a desexualized one... No matter what, though, we are not desirable."[6]

This is one of the reasons why many disability activists were upset about Kylie Jenner's photoshoot for *Interview* magazine in December 2015. Jenner, already a celebrity icon at the time, appeared on the cover of the magazine sitting in a brass-colored wheelchair—sexy, glamorous, and blank. It was fetishization to the nth degree for Jenner, a currently able-bodied person, to use a wheelchair as a prop while wearing a black latex bodysuit. It's "crip drag," as comedian and disability rights activist Caitlin Wood named it.[7] Even if the idea for the photoshoot didn't originate from Jenner, she still participated in it. You'd think someone on her team would have had the foresight to know this was a bad idea. But seeing as how our society treats disabled people as an afterthought, it makes sense that nobody cared to stop it. Do magazines ever showcase physically disabled people being sexy on their covers? It's a rarity. In May of 2023, British *Vogue* put five disabled people on five separate covers. This might have been representation, but it was artificial. The magazine issues are about disability rights, but I would have loved to see a disabled person on a magazine cover for no other

---

6   Kayla Whaley, "Nobody Catcalls The Woman in the Wheelchair," *The Establishment*, August 10, 2018, https://theestablishment.co/nobody-catcalls-the-woman-in-the-wheelchair-82a6e4517f79/index.html.

7   *Bitch Media*, interview with Caitlin Wood, podcast audio, https://soundcloud.com/bitch-media/lets-talk-about-crip-culture, 2015.

reason than they were the model that was chosen. Let's see a disabled person on the cover of a magazine that doesn't even mention their disability. Disabled people don't need to talk about our disabilities all of the time. Our disabilities aren't necessarily our primary interests, even if the issue of disability rights might be. Our disabilities aren't the most interesting thing about us.

According to the Invisible Disabilities Association, approximately 96 percent of people who live with a disability have one that is nonvisible.[8] This includes people with mental health issues. Having a nonvisible disability means having to decide when to disclose, and potentially doing so over and over. It's an exhausting experience. In her article "My Body, My Closet: Invisible Disability and the Limits of Coming-Out Discourse," feminist disability scholar Ellen Samuels discusses how, as individuals with nonvisible disabilities, we are often engaging in a "self-destroying tension between appearance and identity."[9] In this way, having a nonvisible disability as part of one's identity is always up for debate and there are always demands for its legitimacy.

By the time I was seventeen, I had even more disability diagnoses. After having been bullied by my friends and subsequently unable to function, my parents had me see a Cognitive Behavioral therapist and I was put on Zoloft. I started to see a psychiatrist, too, who diagnosed me with various acronyms: GAD, PMDD, PTSD, SPD.[10] I constantly consider the implications of disclosing my disabilities and how I will inevitably feel inadequate and a "problem child." If you need accommodations for work or school, you will most likely need to disclose formally. Some workplaces allow a person to disclose informally, and depending on the accommodation, this can be worked out between the employee and their supervisor. Disclosing formally is supposed to be better protection for the disabled employee. However, in either circumstance, if you disclose, you are looked at differently, and often

---

8   Invisible Illness Awareness Week, October 12, 2023, http://www.invisibleillnessweek.com/.

9   Ellen J. Samuels, "My Body, My Closet: Invisible Disability and the Limits of Coming Out," *The Disability Studies Reader*, May 2, 2013, 321—37, https://doi.org/10.4324/9780203077887-34.

10   Author's Note: Generalized Anxiety Disorder, Premenstrual Dysphoric Disorder, Post Traumatic Stress Disorder, Sensory Processing Disorder

questioned by colleagues, coworkers, and supervisors. Reporter Alecia M. Santuzzi of *Psychology Today* writes, "Without knowing that a disability is involved, teachers, supervisors, and co-workers are left to assume that unexpected poor or inconsistent performance accurately reflects the person's ability to do the tasks."[11]

In 2017, I started a second graduate program in Library and Information Science. Before starting classes, I navigated my way through the university's disability services—something I hadn't done in nearly a decade. Because of all of my disabilities, I figured I should look into accommodations. The summer before I started school, I met with an amazing disability services counselor. He gave me so much information and a listing of various types of accommodations I could ask for. What didn't go well, and what is still difficult, are the terms with which I received accommodations at the university.

Because my learning disability testing is considered outdated[12], my accommodations did not go towards my learning disabilities, but instead towards my mental illnesses and neurological disorder. To non-disabled, neurotypical folks, this might seem inconsequential. However, it's problematic because, while my dyscalculia is not necessarily a daily issue (numbers, math), my Language Processing Disorder *is* a daily issue. I can't adequately articulate this disorder of mine, because language use and recall are major parts of the disorder[13]. The point is I chronically struggle with processing language. When I had to work on assignments for school, it took me longer, it was more challenging, and much more frustrating. The accommodations I received for this second grad program did not speak to my learning disabilities at all.

There are so many access issues in regards to disability testing. Ableism, classism, racism, sexism are all at the root. I could have gotten retested, but I didn't have the time nor the money. It costs hundreds, sometimes thousands of dollars to get testing done. There is

---

11   Alecia M. Santuzzi, "Invisible Disabilities," Psychology Today, June 26, 2013, http://www.psychologytoday.com/intl/blog/the-wide-wide-world-of-psychology/201306/invisible-disabilities.

12   AUTHOR'S NOTE: It needs to be within the last five years, and mine is from college between 2004-2008.

13   AUTHOR'S NOTE: Writing a book with this is intense and slow.

also usually a waitlist, and once you *do* get in, you need to go in for 3-hour time periods. It's grueling, difficult to schedule, inconvenient, and costly. Not to mention traumatizing, or in my case, re-traumatizing. It does not prioritize the working class. Disability and classism are inextricably linked whether it's a visible or nonvisible disability. Accessibility is an essential disability rights issue. Mia Mingus, a disability justice organizer writes, "Accessibility is concrete resistance to the isolation of disabled people."[14]

If I would have had access to learning disability testing during my second graduate program, this wouldn't fix the greater issue of the perpetual disbelief in/of disabled people and our diagnoses (whether these diagnoses are self-diagnosed or doctor-diagnosed). Getting accommodations is essential for those of us who need them. Too many of us have had to go without due to access issues, internalized ableism, or the system's unwillingness to provide for us in any meaningful way. This experience parallels with how I had to get a medical accommodation for the first year and a half of the pandemic so I could work remotely. Navigating a medical accommodation is also a bureaucratic level of hell I don't wish on anyone.

It still angers me that I didn't receive accommodations for disabilities that I have solely because I didn't have the funds to get retested. It angers me that even if I did, it would be an incredibly re-traumatizing experience, all for the sole purpose of "proving" to academia that I'm "impaired." I'm also still angry that I needed to get a medical accommodation to do my job remotely during a deadly pandemic—a job that didn't need to be done in person.

There have been countless times where the authenticity of my disabilities was questioned. I had a science teacher in middle school who told me I was using my disability status as a "crutch." I spent a lot of time and energy learning how to think like a neurotypical person and I resented it. I badly wanted to fit in. I badly wanted things to come easier for me. What is teenage life if not the incessant desire to fit in? What is life, regardless of age, if anything but the desire for love and

---

14   Mia Mingus, "Access Intimacy, Interdependence and Disability Justice," Leaving Evidence, April 27, 2018, https://leavingevidence.wordpress.com/2017/04/12/access-intimacy-interdependence-and-disability-justice/.

belonging?

As I grew older, I continued to obsess over the idea that my nonvisible disabilities made me undesirable. At first, I understood it in terms of teacher/student relationships, and then I began to understand it in romantic/sexual terms. Anytime I had a crush on a boy, "disabled = non-desirable" ran through my head, taunting me. I had tried to "pass" as neurotypical, as non-disabled. I had tried often to neglect my own needs and accommodations. I had tried hard (and failed) to assimilate. This was an ultimate betrayal of myself. I didn't like feeling like a sell-out. I didn't like feeling like I was embarrassed to be disabled and neurodivergent. I felt loathsome for claiming a feminist identity when I was overly concerned with how cis, straight men were perceiving me.

During my first year of college, I thought I had finally left the headspace that told me my disabilities made me undesirable. I thought I had stopped caring. How I did this was not the best or healthiest way for me. I did it by sleeping around. The power I felt I had as a slut[15] was intoxicating. It didn't matter whether I was smart or stupid. I didn't care. I only wanted to be seen as sexy so I could have a moment of feeling undeniably craved. I rarely told any of these people of my secret disability shame. I didn't want to be looked at differently. I didn't want to be seen as anything other than alluring.

During my first round of grad school, majoring in Women's and Gender Studies, I thought my issues with desirability were finally resolved. I felt like a "bad" feminist to care so much about being thought of as desirable, so I gradually unpacked these feelings and was able to stop caring. For the first time, I was having conversations with the people, mostly men, that I slept with about having learning disabilities. None of them cared, which at the time made me feel great. Finally, I was sleeping around because I wanted to, not because I needed proof of anything. I still felt like a fraud, though. Did I now need to *perform* my disabilities in order for them to believe me? Did I need to *perform* my sexuality to make up for the fact that I was disabled? I became more confused. I felt wanted, at least. I felt a type of belonging I hadn't felt before. I felt beautiful.

------

15   AUTHOR'S NOTE: In the reclamation of the word way, not the derogatory way.

Where I didn't feel this belonging was online. Often, when I would post things on *Guerrilla Feminism* about my disabilities, people would ask seemingly harmless questions like, "When were you diagnosed?" or "Did you have testing done?" Both questions I could easily answer, but it irked me that I knew people wouldn't believe I had disabilities if I hadn't received a formal diagnosis or had testing done. It's important to note that many people self-diagnose these days and that can be just as valid, especially since there are so many barriers to getting a formal diagnosis. It seemed like people online were trying to find holes in my story. The tables had turned. I used to be the one trying to find "proof" of my desirability. Now, people I didn't even know online were trying to find "proof" that I had disabilities—that I belonged to that community. I finally got to the point where I not only accepted my disabilities, but I appreciated them, and yet, people online didn't believe me. They seemed to think it was an identity I was falsely using. I was now worried about being trusted in an online community I created. I stopped worrying about my desirability.

This changed when a doctor diagnosed me with herpes—a souvenir from an ex-boyfriend. The diagnosis shocked me. Never before had I had a sexually transmitted infection, and suddenly I had one of the few incurable ones. Like my learning disabilities, my STI-positive status is mostly a nonvisible one. Nobody knows I have herpes until I disclose. The process of disclosure, similar to disclosing my disabilities, creates an atmosphere thick with vulnerability. This vulnerability can lead to supportive and affirmative experiences, but STIs are still considered an "undesirable" status.

I now had two undesirable identities under my belt (one, literally). As a woman who was learning disabled, I felt desexualized, but now that I had herpes, I was oversexualized. When I told people I had herpes, some would ask incredulously, "How many people have you slept with?!" Having herpes was clear proof that I was "dirty," "disgusting," and "slutty." This diagnosis pushed me out of the "desirable" category that I occupied so briefly. I know that men deal with a certain amount of stigma for being disabled and/or STI-positive as well, but if you're a woman with these identities, you are subverting mainstream notions of desirability. It's okay for men to have sex; to sleep around. It's okay for men to even have an STI—it's almost expected. This is not the case for women. Society doesn't like when there is proof that a woman had sex, especially with multiple partners.

Contracting herpes was a turning point for me regarding my desirability. It took having something physical and visual for me to come to terms with the non-physical and nonvisible disabilities that had affected my self-esteem for so long. The herpes felt much worse, because I couldn't hide it like I could the learning disabilities. I could mask being neurotypical. I was used to hiding my "brain" issues—it came natural to me, even if it drained me. I couldn't easily hide the herpes, unless I never wanted to have sex again. After the diagnosis, I felt an overpowering impulse to find someone, anyone, who would fuck me now as an STI-positive woman. I needed proof again that I was desirable, lovable.

I went back to my old patterns with sex. After disclosing my STI status to partners, I slept with them, or more accurately, let them sleep with me. Once again I sought proof of my worthiness. I always received the same so-called proof. Men would fuck me carelessly. They would never initiate the "have you been tested?" conversation. It made me realize two things: 1) many men don't give a shit about their health or the health of who they're sleeping with, and 2) herpes is not a big deal. Similar to "outing" myself as having learning disabilities, the people I "outed" my STI status to didn't seem to care. I was still coveted, but it didn't feel good. If getting people to sleep with me was how I measured desirability, then yes, I was desirable. But once I had this, I didn't like it. I wanted something more.

To be desired is to be wanted, but not just in a sexual way. Being desired is about being loved and accepted for all that you are. It's a positive thing, but the people I was dating and the sex I was having didn't feel positive. It didn't feel gratifying. It felt sluggish, boring, and stale. Most of the time, it didn't feel like I was even in the room. I had to cut myself off. I finally stopped having sex that I didn't truly want. It wasn't easy, but I knew what I had been doing was self-destructive. I remember asking myself at the time, "How is this fulfilling when it doesn't feel good?" I had to break the pattern.

Desirability, for me, is too often based on appearance. When I visualized the entirety of my identities, I would linger on the undesirable ones and would feel my attractiveness vanish. At the intersection of STI-positive and learning disabled is a bottomless feeling of isolation and invisibility. There lies the impulse to be perceived and not be perceived in a society where visible "proof" is always required to be taken seriously, and to be considered desirable.

I still worry about my level of desirability, but in a new way: do I desire myself? Do I want myself? Do I love (or at least accept) myself? These questions are more important to me than the old ones. If someone doesn't find me desirable, whether it's because of my STI-positive status, my learning disabilities, or something else entirely, that hurts for a few days, but if I don't want me, I'm hurt for as long as I'm alive.

I have to choose to desire myself each moment of each day. Desiring myself means I practice radical self-care. It means I take "selfies for survival," which is what I did when I created the tag (#selfies4survival) on Instagram, and others started posting their own. Again, an online community was there for me. Choosing to desire myself means I self-advocate aggressively, ask for the accommodations I need without apology, ask for what I want from partners, ask for what I desire from the world. I can't live with myself if I don't desire myself. I may not desire myself all the time every day, but I try. In the words of one of my favorite poets, Nayyirah Waheed: "If someone does not want me it is not the end of the world. But if I do not want me, the world is nothing but endings."[16]

My learning disabilities, neurological disorder, mental illnesses, and herpes may be unwanted, but they each add a texture of brilliance to my personhood. My time in Special Ed wasn't all bad, I had some damn good pizza.

---

16   Nayyirah Waheed, *Salt* (CreateSpace Independent Publishing Platform, 2013), 163.

A BODY HAUNTED BY MEN: THE HERPES OF IT ALL

...your scars not only mark a cut, they commemorate a joining... Scar tissue does more than flaunt its strength by chronicling the assaults it has withstood. Scar tissue is new growth. And it is tougher than skin innocent of the blade.

—SHELLEY JACKSON, *Patchwork Girl*

HE ENDED UP BRANDING ME TWICE in the end: one colorful tattoo and one incurable STI. He made sure to leave his mark. The pain he inflicted on me cut through to my soul. He was the first to kiss the pot-hole scar on my back. My love for him still exists in small, discrete, fragmented pieces in my heart. That love is not just there for him—it's there for me, too. How fortunate he was to experience my love. Believing he is some kind of "monster" may be more convenient, and more socially acceptable, but I cared for him so deeply that dehumanizing him would mean dehumanizing me. I was a different person before and after him. Before him, I envisioned heartbreak to be a sort of shattering, but after him, I felt it as a pulsating, oozing wound. It was a bloody, messy open lesion. I don't want this story to be about him, but it is, at least, in part.

I am no stranger to scars. I got my first one when I was three. I had to get a precancerous mole removed from the center of my back. I vaguely remember being held down while I lay on my stomach and crying. I didn't understand what was happening. The plastic surgeon who removed the mole didn't do it properly (he now has a reputation), so I have a deep permanent indentation in the mole's absence. I often refer to this as my "pot-hole scar." The scar, as Clarissa Pinkola Estés writes, is a door.[1] This particular scar is a door to parts unseen. This man liked to place a finger on it.

I met Daniel at the local co-op, but the art teacher we both had in high school formally introduced us later. Daniel was a tattoo artist. He was the bad boy of my dreams—the bad boy I could never get in high school. He was seven years older than me, so we never knew each other in school. At five foot six inches, he was short and muscular with dark short hair and dark brown eyes. I pursued him. I would make sure to be in his check-out lane at the co-op and one day was brazen enough to ask for his number. I initiated the flirting through texting. Eventually, he asked me out. We had a drink at a bar and went to see "Gravity," the space movie starring Sandra Bullock and George Clooney. He walked me to my car and didn't kiss me, but I had hoped he would try. After he cooked dinner for us at his place on our third date, we were sitting on his couch with the tv on in the background. He asked if he could kiss me. I tried to smile meekly to contain my excitement. I said yes. Daniel was sweet, charming, and kind. He had a boyish quality to him that made him fun, but also a bit dangerous. His personality was not great for someone like myself who had trauma and an anxious attachment style, but I liked that I could lose myself in him. I didn't know how dangerous that would end up being. I fell in love with him almost immediately. Before him, I had never loved anyone as intensely. It simultaneously felt like breathing and drowning. My lungs nearly sprinted out of my chest. The butterflies in my belly fluttered daily, not even stopping to rest as I slept.

I had very low, if any, standards at this time. The last long-term relationship I had was in my early twenties in college. I had countless situationships, but nothing concrete, nothing as hypnotizing as this. The fact that Daniel treated me with kindness and desired me was more than I could hope for. He wasn't great at making plans or texting me back. I didn't care—I was already tangled up in him. I lapped up every word, every glance, every touch. I began to make a home in him. However, as the poet Warsan Shire writes, "You can't make homes out

---

1   Clarissa Pinkola Estés, *Women Who Run With The Wolves: Myths and Stories of the Wild Woman Archetype*, (London, UK: Rider, 2022), 19.

of human beings."[2]

Unfortunately, I knew early on that the relationship was not a good one, but I didn't want to stop the feeling of love—mine or his. I wanted to stay in this place for a while—stretch into it, hold onto it. However, on a grey October day, only the second month of dating, Daniel sexually assaulted me. This was the second time in my life that I had been assaulted (the first, a drunken night when I was eighteen). This time, I was also under the influence. Daniel knew about my previous assault. I had discussed it with him prior, and said I needed to feel safe with whomever I was with in order to drink or smoke weed. I felt safe with him—a safety that I hadn't felt for a long time—a safety I desperately wanted to be real.

We were both high, although I was much more sensitive to weed (and any drug) compared to him. We began kissing, slow and long— the kind of kiss that makes your entire body bend and quake with pleasure. We were making out on his couch, our clothes a pile on the floor. He kissed the scar on my back. His eyes were kind and dark. It was enjoyable and sexy. He smelled of autumn—woodsy with a hint of cinnamon. I drifted off deeper into his scent. Then he was on top of me. Then he was inside of me without a condom—something that he knew was not allowed. I didn't have my IUD yet and I was extremely anxious about accidental pregnancies. I started to cry. I couldn't physically push him off of me, which made me cry more. The weed weighed me down deeper into the couch. I felt a paralysis I hadn't known before. Daniel eventually stopped. Through tears, I apologized to him for ruining the mood. He left the room to grab a drink in the kitchen. I was alone, naked and crying. I slowly grabbed my clothes and went to the bathroom to get dressed and try to calm down. I spent the rest of the afternoon asking for his reassurance that he still wanted to be with me. I kept thinking I was incredibly fucked up. I didn't even tell anyone what had happened. If I did say anything, it was: "I think I had a bad trip." I blamed the weed and my low tolerance instead of him. I wanted to convince myself that what happened didn't happen. I wanted to continue dating this man I loved. I didn't want to think he could hurt me like he did. I didn't want to believe he could do that

---

2   Warsan Shire, *Teaching My Mother How to Give Birth*, (United Kingdom: Mouthmark, 2011).

to anyone. If I would have told someone what actually happened, the mirror they would have held up to me would have made me see too clearly. I would have shattered. I would have ended it. I'll never know for sure, though.

That December, Daniel tattooed me. I had wanted to get a large arm tattoo of Joan of Arc in the traditional style, a la Dutch tattoo artist and painter, Angelique Houtkamp. He designed and tattooed a gorgeous rendition of Joan. He would have given me the "girlfriend discount" and done it for free, but I insisted on paying for it. I didn't want it to be a gift, especially if we were to ever break up. On December twelfth, Daniel told me he loved me. It was my birthday and we were seated at a big table with my friends at a restaurant downtown. He was drunk and quickly said into my ear, "I love you." I looked into his eyes, not knowing if he was kidding. For years, I had thought most people lied to me when they told me they loved me or even liked me. His eyes were red and glossy. I forced a smile. I didn't know whether to feel happy or sad. The next morning I asked if he remembered what he said to me. He said, "Of course! I love you." That made it all okay. However, just a few weeks later, he texted to say he needed some time and space. I should have ended the relationship then. I should have killed the butterflies in my belly. I should have let him go. I would have been spared from even more grief.

After New Year's, Daniel texted me, "I miss you." I was so happy to hear from him. He wanted to see me as soon as possible. I went to his apartment and he embraced me passionately. It was like we never took a break from each other. His smell, his voice returned me to him. We were back on track. I thought perhaps the break was good. He seemed more sure about me, more thoughtful. There was still a small voice in my head that kept saying, "be careful," but I ignored her. I ignored most of my instincts when I was with him and I think he knew this.

In late March, I was diagnosed with herpes. I thought of the sexual assault, and felt disgusted in myself for still being with Daniel, but I certainly couldn't leave him now. I thought about how he nearly ended things in late December, but then came back, and how I could have gotten out of the relationship without the herpes of it all. I didn't identify what he did to me as sexual assault when it happened nor when I got my herpes diagnosis. I couldn't, because that would bring with it too much heaviness—a meaty, ugly thing that I couldn't process. I still didn't want to lose him. I still didn't want to believe he could hurt me the way he did—in any of the ways he did.

When I found my first herpes outbreak: a single blister-like sore above the entrance to my vagina, I was scared and confused. The pain of this tiny thing was agonizing. I could barely walk or pee. The sore was unlike anything I had seen on my body before. As someone who had struggled deeply with health anxiety and sensory processing disorder, I was used to over analyzing every section, every crevice of my body for cuts, scrapes, bruises, injuries—anything that may need further attention. This behavior, called Body Checking, is associated with OCD and was as familiar to me as breathing. On a good day, my body was something I could ignore—something I just happened to walk around in. I didn't poke and prod at it. I didn't notice each sensation or each random bruise or cut. My body hadn't been my own for a long time—and that was fine with me at the time. When I found the herpes sore, I was startled and in shock. It looked like an open wound with a deep red that was captivating. I didn't want to look at it, and yet, I wanted to look at it all the time. My health anxiety forced me to have one foot in the present and one foot in the past at all times. Poet Sophie Strand writes about pain keeping us present saying:

In moments of extreme pain, physical or psychological, we become stitched to the present moment. It becomes impossible not to be radically present. We can no longer count on a future. And our bright-minded, able-bodied pasts don't feel like they belong to us anymore. Often the pain is so intense that there is no escape in any direction.

I was used to feeling this internal paralysis. I was used to my futures disappearing. I made an appointment with my gynecologist for the following day. I was hoping this sore was nothing, but I knew better.

As I lay with my legs in the familiar stirrups, my doctor swabbed the sore. I winced, but it was over quickly. She told me to get dressed and that they should be able to tell me the results very soon. My doctor left the room and I slowly got off the table, put my clothes on, and sat down in a chair. The wait felt excruciating. I lost all sense of time. I was left with my thoughts about Daniel, my health, and what I was going to do next. Finally, there was a knock at the door. My doctor sat down across from me and told me, "The swab came back positive for genital herpes, type 1." I couldn't breathe. I started crying. My brain was unable to process what she just said. A loud swirl of thoughts took over, "Am I different now? What am I going to do? I knew I was unhealthy!" I began to feel irrationally angry at my doctor, sitting there with her impeccable blonde bob haircut. I envisioned her perfect little life that probably didn't include herpes or a partner who had assaulted her. I was angry at the messenger. I was angry at the world. I asked through sobs, "How!?" I knew nothing about herpes—just that it was incurable; just that if you were going to get an STI, this was one of few to try your damndest not to get. My doctor talked to me about it, printed off some medical information, wrote me a prescription for Valtrex, and sent me on my way.

I was confused by my diagnosis. I did everything "right" when it came to sex (or so I thought). I got tested for STI's annually. My partners always wore condoms. I had open and, as far as I knew, honest conversations with partners about sexual health. My feminism had supplied me with the understanding that everyone is worthy of love and pleasure, and yet, here I was convinced that my life was probably over. I only knew people who had oral herpes (cold sores), and that was considered not a big deal compared to the kind I had.

My doctor informed me that a standard STI[3] panel doesn't include a herpes test. She explained that most doctors don't like to test for it unless a patient has a visible sore that can be swabbed. Blood testing is not recommended due to potential false positives, and for the possibility that a person might have herpes, but might never have an outbreak. I understood that people could contract herpes from unprotected sex, but I didn't know there was still the possibility to contract it when using a condom. I also learned that there are two types. HSV-1 is typically referred to as oral herpes (or cold sores), whereas HSV-2 is called genital herpes. However, you can contract HSV-1 genitally by

---

3   AUTHOR'S NOTE: I use "STI" instead of "STD" because the former is more correct and carries less stigma

receiving oral sex from someone with oral herpes (like I did), or more rarely, from unprotected vaginal sex.

I filled my prescription for Valtrex the same day. The typical regimen is to take quite a bit of this medication during the primary outbreak. Perhaps you've seen the commercials about this drug: a woman talking about how great her life is now that she's taking an intense antiviral medication; couples frolicking while cheesy easy listening music plays. The commercial has you thinking: "Maybe life *is* actually better with herpes!" I didn't feel like frolicking the first time I took Valtrex. It made me so tired I could barely keep my eyes open. Though, the fatigue was a welcome reprieve from the intense anxiety I was feeling.

The diagnosis left me feeling dirty, ashamed, and ugly. The worst thing about herpes is the stigma—and it's everywhere. The same, tired "jokes" are told incessantly: "herpes is the glitter of the craftworld" or "Love isn't forever, but herpes is." People tend to joke about things they don't understand or things they're uncomfortable with, and people are *very* uncomfortable with herpes, and STIs in general. If a person has oral herpes, they can refer to them as "cold sores." In fact, many doctors don't even advise disclosing oral herpes to sexual partners, since oral herpes was initially thought to only be contracted non-sexually. Typically, children get oral herpes when an adult with oral herpes kisses them on the lips. Because it was thought to never be sexually contracted, oral herpes is considered morally "better." Since I contracted herpes sexually, I'm a "slut," "whore," and "tramp." Those of us with vaginas have started contracting herpes type 1 genitally more frequently in the last decade. The intensity of herpes stigma is why conversations about safer sex don't happen. People are too embarrassed to talk about it, even though a majority have at least one type.

As if the stigma wasn't awful enough, I also felt like a horrible girlfriend. I was sure it was somehow my fault. In fact, my initial concern was, "What if Daniel thinks I cheated?" He knew I was going to my doctor. He knew what I had found on my body. He told me to keep him updated. After the doctor's appointment, I went to the co-op where he worked, probably not the best idea, but I didn't want to be alone in this any longer. Red-faced and bleary-eyed, I approached him while he was putting out fresh produce. His smile quickly shifted, and he said: "I have a break in ten. Go to my place and I'll meet you there." He lived very close to the store, so he was often able to go back to his place for his breaks. Sitting alone in his apartment, I wondered: "Is this it? Is this how our relationship dies?" When he got home, I started crying again. I told him what had happened:

"I have herpes, and I don't know how."

"It's okay. We'll be okay."

"Do you have herpes? Have you been with anyone who has?"

"No. I don't have it, and I've never been with anyone who has—as far as I know."

He held me as I cried. He told me he loved me. I looked out the window at the blue sky and felt like everything might be okay. Maybe this was bringing us closer.

Finding out I had herpes heightened my insecurities as a partner and sexual person. I was consumed with so much guilt and shame that I gave Daniel a sleepy blow job while I was still recovering from my first outbreak. I was weary from the Valtrex, but wanted to make sure he still desired me. Once the herpes sore became a faded scar, we began having sex again. We used condoms a couple of times, but then went back to no condoms. I had an IUD and Daniel didn't seem concerned about my herpes. I thought this was a good sign. It provided reassurance that I was still sexy and worthy. I thought everything was returning to normal.

It was now May, and I hadn't seen Daniel all week. He said this was because his older brother was in town. Daniel seemed a bit distant—physically and emotionally. At one point, I texted him while walking to my car from work asking, "Do you still love me?" He responded back immediately, "Of course!" with a kissy face emoji. I sensed something was different. I *knew* something was different, because I wouldn't have asked him if he still loved me otherwise. He made plans to see me over the weekend. On a particularly warm Saturday, I wore my favorite Betsy Johnson dress—a short, black lace floral number. I excitedly headed to Daniel's apartment.

He broke up with me on the couch where he assaulted me while shoving a Taco Bell burrito into his mouth. After dating for seven months, he said he didn't have the time for a relationship. I was con-fused, but knew I should have listened to my gut. I looked at him crazed with disbelief. He attempted to smooth away my tears with his Taco Bell-laced fingers. I stopped him and said through shaky sobs: "I... can't... believe... this..." Through my tears, I yelled, "I have herpes! What am I supposed to do now?!" I got up to leave. He seemed angry and followed me out the door. He got in his truck and sped off. I got in my hand-me-down green Toyota Rav-4, and drove to my dad's house nearby. My dad was a wreck by how much of a wreck I was. He waved a bottle of water in my face as if hydration would help anything at that moment. I told him what happened, and he hugged me and let me convulsively cry. I drove home, back to my mom's house. It was now her turn to hold me as I cried. The rest of the day was a blur of tears, hot anger, and an emptiness I had never felt before. My Joan of Arc tattoo suddenly had an enormous, red pimple right on her nose. My mom commented, "She's mad at him."

A week later, before I headed to work, Daniel messaged me on Facebook saying he missed me. I was again confused and angry. Yet, I wrote back, "I miss you, too." I asked him if he cheated on me. He emphatically denied it saying, "No, I would never ever do that. I'm not that type of person." He told me he still loved me. I told him that didn't seem to be the case. Daniel responded: "You'll understand it when you're older."

A few months after the breakup, I found out through a friend of a friend that Daniel had, in fact, cheated on me for at least two months. While he sat with my parents and I for Easter brunch, he was cheating on me with a 21-year-old bartender. I also found out he had been in an active addiction, using coke—a lot of it. I had no idea, and felt in-credibly stupid and even more wounded. I now had two reminders of my ex: my tattoo of Joan of Arc and an incurable virus. Two wounds with two ecosystems of heartbreak. With each outbreak, I would imag-ine Daniel saying with a Cheshire Cat smile, "You'll never get rid of me." He branded me and every lover after will know about him. I was haunted by him. I lived in a body haunted by men. I was now also haunted by my new health condition.

I ended up sending a Facebook friend request to the woman

Daniel cheated on me with because I wanted her to see my incoming message. This was not to project my anger onto her. Everyone always blames the "other woman," and rarely the man at the center of it all. I wanted to offer some camaraderie, some compassion. I didn't even have to tell her about the herpes, because the friend of a friend who knew her had told her (even though that wasn't this person's information to tell). I felt sorry for the "other woman." I found out that Daniel had lied to her about being single. He went for her because she had money and material possessions that he later sold for money for coke. In my message to her I said: "I'm sorry Daniel hurt you. He hurt me, too." I wasn't sure what I expected. She blocked me as soon as she received the message.

I wanted to help this 21-year-old woman; this baby who was intoxicated by a then 36-year-old man who had his shit together from the outside. I felt immense compassion for her. I don't know why. Maybe it was just because this man fucked me, and then went and fucked her, and vice versa. Maybe I felt her there still lingering. People rarely have compassion for "the other woman." She is to be hated. But how could I hate someone who was also being lied to? If I'm going to hate anyone, it's him. He broke my trust. He broke it all. She was just along for the coke-fueled ride.

Minutes after I messaged this woman, I received a threatening text from Daniel, which made my heart jump and my belly nauseous. Clearly the other woman told him. He said, "Don't talk to my friends. Stay clear." He meant, "steer" instead of "stay," but regardless his point was made. I texted him back: "I really, really, really hope you get the help you need for your addiction. I'm sorry you felt the need to cheat on me with her for all of April. And don't worry, I won't try to friend request any more your friends. I want nothing to do with you. I hope you get help before you hurt anyone else or yourself." I waited. No response. Then I blocked him from all forms of communication.

For a long time after the breakup, I was sure the cheating and the herpes were my punishment for having had an on again/off again affair with a married man. Even though I wasn't the one who initiated it, and I never interacted with him when I was in a relationship with someone, I couldn't shake the idea that karma had come for me in an abundant way. I spent a lot of time feeling bad for myself asking, "why me?" After the breakup, people kept saying the wrong things to me, both in person and online. Some asked: "What is it like having a tattoo from him? I would feel awful!" Others asked, "Are you going to get the tattoo removed? I would." These questions and the judgment angered me. They assumed I only wanted the tattoo because of him. They assumed I must hate myself because I have a permanent marking from someone who treated me so poorly. I told people over and over: "I had been thinking about getting this for over a year before we met. He gave me the opportunity." Even if this wasn't my reasoning, would it matter? Why? To whom? I tried to understand what had happened to my life. In the meantime, I kept hearing about what my ex was up to and I kept seeing him around town. Seven months after he dumped me, he got married.

I was single and the dust had settled from the breakup, and I did what I normally do in moments where I feel like I don't understand anything: I researched everything I could about genital herpes. At the time, I didn't have any close friends who knew they had it. There was no one I could talk to. I immediately found #Herpblr, the herpes community on Tumblr. Most of the people writing and commenting were much younger than me. Many talked about feeling suicidal after their diagnosis. I felt a kinship with these people I found online. We never shared real names, but they were there for me and I was there for them. People posted about the diy balms they made to put on their sores (typically a mix of coconut oil and tea tree oil). They talked about how they disclosed their herpes-positive status with new partners, and how these disclosures got easier over time. I also came across Ella Dawson, a sex and culture critic who has herpes. She did a TEDX talk titled, "STIs aren't a consequence. They're inevitable." Finding Dawson's work was incredibly helpful and healing for me. I learned more from her and #Herpblr about sexual health than I ever learned in sex ed classes. As a sex ed student in the 90s and early aughts, I was taught how *not* to get an STI, but nothing about how to live with one. No wonder people become suicidal after an incurable STI diagnosis. Most of us were probably taught some variation of "there is no life to live after that."

What I remember most about my first year with herpes was the obsessiveness with which I would check my vulva. Already a pro at Body Checking, vulva checking became constant. Anytime I was naked, I got up close and personal with this part of my body. Sometimes I would need a hand mirror to do a full inspection. I poked, prodded, and spread my skin every which way I could. It was exhausting, and not how I wanted to be in relationship to my body. I became anxious and afraid of getting another outbreak, even after my fifth one. The fear never dissipated. I kept cursing my abusive ex. I'm sure a part of me was hoping it was all a bad dream. I was still getting used to this new medical condition. I was still adjusting to the fracture it created in my reality.

After reading everything I could on herpes and realizing how many people actually have it, I began to feel better about it. At the most, it's a skin irritation that occurs infrequently. It wasn't going to define me; it shouldn't define anyone. Arming myself with facts increased my confidence. I didn't feel ashamed anymore. I didn't feel dirty. Even my doctor said the worst thing about herpes is the stigma, not the virus. Eventually, I started to write publicly in online spaces like *Guerrilla Feminism*, as well as for other media outlets about having herpes and how to disclose an STI-postive status to partners. I was tired of feeling ashamed and embarrassed for things that happened to me that were beyond my control.

In April of 2016, I co-created the hashtag, #ShoutYourStatus for STI Awareness Month with Kayla Axelrod, Ella Dawson, Frankie de la Cretaz. #ShoutYourStatus came about from a conversation the four of us had regarding STI stigma and shame. We are all HSV positive, and since being diagnosed, we all have encountered jokes, harassment, misinformation/miseducation, and more. I was interested in co-creating this hashtag, because it became abundantly clear to me that most people don't know anything about STIs, but specifically about herpes. Through the creation and use of this hashtag, all of us were harassed daily. As a woman online, I am somewhat used to this. Nearly all of the trolling happening within the tag was from uneducated people, including a lot of incels and MRAs.[4] Many continuously tweeted at me to "USE CONDOMS, WHORE!" One woman used a Bea Arthur gif

---

4   AUTHOR'S NOTE: Men's Rights Activists.

from one of my favorite "Golden Girls" episodes that showed Bea Arthur's character exclaiming: "CONDOMS, CONDOMS, CONDOMS!" This person failed to understand that condoms are not one hundred percent effective at preventing STIs, especially HPV and herpes. Then, there were the trolls telling me what a "loose" woman I must be to have contracted an incurable STI. Again, such terribly uneducated souls. You can get an STI from sleeping with *one* person. It was enlightening to see how quickly MRAs could take a hashtag that was meant to empower and instead muddy it. At the time, there were at least four articles that popped up discussing how feminists are now "proud" of having STIs because of our hashtag. The idea that those of us who have STIs should be ashamed comes from a misogynist, sexist place.

People called me "brave" a lot during this time, specifically for sharing about having been raped four times and for having herpes; brave for sharing such enormous "shame," I suppose. It started to grate at me (still does). Bravery has nothing to do with it. Naming it "brave" contributes to the stigma. It also assumes that those who don't share publicly about these things are somehow not brave. I've received hundreds of private messages from well-meaning followers who have said things like, "Wow, you're so brave to say that publicly. I could never do that." It feels like a backhanded compliment. The stories of the things I've experienced are not brave, and I am not brave for speaking about them publicly. When we read others' stories online, we may often deal with the onset of uncomfortable feelings. Often, our *own* shame around something is projected onto the person sharing the story. This comes out by way of comments like, "You're so brave."

I started dating again. I realized I was still worthy of love. I was still worthy of good, pleasurable sex. If someone didn't want to hang out with me or have sex with me because of herpes, they were not someone I wanted. I know there are people who choose to not disclose their STI-positive status, but I could never do that. It became another way for me to build trust in a relationship—even if the relationship was going to be short-lived. I could never take away someone's choice. I had been so accustomed to my own consent being stripped from me to ever consider doing that to another person. Consent was important to me. The first few times I disclosed, I'm sure I was awkward. I leaned heavily into the tired narrative of girl-was-super-in-love/girl-got-cheated-on/girl-got-herpes. I wanted my partners to know it wasn't my fault. I couldn't have prevented it—unless I was abstinent. After reading more from unashamed STI-positive people online, I finally understood that it doesn't matter *how* someone contracts herpes. The *how* is typically the same for all of us: we had sex. Sure, there are variations within that, but the meat of it is the same. I am not somehow morally "better" for getting herpes the way I did. If I would have gotten it from a one-night-stand or from sleeping with several different people, it wouldn't matter. STIs are an inherent risk when having sex—for all of us. Any type of sex is risky, falling in love is risky. We get to decide which risks we're willing to take. In an article by social psychologist and author, Dr. Devon Price, he writes:

> Life is nothing but a negotiation of risk. If a person has gender dysphoria and they want to combat it, they must risk a transition they could one day regret. If an abolitionist wants to take a stand against the police state, they must plan for the possibility of arrest or political repression. When we open our hearts to love, we expose ourselves to grief—our partners will keep changing and growing, sometimes away from us. Each step that we take forward in life closes off potential paths. There is no avoiding this. Instead of chasing after the false promise of "safety," trying to remain completely insulated from harm and challenge forever, we must get better at admitting risk into our lives.[5]

Getting diagnosed with herpes helped me become better acquainted with my own relationship to risk and safety. I had done "everything right" and still managed to get one of few incurable STIs. This diagnosis was a reminder that anything can happen at any time and that I can't live my life with the sole purpose of avoiding risk, harm, or pain.

During this time, I became really good at disclosing. I disclosed in various places: in the car, at a date's apartment, at my apartment, on the phone, via text. It was important for me to disclose where I felt safe and confident, so I could be fully vulnerable. I would make sure I had an exit strategy in case the interaction quickly deteriorated into aggression from my date. It was unfortunate that I thought this way, but I was already used to it from just being a woman who dates men. I was familiar with attempting to prevent men's violence on my body.

5   Devon Price, "There is no safe sex. There is no safe life," August 15, 2024, https://drdevonprice.substack.com/p/there-is-no-safe-sex-there-is-no.

I found it best to disclose on my own turf (at my apartment), so I have more control of my environment. I never liked disclosing in public spaces (restaurant, coffee shop, bar, sidewalk), because it felt more cumbersome with zero privacy. I wanted to be able to express myself freely, and I wanted my partner/s to be able to do the same. They may have a ton of questions or they may be silent. Either way, it felt more helpful to have this conversation in a private, quiet, safe space. After disclosing to new partners, I expected them to flinch, gawk, or ask me to leave, but that never happened. Instead I was met with sympathy, curiosity, nonchalance, and, every so often, "me too." After the few people who disclosed that they, too, had herpes, I wondered if they would have disclosed at all had I not done so first. Speaking about herpes made me feel stronger the more I did it. It made my confidence bloom.

I'm often asked when to disclose an STI-positive status. I have my own rules about this. There are times that are definitely not good to disclose an STI status to a date. The main one being right before you engage in sexual activity. If someone has oral herpes, they should disclose this before they kiss their partner on the mouth. If a person has genital herpes, HPV, or HIV, then disclosing before any type of sex happens (fingering, oral sex, vaginal sex, anal sex) is imperative. I've disclosed via text message when the topic of sex came up saying, "Hey, by the way I have herpes. It's not a big deal, and I'm happy to answer any questions you might have." I've disclosed in person by starting with, "So, tell me about your sexual health history. Have you ever had an STI or do you have one currently?" I prefer to disclose in person, because I like to see the person's immediate reaction, even though this can be scary. I've disclosed on the first date and on the fifth date. It really depends on how I'm feeling about the situation (and how soon I want to have sex). Some people like to get it over with quickly, while others like to wait. Neither way is wrong.

There have been a few times where I felt I had to disclose on the first date, because, for example, one man made a herpes joke. I could have let it slide, or laughed along with him, but I didn't feel like contributing to my own marginalization and oppression. I don't remember the beginning of the "joke," but it ended with, "...and that's how you get something like herpes!" I felt comfortable and safe enough with him to call him out right then and there. I said: "Hey, that's not funny. I have herpes. It's really not a big deal." He ended up feeling bad, and apologized profusely. Later, we had sex.

Contracting herpes—or any STI—is not the end of the world. You will date again. You will have sex again. The virus may change you, but you'll become even more aware of your body and its inner workings. Most people who have herpes know when they have an outbreak coming on. We can then make sure to abstain from sexual activity during this time. It's actually safer to sleep with someone who knows their status compared to someone who doesn't. The majority of the time, the person who doesn't have herpes is not going to contract it, so long as the person who has it knows and listens to their body.

I spent a long time—too long—looking for closure outside of myself for that bruise-colored relationship. I used to fantasize about my ex groveling at my feet apologizing to me. I could almost envision the depth of anguish and atonement in his eyes. I lost sleep as I continued to envision this very specific idea of closure that my sadness and hurt had birthed. Several months after our breakup, I got another tattoo. This one is on the back of Joan, on my inner bicep. It reads: *"si viju lu diavulu non schiantu."* It's in Calabrese—the Italian dialect of my ancestors. It's from a traditional Calabrese women's folk song and translates to: *"If I see the devil, I do not run."* The placement and the saying were deliberate. I saw the devil, wrestled with him, was branded by him, and came out alive. I am forever grateful for my strength and vulnerability. I am forever grateful for my resilience. This felt like closure. This felt like all I needed.

At some point, I wanted to get my Joan of Arc tattoo touched up. The colors had faded. For a long time, people would ask me, "Doesn't it suck having a tattoo that your shitty ex did on you?" That question used to feel so heavy, but I would tell them, "I created this tattoo. I bought this tattoo. I refuse to hate any part of my body because of a man who didn't treat me well." I still felt bugged by the fact that Daniel's steady hands had been the last to ink that arm. I decided to get it re-done; to wash Daniel off of me. I found a woman tattoo artist in Chicago for the occasion. She made Joan look even more beautiful, coloring over some areas with more vibrancy than my ex had. During the touch up, I envisioned Daniel and all of his energy leaving my body. I was still me. This was still *my* body. This was still *my* skin. Daniel didn't live, or love, here anymore. The loss of that home, that seashell, was painful, but losing it pulled me back to my own.

Daniel and the woman he married recently got divorced and there are charges of domestic violence against him. I only know this because I keep tabs on him. Knowing he's alive scares me. Knowing he now lives five minutes away from me feels cruel. He has children. Daniel and I had talked about marriage and having kids. He said he wanted both with me. I consider how this was almost my life. How close I was to more abuse, more fear. I shiver thinking about what could have been—how much worse things could have gotten. Getting herpes from him doesn't seem that bad afterall.

Herpes is an infection that lives in the body forever, but it's less disruptive the longer a person has it. It's a chronic illness, judged more harshly than others because of its associated with sex. It's not good or bad, and it doesn't make a person good or bad, either. It's just a fact of life, a fact of the inherent risk of love and sex. The little volcanoes come and go. They don't scare or scar me anymore. My body might be haunted by Daniel, but my body is haunted by anyone it's come into contact with. How could it not be? My body is an archive of ghosts. I continue to learn how to live amongst them. It's getting easier.

Chapter Four

THE GAMIFICATION OF LOVE AND SEX

There is no hell but the one of memory so what could kill me now?

—CAMONGHNE FELIX

MEN LIKE TO EXPERIENCE ME. They want to fuck me because I'm loud and brash with hips like crescent moons. I have become used to their taking from me, their excavation, and their eventual abandonment after they've licked my bones clean. The song "Outta Me" by Bikini Kill, especially the last verse, plays in my head:

And now I am quite sure you want
Everything, everything, everything, everything
Everything, everything, everything, everything
Outta me

Every man I've ever loved seemed to want everything out of me. I'm an amalgamation of all of them. Maybe it's my Cancer rising, maybe it's remnants of my pockmarked childhood, but ever since I can remember, I have been looking to be discovered, healed, rescued, and I've mostly tried to find these things in the men I've dated. I looked for discovery, but found myself objectified. I looked for healing where instead I found harm. I looked for rescuing, but was endangered instead. No one can save me, but me.

I have been on and off dating apps since I was 23. My online dating experience has been prolific with many made-for-*Lifetime* movie stories. I initially got on dating sites when I moved to Chicago for my first grad school program. I didn't know many people, and thought it would be fun to try online dating. Online dating was still fairly new at the time. I didn't have a smartphone and there weren't apps yet, so I joined OkCupid on their website. I spent far too much time taking personality quizzes that would then show what percentage of compatibility I had with others. I spent an embarrassing amount of time crafting my profile. I agonized over whether to say I had disabilities and that I was neurodivergent. Was I being deceptive if I didn't? In the end, I opted not to. It had been my experience that the "disability conversation" was better in person—most of the time. In *Dateable: Swiping Right, Hooking Up, and Settling Down While Chronically Ill and Disabled* by Jessica Slice and Caroline Cupp write, "Disability adds another layer of complication to the intrinsic vulnerability of dating. There are concrete accessibility issues, of course, but also the mantle of 'otherness' that many of us who were born or came of age with disabilities have assumed since childhood."[1] I was still longing to be desired despite my disabilities. I hadn't yet awakened to my radical disability politic. I still did a heavy amount of *masking* in order to appear neurotypical. If I was paying for the meal, I tried to keep up a conversation while calculating the amount of tip to leave. I didn't want my date to see me working hard to do "simple" addition in my head. I tried not to show myself using *TouchMath*®, where I physically put a touch point on certain spots on the numbers. So, on the number "5," I see five "touch points." On "2," there are two touch points, and so on. This is the only way I can do addition due to my dyscalculia. I felt like I covered up my secrets well.

The amount of times I had a significant vulnerability hangover from a date or dates was too many. It's not that I shared everything on the first date, but I also always felt a gnawing internal fear of "What if they find out about this before I've told them?" This fear increased after I gained an online following and began writing for various publications. I was highly Google-able. My name was too unique. I had no anonymity.

The years I lived in Chicago—four total—are filled with countless first (and last) dates, disappointing hookups, and situations that

---

1   Jessica Slice and Caroline Cupp, *Dateable: Swiping Right, Hooking Up, and Settling Down While Chronically Ill and Disabled* (New York, NY: Hachette Go, 2024), 2.

I'm thankful I got out of alive. This is not hyperbole—I dated, unbeknownst to me at the time—some very unsafe and scary people. I made out with one guy I met from OkCupid behind a bar in Wicker Park, and he wanted to come home with me, but I said no. I looked him up online when I got home only to find that there was a "WANTED" poster out for his arrest due to a violent incident (SIDE NOTE: fuck the police, fuck carcerality—that being said, I will never not be terrified when I read about a white man's penchant for violence against women). Another date that I met for a drink asked me a typical first date question, "When's the last time you had sex?" (This is not, nor should it be, a typical first date question). I answered because I didn't care, and told him I was in a "situationship" with someone, but I had wanted out of it. The man replied, "You sound like a whore." I sat up straight and chugged my gin and tonic. He found our waitress and said, "Check please." I said, "Thanks for the drink," and got up to leave. He yelled after me, "Yeah, get the fuck out of here!" I ran home weightless and sloshy from the alcohol hoping he wasn't following me. In another dating experience, I had a two-month fling with a woman twenty years my senior from work who wanted me to move in on the second date (a true blue "U-Haul" lesbian in the wild). I was all over the place. I was restless. I was looking for love in all the wrong people.

I would often have at least two dates each weekend. Early on, my best friend (and roommate at the time) Audrey would accompany me to a cafe that I would meet a date. She would sit in the background until I gave her a hidden "all clear" sign. Before other dates, I would leave the guy's name and number with Audrey (as well as my friend Anju who was living in San Francisco at the time) in case I went missing. This is just what women must do when single and trying to date. I would get a free meal (and drinks) out of it at the very least. I always felt I needed to give something back in return. The transactional sex I had during this time was never for my benefit or pleasure. I was treated as a hypersexual slut, which wasn't necessarily incorrect, but I resented the men who thought I was easy. I started to think maybe I should start charging.

For a long time I was anti-sex work and anti-porn. I read many essays by the "radical" anti-pornography/anti-sex work feminist Andrea Dworkin early on. Her work formed much of my initial thinking about sex work, unfortunately. It wasn't until my grad program in Women's & Gender Studies that I started to read things by and about sex workers. I began questioning Dworkin's rigid line of thinking. Charlotte Shane, a former sex worker and writer says about the feminist anti-sex work position:

> The end point is men using women's bodies for their own sexual pleasure, violently or at least callously. *Men consume, women are consumed.* This engineered universe circumvents consent by erasing the possibility of no; men are never confronted with denial of sexual gratification because there are endless outlets through which they can purchase it. Money, the story goes, gives the men irrevocable sexual license.[2]

Women are always thought of as the ones who are consumed, never the ones who are doing the consuming. This lack of agency and autonomy is dangerous and undermining. There have been countless times where I have felt consumed by men that were fucking me. I mistook consumption for passion. I wasn't really there. I didn't think about my own pleasure. I didn't experience this in the sex work I did, though. Perhaps my feelings would have been different if I engaged in offline sex work. We're all in the act of consuming each other at different times throughout life.

I was a cam girl and also a findom (financial dominant) briefly. As a poor grad student I needed money, but I also liked the attention. It's important and necessary for me to note that the form of sex work I did was by choice, not survival. It's also important to say that the sex work I did was only online. Though all forms of sex work come with risks, doing this work online versus in person allowed me more protection than an escort might have. Furthermore, I had no bad experiences from sex work and it was the one job I had where I felt the most respected and autonomous.

This private corner of my life helped me take back some of the power I had lost in my offline relationships with men. I could be whomever. I wouldn't say it was empowering—I don't find any labor to be empowering—but this work was important to me. Being a for-

---

2   Charlotte Shane, "Men Consume, Women Are Consumed: 15 Thoughts on the Stigma of Sex Work," *Jezebel*, September 1, 2015, https://jezebel.com/men-consume-women-are-consumed-15-thoughts-on-the-sti-1727924956.

mer sex worker has given me a sense of belonging. In the forward to *A Whore's Manifesto: An Anthology of Writing and Artwork by Sex Workers*, poet and former sex worker, Clementine von Radics writes:

> We, this sorority I imagine, are a heterogeneous riot of voices, less a community of women and more a network of cis women, trans women, and non-binary queers who perform a stylized version of womanhood for the gratification of clients-mostly cis, straight men of means. There are of course cis and trans men in the industry too, and non-binary people who performed a stylized boyhood.[3]

I've always felt safe and comfortable amongst sex workers. This "sorority" is life-long and the networks are endless. Getting hundreds of dollars to call men horrible things was intoxicating. I leaned into cis men's stereotypes of feminists. I became their "man-hater" and they ate it up. Were they consuming me or was I consuming them?

My time as a sex worker was quite separate from my pleasure, which for me was a good thing. Doing cam work was easier for me than the findom stuff, and I liked being watched. I liked being in my own space. I liked doing what *I* wanted to do. I continued to keep this part of my life private—not even telling friends at the time. Though I felt I belonged amongst sex workers—many of whom were feminists—I didn't feel this belonging with certain feminists.[4] Even after I had stopped doing this work, I would only covertly mention it in online spaces. I would often allude to it here and there, but I never made a public post proclaiming it. I wasn't embarrassed. I just didn't want my family to know. I also knew I would be rejected by feminists and from feminist spaces. These weren't necessarily people or spaces I wanted to be around, but losing access to anything and the potential for rejection made me nervous. At one point, I was outed by someone who used to work with me on *Guerrilla Feminism*. They were also a sex worker and because of that, I had mentioned to them that I had done sex work in the past. They later used this against me. They tried to say I was a liar. It didn't get much traction, but it scared me and was enough to silence me.

---

3   Clementine von Radics, *A Whore's Manifesto: An Anthology of Writing and Artwork By Sex Workers*, ed. by Kay Kassirer (Portland, OR: Thorntree Press, 2019).

4   AUTHOR'S NOTE: Namely SWERFs (sex worker exclusionary radical feminists).

My sex worker life was completely separate from my offline life where I felt small and desperate for attention from men. Acting as a findom was outside of my own personal sexual interests as a tried and true submissive. In my offline personal life, I only liked being fucked by Doms, or at the very least, those who were aggressive and rough with my body. I was bisexual, but I gravitated towards men. I was still trying to not feel like a "bad feminist" for my sexual submissiveness. I was still early on in my kink education. I wanted hickies and bruises. I wanted tangible things I could see that showed me how much someone liked me, wanted me. I walked around wearing these souvenirs like a pageant queen. In college, I met Gloria Steinem briefly and was assigned to write about her visit for the student newspaper. The picture we took was quick. A friend on the paper had to use Photoshop to erase the hickey on my neck before publication.

In dating, I didn't have standards because I didn't imagine myself worthy of them. I had a "situationship" with a man who showed up drunk to our very first date. In the rain that night, he kissed me abruptly the second he saw me. We began seeing each other off and on. I drove from Chicago to Evanston for dick even though the man attached to said dick treated me like shit. He fucked me roughly and it made me feel wanted, even if it was all pretend. I didn't care that he only ever texted me between the hours of 10pm and 12am. I didn't care that I hid parts of myself so he would barely know my personality. He knew my body, and that was good enough for me. He *wanted* my body, and that was plenty. I didn't really know his personality either. When I pressed him about the status of our "relationship" and whether there was potential for it to be more, he shirked any responsibility he had with my heart. He said to me, "You want too much. *You're* too much." My tears fell like snowflakes, cooling my warm cheeks. I responded with a meek, "I'm sorry." I'm not sure if I was apologizing to him or to myself. This was the same man who had told me months earlier that he never considered a real relationship with me because I slept with him on the first date. Unfortunately, I dated too many men like this. They each meant something to me while I meant nothing to them.

During this situationship, I dated a variety of people. I started seeing a woman who was twenty years older than me. This was my first relationship with a woman. I had messed around with women in the past, but never had a relationship with one. I barely noticed the age difference or the power dynamic installed within it. She wanted all of my time. She wanted me to move into her condo within two weeks of dating. I started to feel smothered, scared, and anxious by how much she seemed to like me. I broke things off and felt like it was brutally unfair that her heart was broken and mine wasn't. I was so used to being the one left; the one with their heart in ashes.

I ended up moving home to Madison after four years of being in Chicago. The job I had, essentially a call center for a tutoring company, fired me due to what they labeled, "personality reasons." I had never been fired before, but it came as sweet relief. I spent the next several months looking for a new job as my money started to drain. I applied to hundreds, maybe even thousands of jobs, but nothing came through. My time in Chicago had come to an end. The only thing that was upsetting about this was the feeling that I couldn't "make it" on my own like other people my age. I wasn't upset about moving home, though. Truthfully, Chicago never felt like home; never felt like something I could rest into. I also felt like I had dated nearly every person available in the Windy City, and none of it was good, so a move seemed positive.

I moved home in the summer of 2012 and immediately was back on OkCupid, and then later Tinder, Bumble, and Hinge when I got a smartphone. The prospect of seeing new faces felt exciting. The first man I met was, unbeknownst to me, out on parole after being released from prison for a domestic violence incident. Then I dated a vegan man with glasses. He was tall and moody and liked good music. After one drunken night downtown, we got slices of pizza as big as our faces. Attempting to be considerate, I asked if he was okay with me getting a slice of pepperoni. He said that was fine. When we got outside, he was silent, brooding. I asked, "What's wrong, babe?" He responded coldly, "I just can't stand the smell of cooked animal flesh." I threw out my pizza when I should have thrown him out instead. I felt like I was incapable of trusting people. I was raised to accept everyone. I was raised with the understanding that people were neither all "bad" nor all "good"—that they were human and their humanity was always complicated.

I've met various people through these apps over the years. I mentioned my feminism in every bio, but learned later how that would be used against me. This usually meant that men expected me to go half on meals or half on everything in the relationship, even if they made more money than I did (which they alway did). I saw some people mention their herpes status. Props to them, but I didn't want that to be the thing that set me apart. At one point, I received an email from the people at Positive Singles, the herpes-only dating site, asking if I would be willing to hawk their product on my Instagram. I declined. I wasn't about to limit myself (or the love I had to give) just because I happened to have herpes (and knew my status). Most people have herpes, they just don't know it. No amount of money was going to make me advertise for segregated dating apps, or any dating apps for that matter.

Dating apps are a problem, but how else can we safely meet people during a global pandemic? The exhaustion I feel from creating accounts, swiping, starting and stopping conversations is enormous. Sarah Jaffe writes, "Dating apps are the gig work of romance, where we are both worker and product. The skills and lifestyles of today's networked, job-hopping worker, in the low- or mid-wage economy, are colossally unsuited to healthy relationships."[5] I am exhausted from being both worker and product. I am exhausted from being both spectator and spectacle. I am exhausted from the capitalism of it all. Perhaps it's also exhausting because three out of the four men who raped me were people I met from Tinder and Bumble.

In my mid to late twenties, I realized how much I liked being someone's "good girl." I may not have grown up with any repressive religious beliefs, but as an adult I moved in circles that constantly said BDSM was "anti-feminist." I knew it wasn't, but I also felt weird about it. I didn't feel like I could be open and honest about being "kinky" with anyone other than my sexual partners. Even then, after I would speak of my predilections, I would often be met with, "Whoa, really? But aren't you a feminist?" I had an inner knowing that my feminism didn't contradict with my sexual interests, but I still felt weird about it. When we decide to judge or policy other people's sex lives, we aren't

---

5   Sarah Jaffe, "This Valentine's Day, Let's Look to Marxists to Reimagine Love, Romance and Sex," *In These Times*, February 13, 2023, https://inthesetimes.com/article/this-valentines-day-lets-look-to-marxists-to-reimagine-love-romance-and-sex.

being feminist. Gayle Rubin, a cultural anthropologist, theorist and activist writes:

> Most people find it difficult to grasp that whatever they like to do sexually will be thoroughly repulsive to someone else, and that whatever repels them sexually will be the most treasured delight of someone, somewhere. One need not like or perform a particular sex act in order to recognize that someone else will, and that this difference does not indicate a lack of good taste, mental health, or intelligence in either party. Most people mistake their sexual preferences for a universal system that will or should work for everyone.[6]

Because of my sexual proclivities, I didn't feel like I belonged in many circles of feminism. In 2013, I wrote a blog post called, "BDSM & Feminism: The Two Can Coexist," and I received a lot of criticism from various feminists online. I resented the comments that I was somehow "contributing" to my own "oppression" by having the kind of sex I wanted to have. I felt gaslit. How was engaging in consensual sexual acts anti-feminist?

I began experimenting with Dom/sub dynamics in relationships/situationships. As a baby sub, I had no idea about "fake Doms" (men who say they're Doms but actually know nothing about enthusiastic consent). I didn't have anyone to ask about this, and even if I did, I would have been too embarrassed. I hadn't yet found feminist pro-BDSM spaces. This is part of why I didn't tell anyone about being sexually assaulted by a man claiming to be a "Dom."

This assault was the most physically violent one I had experienced. I met Jacob on OkCupid. He was tall, conventionally attractive. Jacob was a teaching assistant at the local university getting his PhD in Sociology. He was also doing sexual violence prevention work on campus. We met at Tempest Oyster Bar downtown Madison. I vividly remember the nautical seashell vibe. I got a martini and only drank half of it. Even at that point, I rarely had a drink around strangers—a behavior I started after being assaulted when I was eighteen. Jacob had two martinis. We had a witty banter, laughed about the horrors of grad school, and talked about how ridiculously racist Madison was. He

---

6   Gayle Rubin, "Thinking Sex: Notes for a Radical Theory of the Politics of Sexuality," *Deviations: A Gayle Rubin Reader*, 137—81, (Durham, NC: Duke University Press, 2011), 154.

walked to the bar from his place, not terribly far, but quite a long walk in the below zero Wisconsin cold. I offered to drive him home. I initially was not going to take his offer to "come inside," but when I saw where he lived I changed my mind. He happened to live in the house a boyfriend from two summers ago lived in. I thought, "This is too fucking ridiculous. I can't NOT go inside." Luckily, Jacob was not living in my ex's old room—that would have been far too weird. We walked up the stairs to his bedroom, sat on the floor—he barely had any furniture. It looked like he was just moving in or just about to move out. I sat on the floor. He sat across from me. The owner of the house's cat was purring between us. He moved the cat out of the way to kiss me. It was nice. It was passionate. It got aggressive quickly. We moved to his bed, which was a twin-size air mattress. He rushed to shed me of my clothes. I didn't mind. He stayed clothed, which I remember thinking was a bit odd. He was on top of me. He held me down for a bit, and made out with me. I pushed him away at one point to ask: "So, what are you into? Are you a Dom?" He responded with: "I'm into a lot of things. Yes, I'm Dom, how could you tell?" He laughed sheepishly and responded, "And I know you're a sub." He asked me: "Do you like being slapped?" I thought he meant on my ass. I thought he meant spanking. I said, "Yes, very much so." He held my throat for a moment, and then slapped me hard across the face. This was the first time I had experienced that. I didn't necessarily dislike it, but I didn't like it or want it from him. I didn't know what to do. I didn't know where this was going. I suddenly could not speak, and my body went limp. He slapped my face a few more times. Then he took my underwear off. And he slid his fingers inside. Slow at first, but eventually, quick and hard and painful. He was still fully clothed, kneeling on top of me. I didn't know what to do or how to get away. He noticed I was bleeding, and then stopped. I felt lightheaded.

He said we could keep going, but I lied and said I needed to get home. It was late after all. I just knew I needed to get out of there alive. He flung my bra at me. I must have scoffed at this, because he said: "What? You seem really uncomfortable." Scared and shaken, I said to him: "No, I'm just really tired. That's all. I should go." I put my clothes on, and he walked me downstairs to the front door. He leaned in to kiss me goodbye. As I left, I noticed he still hadn't washed my blood off of his fingers. And then he said to me, "You better believe I'm going to jerk off to you now." His orgasm was my pain.

I texted a good friend afterwards saying I had really aggressive hot sex. I had to lie to myself (and to her) about what really happened because I couldn't process it. A week later, I talked to my mom about it. She gently said, "It sounds like an assault." She was right. I was terrified. At some point, I posted about this experience online. I received a lot of kindness and care. I blamed myself. Months later I walked right past Jacob on campus. He pretended not to know me and I did the same. I felt physically ill afterwards.

After some time and after I had read more about BDSM, I figured out how to gauge whether someone is a *real* Dom or not. Part of the beauty of BDSM is that it's based in enthusiastic consent and care. I now know to have extensive conversations about hard and soft limits prior to engaging in any sexual activity. However, we can know all of the things about BDSM and the person we're sleeping with, and they can still end up hurting us.

Dating apps have not been all terror for me. I did manage to have two two-and-a-half year-long relationships with people I met on Bumble and Tinder. Each time, I felt like I had glitched the algorithm to work in my favor. I had found two amazing humans! Though these relationships ended rather horribly, they taught me a lot.

I have an intensely structured breakup routine. Once a relationship ends (often an hour or less after it happens), I delete all pictures of us on my phone. I unfriend or unfollow on social media platforms. I purge any ephemera I may have received throughout the course of the relationship. Some things take more time to get rid of, especially if they're expensive. One ex gifted me a pair of Frye boots (that I wore twice because the fit was odd), and I had to keep the shoes in their box deep in my closet until I could find someone to take them. When I finally found someone to give them to, my body felt relieved. It was as if I was holding on to a shoebox of his ashes. I've also gotten rid of earrings, an Apple Watch (it was nearly dead anyways), and an Ember Mug (also nearly dead). I can't stand to keep any ephemera from an ex because keeping it continues to connect me to them. It feels cancerous. I prefer a quick severing; a clean cut.

I met Luke on Bumble in late December of 2016. He was nerdy, booksmart, and introverted—very different from past people I dated. I wasn't initially physically attracted to him, but that came later after I fell in love with his personality. He was the first person I was in a relationship with after dating my abusive ex, Daniel. I had zero standards and the fact that Luke was decent to me was all that mattered. I settled for crumbs, because I didn't know I could demand more for myself. Our sex life was timid and kind. Luke and I had various problems, but nothing I didn't think we could work on. Right before we were potentially slated to move in together out of state, he called me. I hadn't heard from him all day, which was odd. He said, in what felt like a stream of consciousness, "Hi, I don't want to marry you. When I think about living with you, I don't feel excited." I was taken aback. At the time, I was driving to the gym to workout. I immediately turned my car around as I felt the tightness in my chest followed by tears. I was so thoroughly disoriented and confused by what he was saying. We had only ever talked about marriage in an abstract way—nothing to suggest we were at all close to making a decision either way. He started to cry after he heard me crying. I asked him what was going on. He couldn't (or wouldn't) tell me. I told him, "Well, I'm not going to break up with myself for you, so you need to do it." Finally, he said, "Okay, I guess I think we should break up."

We hung up and then I started to worry about his mental health and whether he was suicidal. He had been dealing with depression and had been suicidal in the past. He pushed all of his friends away, and now he was pushing me away. I called him back, because I was concerned he might hurt himself. I asked him if he was safe; if he was okay. He assured me he was. I spent exactly two days mourning this relationship. Not because I had a deadline for myself, but because that's all the time I needed. I felt waves of relief wash over me after that phone call with Luke. I was no longer tasked with carrying all of his heavy emotions or attempting to get him to open up to me. I was glad it was over.

I was on the dating apps a week later and came across my ex. The audacity of this man being back on the apps when he so clearly didn't even know what we wanted. He looked terrible, which was a small comfort to me. I swiped left. I felt yet again hopeless by the dating scene; by the apps. I was jaded and I didn't want to be. I was slated to officiate my brother's wedding later that month in New Orleans. I decided I needed to take a break from the dating app game. The break was short-lived. Those damn dating app slot machines called me back.

A psychic I saw in October of 2019 told me "This is it. He is it." I wanted to trust her so badly—so I did. I had just gotten out of the relationship with Luke a month prior. When the psychic told me this good news about my new relationship, which was in its infancy, I was so excited. I'm not someone who lives their life by astrology, but sometimes I use it to soothe the daily buzzing of my anxiety. Sometimes I need "woo" things to feel held. Plus, I am someone who has an abundance of hope and always believes in magic and miracles. I met Rob on Tinder. He seemed stable, reliable, a real adult. He had a teenage kid, was divorced, well traveled—he had lived and experienced things. On our first date up until things got bad, I wanted him in a way I had never experienced before.

We had a sexual relationship that was intoxicating. It was one of my first truly satisfying Dom/sub relationships. I liked being *his*. I liked giving myself to him over and over again. He liked it, too. He was newer to actually doing BDSM, but had always known he was into it. His Dom tendencies were there waiting to come out and play. I, on the other hand, had known (and practiced) being submissive in the bedroom for several years by then. He slapped my face, spanked my ass, tied me up, and made me beg. The pain felt good. When I found Rob, it seemed like I had finally found my match sexually. There was gentleness and aftercare there, too. We weren't Dom/sub twenty-four seven, but it quickly became my favorite part of our relationship. It was the only time I felt like Rob really loved me. When I think about it now, I see that it wasn't love—it was his excitement of domming me, and that excitement waned. I became the discarded toy and he was done playing with me.

Rob and I had, what I thought at the time, was a great relationship. However, I look back now and see what I couldn't see before. It's clear that I wanted to be with him more than he wanted to be with me. He was excited that I would let him do almost anything to me. He still had Catholic guilt about liking domming. Our sex was his exorcism.

I made things easy for him. *I* was easy for him—not just sexually. I appeased him. I acquiesced to him. I started being his sub outside of the bedroom without either of our consent. I'm not sure when exactly things shifted, but at some point, I felt my place with him fading. No amount of sexual prowess could bring him back to me; could excite him about me again. I felt like a ghost around him—lovingly haunting him, praying he would notice me again.

When a crisis involving his kid came up, Rob pushed me away. We had been together for two and a half years at this point, but he abruptly stopped talking to me; only texting randomly instead. I told him it was fine—anything to hang on to him. I made excuses as to why he couldn't, at the very least, call me. We were supposed to finally see each other, but Rob texted last minute saying, "Thinking about seeing you almost gives me a panic attack." He couldn't (or wouldn't) explain why. Was he cheating? Was he about to? Was he having a breakdown? I'll never know. He went away for a weekend, and said he needed to think about his feelings for me (and everything). I felt like I created this dynamic: Rob thinking he could sit me somewhere and I would wait for him to come back whenever he wanted. It was like emotional domming. My body was bound, my mouth was gagged. I would wait. Not this time, though. I could have waited to see what he decided about me after his weekend away, but I knew that would deny my own integrity. I also didn't want to know what decision he would make about me. I knew that doing so would be of great harm to myself. How many times in the past have I waited around for someone to decide about me? Too many to count. I needed to break the pattern. I texted him: "It seems like you need your space, so I'm going to remove myself from this situation."

Rob waited two days to text me back. His wall of text began, "Hey. I'm sorry I didn't reply sooner. I didn't know what to say. I still don't. I also didn't want to ghost you so I'll try and share a few things." I guess he didn't know *I* was the ghost in the relationship, not him. Rob said the relationship was adding to his stress. It was over. He ended with, "I know this isn't what you want to hear, and it's not what I want to feel, but it's not fair to either of us. At some point when I'm in a better place I'd like to catch-up if you're ok with that, but I also understand if you'd rather not." The neon anger that bloomed inside me was too much to bear.

Throughout my life, I've always been amazed at how big and strong an emotion can grow inside of me. I used to think anger was a useful emotion. I preferred it over sadness. Anger felt like movement, while sadness felt like stagnation. I now realize that anger—the slow burn kind—is just too much love with nowhere to go. It no longer feels like movement to me. It feels like a deep, heavy sludge that I have to crawl through. Rob's text is tattooed into my memory. I could do an interpretive dance to that text like women on TikTok do to their exes voice messages. My anger after receiving that text swells in my mind like a third-degree burn.

It feels like Rob is dead. That sounds macabre, but when we broke up, I hadn't seen him for over a month. I lessened any expectations I had for him because I knew he was dealing with something traumatic with his kid. Instead of leaning on me, his partner, for support—he pushed me away. I guess this may have been the worst thing that has ever happened to him, and so he truly didn't know how to handle it. It still doesn't excuse his ability to easily dispose of me and our relationship.

Rob showed me a level of consistency and stability that I never had before and, honestly, never knew I needed or wanted. But he wasn't all that stable. He was a "looks good on paper" guy. Emotionally, he was stunted. I can never know how someone will act when something unexpected happens in their life. I can think I know someone, but find out years later they aren't who I thought they were. I might not be who people think I am either. I am in awe of the fact that so many of us can continue to live in our bodies which remain as archives of pain, grief, and anger until we die. There's joy in there, too, somewhere. The body remembers.

After our breakup, I took six months off from online dating. Tinder, Bumble, Hinge would all be there for me whenever I decided to venture back to the gamified world of love. I never wanted to do the online dating thing again, but it's difficult to meet people organically, especially when I don't like to leave the house all that much.

I rejoined the dating app world in November 2022, and almost immediately any excitement to see what's out there wore off, and I felt left with a heavy sadness and a dash of hopelessness. I looked at all genders and to no one's surprise, it's the straight white men who have the scariest profiles. They have one of four kinds of pictures: 1) a selfie that shows the innermost recesses of their nostrils, 2) a shirtless pic, 3) a pic of them posing with a dead animal they killed, and 4) a pic of them and their gun. It's bleak. Everyone is now into "ethical non-monogamy," which is all fine and good, but it leaves very few people for those of us who are still looking for a monogamous partner. I eventually came across my ex, Rob, on Tinder and felt immediately irritated by his profile claiming he was "happy and healthy," when I knew the truth.

Being on the apps again made me understand more and more why people settle for the crumbs they have, because it might be a sliver better than having to be on these horrendous apps. It might be slightly better than who is out there. Swiping left and right feels trivial, because it is. It's like any other game app on our phone. It may as well be another version of Candy Crush. We are all so desensitized by it that we forget real people are behind the photos we see. We forget each other's humanness.

For three months, I dated someone who went to weekly therapy (and even put it in his Hinge profile like a badge of honor). He love-bombed me from the beginning, and the entire time we dated, it felt off, but I couldn't pinpoint why. He was *so* nice. Now I see it very clearly: sure, he was nice, but he was completely inauthentic. He said a bunch of shit about his "attachment style" and how open and honest he was in his therapy sessions. Early on in our relationship, he admitted he could be manipulative. I filed this red flag away—not to ignore it, but to see when or how it may come up. Later, I found out he was using so much weed that he couldn't hang out with me sober, nor could he even get the things done that he needed to get done. I asked if he had talked to his therapist about it. He responded, "No, because then I'd have to tell her about my weed use in general, and I just don't want to go there."

It was clear to me that he was not actually processing much in therapy. He was simply learning the language, because he knew women would appreciate it. I don't believe he did this maliciously, nor do

I think all men do this maliciously, but I think there's a real societal problem with men (primarily) doing something to look "good" or get "credit" for it with women.

It reminds me of when I started seeing men self-identify as "feminist" in their dating app profiles over a decade ago. It initially made me feel safer. However, many of these men used the word to lure women. I dated a few of them, and their actions were most certainly not "feminist." I see this, too, in how many of us white people want to self-identify as "allies" to people of color. To me, there is no need to self-identify as an "ally." Either we do the work the work requested of us or we don't. It's up to members of those communities to bestow that label upon us if they choose to do so. I would say this goes the same for cis men who want to identify as "feminist."

I have dated so many men who craved adrenaline. They enjoyed skydiving, mountain biking on impossible terrain, or using copious amounts of drugs. They seemed fearless or uncaring of what would happen to them. I was used to being called "boring" and "adventure-less." I didn't know how to tell them I didn't crave adrenaline, because it was within me every second of my life. Men seem to be less acquainted with pain and death compared to women. I never craved danger or chaos because I lived it and suffered greatly from it.

Dating apps have increased our convenience to each other, but they have also increased our screen time. I could spend several minutes, and even hours, on a dating app. Depending on my distance preference, I could swipe forever. Then I could also spend an inordinate amount of time crafting my bio and deciding which photos to add. I am beholden to a tiny screen playing a tiny game. I match with someone and most of the time nobody sends a message. It's too much effort. I have a match so I've beat the game, right? That's it. I will sometimes send a message to a person I match with only to be met with no response or the conversation dies a quick death. I am tired of making the first move. I am tired of being the initiator in all things. Looking through dating apps is a dizzying experience where everyone's photo blurs into one. I see people and wonder, "Where do I know them from?" I know them from being on these damn apps. I've seen various iterations of their profiles throughout the years, and they've seen mine. We're all a bunch of heartbroken ghosts trying to find love on the internet.

Part of the issue with dating apps is that there isn't a lot to go on. Of course, it's an exercise in vanity. A person's photos speak the loudest online. Sometimes people don't bother writing anything in their profile so that only leaves pictures. I have seen some very physically attractive people on Tinder, but this doesn't mean a whole lot. For me, personality and looks matter about the same. I would say most people feel this way. In such an inorganic space like a dating app, how can anyone grow a connection? Is it even possible?

The days of a darling meet-cute at a local bookstore are not completely lost, but they do seem much less likely than before. For those of us who wear a mask when we go in and out of stores, this probably cuts down on the potential for a random flirtation. There just isn't a great way to date or meet people these days. Online apps seem to be the most convenient and accessible. However, when potential suitors see "feminist" in online dating profiles, I know many keep swiping left. In the mid aughts, I had many men message me on OkCupid telling me they would be interested in me if I wasn't a feminist. One man's first message to me simply asked, "Are you a man-hating feminist?" I got really tired of explaining what feminism was to men. I expected asinine questions from conservative dudes, but I didn't expect them from liberals and leftists. Looking back, I should have. Even leftist men need to continuously work on unlearning patriarchy. I interacted, albeit briefly, with self-identified leftists who were still obviously threatened by feminism and their misunderstanding of it.

Dating as a feminist shouldn't be an issue these days. However, now the "feminist" in my profile attracts men who take this to mean I'm up for anything. Where men once saw me as a potentially frigid "man-hater," they now see me as a quick, super kinky lay. Throw in my bisexuality, and I receive countless propositions from couples looking for a third. If I was looking for that, I would be less upset by it. However, I'm monogamous, and feel too tired for the casual sex of my 20s and early 30s.

In order to get anywhere close to a relationship, dating has to become a full-time job. I don't care enough to do this. Perhaps I did in my 20s, but I have (thankfully) outgrown the all-encompassing yearning of being in a relationship that I once had. My time is much more important to me these days. Also, because I have already had a lifetime's worth of relationship-specific trauma, deciding to go on a spontaneous first date is out of the question. Since the pandemic began, my social anxiety has increased; something I previously never had to deal with much. I am still getting myself back out into the world (masked). The risk of Covid is sometimes not worth it to me. Trying to date during a global pandemic feels so incredibly dystopian. I can't help but feel like there isn't a point. If I weren't so interested in falling/growing in love, then I would just quit dating. Alas, I still very much believe in love and still very much want it. So I trot back to these dating games. I trot back to love that is close, but so out of reach.

Meanwhile, coupled-up people want us single folks to regale them with our juicy and depressing online dating horror stories. I've played that game for a while now. I'm tired of singing for my supper. The couples who sit on the edge of their seat listening to my stories audibly gasp and ooh and ahh. They say things like, "I'm so glad I'm not single!" or "Thank god I don't have to use a dating app!" Sometimes I wonder what that level of safety feels like. Must be nice.

If we didn't live in a society that praised romantic relationships over all else, then perhaps things would be different; better. As a woman in her late 30s, I feel at times like an outcast since I'm unmarried, even if marriage is not something I necessarily want. The pressure to marry is so ingrained in me that it's difficult to feel the texture of where I begin and where society begins. I grew up thinking my life would look very different at the age I'm at now, but whose dream was that? Was it mine? Was it society's?

Many women are finding that they are happier being single or unmarried. Many of us are seeing the freedom this offers us. We have standards that we are unwilling to break. The older I get, the higher my standards, and I'm grateful for that. But this also means, there are fewer and fewer people available to me. It's still frustrating to see how well dating apps have worked out for others. It has taken so much of my energy to mute the voice deep inside that says something is wrong with me. At my big age, I have enough wisdom and experience to know this is untrue, but that voice still creeps in sometimes.

How does anyone date anymore? How does anyone find anyone anymore? My social activity tolerance has drastically lowered since the pandemic began. I'm mostly fine with that, but it makes it harder to meet people. I'm not convinced that anyone else knows how to be social anymore either, though. Some are better at faking it. Some are lying to themselves. I'm incapable of doing either. I am tired of the gamification of love, of dating, of sex.

I should probably delete all of my dating apps. I should probably just get off the nauseating Tilt-A-Whirl ride of new faces and patterned behaviors. There is still this small voice of hope whispering, "Wait, what if?"

Hearts are not for playing with, but for holding with an open palm: gentle, relaxed, free. I wonder if anyone will be able to hold mine someday.

Chapter Five

TRAUMA STORYTELLING AS CURRENCY AND COMMODITY

There is no life without trauma. There is no history without trauma... Trauma as a mode of being violently halts the flow of time, fractures the self, and punctures memory and language.

—GABRIELE M. SCHWAB

"HI! GIRL POWER! I'M GERI!"

This is how Geri "Ginger" Spice introduced herself on a 1998 episode of *The Oprah Winfrey Show*.[1] As a child who was a huge Spice Girls fan, I vividly remember "Girl Power" slogans everywhere, from clothing to journals to random posters at Bed Bath & Beyond. My teenage girlhood was groped by this phrase. At the time, I had no idea that "Girl Power" had been capitalized on and was, in essence, selling a mutilated feminism back to me. Bikini Kill, the 90s Riot Grrrl band, is credited with creating the phrase as a joke and using it in their zine, *Bikini Kill #2: Girl Power* in 1991.[2] Kathleen Hanna, lead singer of Bikini Kill notes that she and Tobi Vail (Bikini Kill's drummer) came up with the title for their second zine by "...discussing what word just felt totally wrong next to girl... And we came up with power." The "Girl Power" slogan was big in the punk scene and was not created to be a marketing tactic. The Spice Girls' (and their managers') were not

---

1   "The Spice Girls Visit The Oprah Winfrey Show," Episode, *The Oprah Winfrey Show* 12, no. 1, (Chicago, IL: Harpo Productions, January 13, 1998).

2   Kathleen Hanna and Tobi Vail, *Bikini Kill Zine*, vol. 2 (New York, NY: Kathleen Hanna, 1991).

in on the joke. If they were, I doubt they would have cared.

Feminism has consistently been commodified, repackaged, and sold back to us. Ginger Spice also declared Margaret Thatcher "our 1st Lady of Girl Power."[3] If we're going with Bikini Kill's original joke, then this fits quite well. I don't think that's what Ginger Spice meant, though. Depending on what type of feminist is asked about the commodification of feminism, some might say it's fine or not a big deal. Liberal capitalist feminists circa 2014 really thrived during the "Girl Boss" era, afterall. These so-called feminists loved Hillary Clinton, but what they loved even more was work culture and "making it." These "Girl Bosses" flew too close to the sun, though, and we're (thankfully) in a post-Girl Boss era now. This doesn't mean there aren't feminists who continue to engage uncritically with capitalism. They still preach about the "importance" of getting money and power just like men. This is why I have said for years on my social media platforms that I don't support "all" women. Capitalism and classism are antithetical to feminism. I don't personally want equality with men. I don't want the ability to bomb countries or kill people "just like men." I want liberation from men, from patriarchy, from the kyriarchy. I want all people to have this liberation. Feminism does not, and should not, align with capitalism in any way. In her book, *Ain't I a Woman: Black Women and Feminism*, bell hooks writes: "To me feminism is not simply a struggle to end male chauvinism or a movement to ensure that women will have equal rights with men; it is a commitment to eradicating the ideology of domination that permeates Western culture on various levels—sex, race, and class."[4] In this way, feminism is liberatory and not aligned with maintaining the status quo, including the maintenance of capitalist societies.

In online spaces, we're seeing commodification of feminism from brands to influencers to celebrities. In 2017, high-fashion brand Dior created a simple white cotton t-shirt that read, "We should all be feminists," a book title from writer Chimamanda Ngozi Adichie. The shirt

---

3   Peter Wilkinson, "Thatcher: Revered and Reviled, in Death as in Life," CNN, April 15, 2013, https://www.cnn.com/2013/04/12/world/europe/thatcher-divisive-force/index.html.

4   bell hooks, *Ain't I A Woman: Black Women and Feminism*, 2nd ed, (New York: Routledge, 2014), 194.

retailed for $710 with only a small percentage going to charity. Taylor Swift, a repeat offender of feminist commodification, continues to put out albums drenched in white girl sanctimonious victimhood, yelling "Fuck the patriarchy" during her Eras Tour. She has yet to say anything about the Palestinian genocide, of course. This is typical of most white celebrity feminists. They dissect feminism and only use the pieces they feel comfortable with. They aren't always selling a physical item, but they're still selling their lukewarm concept of feminism.

Some of us are also engaging in this commodification. We're not necessarily commodifying feminism, but we're selling our stories. Capitalism has forced our hand at this. We're all just trying to survive and most of us don't have nearly enough money to do so. Our stories, the more heinous the better, make our Instagram posts seen more by followers and non-followers. We receive "hearts" for sharing the most painful things that have happened to us. We receive visibility, which can sometimes lead to national, or international, media attention. The proximity to fame and the promise of wealth can be intoxicating. On social media, our words and images are our currency and our morbid marketing tactics. Cue trauma storytelling.

The first time I had sex was a rape. For a long time, I tried to pretend that this wasn't true. I was eighteen and it was with an acquaintance of my brother. Tristan was older, which is what initially attracted me to him. I pursued him. I didn't mind that anytime we hung out he would ply me with alcohol. I didn't mind that I would pass out at his place and he would do things to my body. During one particular debaucherous night, we were at The Angelic—a bar downtown where many university students would frequent. Tristan bought the first pitcher of beer. Once I was wasted from that, he had me buy the next one. In my drunken haze, I remember him showing me where to sign on the receipt. I got drunker and drunker. I went to the bathroom and threw up. Kind, anonymous women surrounded me asking, "Are you okay, hun?" I said I was fine and left. I had to get back to Tristan. I sat back down and rested my head on the table. A server came by telling Tristan, "She can't be passed out here. She has to get up or you guys need to leave." I lifted my heavy head. We left. Tristan drove us back to his place blaring Metric's *Combat Baby*. I haven't been able to listen to that song or that album since.

I'm a 4-time rape survivor. Whenever I say it like that, it sounds like I won a prize. But obviously there is no prize. I'm just in a club that nobody wants to be in. I don't remember the first time I posted about this online, but I do recall a specific time I shared it in an Instagram caption. I was met with comments of solidarity in the form of "me too" and "I'm so sorry." Then came the trolls:

"Wait, how were *you* raped FOUR times?"

"You're too ugly to be raped."

"FOUR times? That seems like a YOU problem."

As a seasoned online feminist, I'm not stranger to trolls, rape threats, or death threats. However, reading these words on that particular day was arduous. It took a lot of courage to write, "I'm a 4-time rape survivor" in a grid post caption on Instagram. I knew I would get shit for it from some people, but I had talked myself into thinking it wouldn't bother me. I was in disbelief at how embarrassed and small I could feel in an online space. I did it and I don't regret it. Telling my various stories is part of my healing.

Many cultures throughout the world depend on the oral traditions of storytelling. In Italian culture, women's storytelling is integral to relating acts of activism and resistance. Writer, historian and associate professor at Smith College, Jennifer Guglielmo says: "Stories of women's resistance were often a part of a storyteller's repertoire, helping female rebels in particular to become folk heroines."[5] These bitesize activisms allow for knowledge exchange. Storytelling in Indigenous communities is integral to maintaining and archiving their histories. In West African cultures, Griots are storytellers who protect and preserve a society's history.[6] We find camaraderie by listening to others' stories. We find belonging by telling our own.

In March of 2017, four women came forward to report that actor Danny Masterson raped them, and in late December of that same year,

---

5   Jennifer Guglielmo, *Living the Revolution: Italian Women's Resistance and Radicalism in New York City, 1880-1945* (Chapel Hill, NC: University Of North Carolina Press, 2012), 20.

6   Charity Wacera, "Griots: Living Historians and Musicians of West Africa," *Our Ancestories*, October 6, 2023, https://our-ancestories.com/blogs/news/griots-living-historians-and-musicians-of-west-africa.

a fifth woman came forward. Society loves to point out the camaraderie of survivors as though it's a bad thing; as somehow "proof" that what happened to them is make-believe; that they conspired to create a false story. In May of 2024, Masterson was convicted of raping two of the five women back in the early 2000s. He was sentenced to 30 years to life in prison.[7] Chrissie Bixler, one of the survivors of Masterson, shared the truth of what happened to her and the other survivors on her Instagram stories. Many people then questioned, "Why is she doing this now?" These people don't understand survivorship and they definitely don't understand the stifling that happens with legal proceedings in place. Once Masterson was sentenced, I imagine that Bixler felt like she could speak out—on her terms. Bixler finally had control of the narrative. She told us, the public, the story of what happened to her and how it affected her life. Women's talk is very much a good thing. Women's stories have power. That power scares society, for good reason.

Storytelling has been an important tool for those of us in marginalized communities for centuries. We find out who we are by listening to others' stories and telling our own. Italian feminist philosopher Adriana Cavarero surmises that our identities are shaped and reshaped by witnessing our stories narrated by others.[8] The early use of blogs and message boards, and now social media, has increased the rate at which we are able to tell our own stories. It has allowed us a sense of control and care over our own narrative. It has also increased the potential that those in power will listen, or at the very least, see/hear what we are saying. Using social media to tell our stories can get us global attention.

I have told various stories in onlines spaces. Some humorous,

---

7   Author's Note: As a prison abolitionist, I am never excited about people going to prison. I also don't personally see it as "justice," but I know that many other survivors do see it as justice and I'm not about to tell them they're "wrong." What's hard is, rarely do we see rapists getting any amount of jail time so when one does, especially a white man who is a celebrity. So, this case is sort of a big deal. I am always envisioning alternative ways of justice and what an end to rape culture would actually look like, feel like, and how we might get there.

8   Adriana Cavarero, *Relating Narratives: Storytelling and Selfhood* (Hoboken, NJ: Taylor and Francis, 2014), xiv.

some tragic. I have talked about having been raped. I have talked about contracting genital herpes. I have talked about my disabilities, including my struggle with mental illness. With each story I decide to share, like a tiny prayer I take a deep breath before hitting "Post." It never gets easier. It often starts to feel like I'm not exhibiting the "correct" amount of terror in the language I use in an Instagram caption. It feels like people want me to perform the many traumatized selves that exist within me. On a good day, I know that I'm not just my trauma and I have spent decades getting to that point. On not so good days, I feel too exhausted by it all that dissociation is preferable. People inevitably call me "brave," which feels like another way to say, "how are you still alive?"

The public sharing of vulnerable stories de-stigmatizes shame and can facilitate a sense of belonging. Perhaps that's why I did it so often—the dopamine hit of feeling understood and like I belonged for a brief moment in time. Even if this is not an easy task, I have never regretted sharing something online. When I don't share my truth, I can feel it metastasize in real time. However, the desire I have to share can start to feel compulsive. Part of this is most likely due to my OCD. Part of this is the "content farming" urge to *hurry up* and find something to post to get seen by the algorithm.

Apps instill fear and urgency in those of us with followings in order to keep us posting on social media. Instagram uses data analytics to keep us scrolling. This is how they keep us on the app. Paid posts are seen more quickly and frequently. How a user interacts with a post, whether they "like" it, share it, or save it, are all things that help a post get seen more[9]. If people aren't interacting with my posts, then my posts don't get seen. Instagram will tell me it's my fault if a post doesn't get seen, because it means people aren't interacting with them. However, many people from marginalized identities have surmised that Instagram's algorithm will simply not show these posts to followers. Thus, the drive to keep sharing, keep posting to see what sticks becomes incessant. The issues of sharing "too much" or sharing compulsively, as well as feeling like we *have* to share trauma to get likes, follows, and

---

9   Julia Kalanik, "How Instagram Keeps Users Scrolling for More," Digital Innovation and Transformation, March 22, 2021, https://d3.harvard.edu/platform-digit/submission/how-instagram-keeps-users-scrolling-for-more/.

perhaps a brand deal are rampant. I am concerned about this. I am concerned with becoming a spectacle. I am concerned with my lived experiences becoming commodified by others or myself. Trauma sells on websites and social media platforms, afterall. This is dangerous if the writer has not even begun to process their trauma before deciding to write and sell a piece to a website or post about haphazardly on Instagram. As Dorothy Allison says, "You have to have found a way to live with your own story before you make a story you can give other people."[10]

Writing about trauma is not new, but the commodification of it didn't begin until websites started seeing it as lucrative and click-worthy. Confessional essays published online began around 2008[11]. Many of these posts were written by everyday people, primarily women, and they weren't necessarily "professional" freelance writers. They were women who wanted to get their story out there. They were women who needed some extra cash. They were women searching for online virality. Everyone's reason for writing the confessional essay was different. The common thread for why online websites published these essays was to create a spectacle. The writer, and by extension the publisher, would be gawked at. The now-defunct website, *xoJane*, became most notable for this. They were known for their column, "It Happened To Me," which published a variety of confessional essays with titles like, "It Happened to Me: My Friend Joined ISIS"[12] or "It Happened To Me: My Former Friend's Death Was a Blessing.[13]" I even

---

10   Dorothy Allison, "A Cure For Bitterness," *Critical Trauma Studies: Understanding Violence, Conflict, and Memory in Everyday Life* (New York, NY: NYU Press, 2016), 244—56.

11   Jia Tolentino, "The Personal-Essay Boom Is Over," The New Yorker, May 18, 2017,   https://www.newyorker.com/culture/jia-tolentino/the-personal-essay-boom-is-over#:~:text=These%20essays%20began%20to%20proliferate,she%20gained%20and%20lost%20from.

12   Chelsea Hassler, "XoJane Actually Just Published a Personal Essay Called 'It Happened to Me: My Friend Joined ISIS,'" Slate Magazine, August 23, 2016, https://slate.com/human-interest/2016/08/xojane-actually-just-published-a-personal-essay-called-it-happened-to-me-my-friend-joined-isis.html.

13   Mary Elizabeth Williams, "Worst Personal Essay Ever? Xojane Scrapes the Bottom of the Hate-Read Barrel," Salon, May 23, 2016, https://www.salon.com/2016/05/20/worst_personal_essay_ever_xojane_scrapes_the_bottom_of_the_

wrote my own "It Happened To Me" about being in Special Ed. I remember the payment I received was not nearly enough for the story I shared nor for the vitriolic comments I received.

For those of us who belong to any marginalized groups, it's expected of us to write about our experience in said groups. I write about facets of my identities because it's what I know best, but I don't want it to be expected from me. It's important to write about our lived experiences within our lived identities, but when it's *expected* from us, when it's the only thing people want to hear from us, it starts to gnaw. That being said, this is not necessarily the same for white writers who can easily "opt out" of our more invisible identities. Writer and artist, Sophia Giovannitti says:

> ...white writers and artists on the left gain platforms and credibility in leaning on any marginalized aspects of their identities and can opt in and out of these identities at will, enjoying different forms of legibility in different spaces. Writers of color can't opt out and often aren't assigned pieces beyond identity politics, particularly if they do not also have the right socio-economic or academic background.[14]

My whiteness has afforded me an easier time at gaining followers, a platform. My invisible marginalized identities can set me apart from other white women if and when I *choose* to lean into them. There is something sinister, manipulative even, about this choice that white women and white people, in general, have. While all of our stories can be important and helpful to others, it's necessary to consider how those of us who are white have immediate credibility in online spaces.

People everywhere can share their stories on the internet. These stories become representative of entire communities. Giovannitti says opportunities are then "dangled" to people in marginalized groups with some sort of promise that will lead to change. Telling one's stories can, however, work to destigmatize issues as well as bring visibility and camaraderie to the cause. This style of activism can lead to transformation and change. For example, it was powerful to witness each survivor who tacked on their piece of trauma to the MeToo hashtag created by Tarana Burke. It was like a big, global fuck-you to those

---

hate_read_barrel/.

14   Sophia Giovannitti, *Working Girl: On Selling Art and Selling Sex* (New York, NY: Verso Books, 2024), 100.

who would rather leave sexual assault in the shadows. Hashtags catalog personal stories, and can act as consciousness-raising. Clicking on a hashtag can bring anyone into a conversation, a discussion, and a reading list of stories. In her forward to *Hashtag Activism*, writer and activist Genie Lauren describes the use and importance of hashtags:

> ...I have found hashtag activism to be irreplaceable. It is both a means to an end, a tool to consolidate information, and way to share a call to action, it is used to share examples of the injustice and oppression that users have experienced. While there are several ways to deliver information, none are as compact, mobile, and easily digestible as a hashtag. While hashtag activism isn't the whole of any resistance movement, it is the arterial network of any movement that seeks to gain national support and impact.[15]

Similarly, people have been using Instagram as a sort of micro-blogging platform by typing out long captions under each image posted, and adding specific hashtags. On my own Instagram, I sometimes do this to speak on issues like white women's fragility/violence, sexual violence, sexism, ableism, and more. The "collage" style of Instagram allows for images, whether blank, text, or otherwise, to gain traction. Not every user likes to read a long caption, but there are many who appreciate this use of Instagram. This seems to be something that is dependent on a person's follower demographics[16]. Though the platform was created to prioritize visuals, a lengthy caption can be more accessible and informative. Including hashtags is paramount if a user wants their post to show up on various feeds. These hashtags have become subversive in their archiving of people's stories.

One incredibly clever and powerful example of storytelling activism is how feminists in China added their own stories of sexual violence to the MeToo Movement. After Sina Weibo, a Chinese Twitter-like platform, blocked the MeToo hashtag, feminists began using the rice and bunny emojis to continue the conversation. Regarding this activism that circumvented censorship, Margaret Andersen for *Wired* wrote at the time:

---

15   Sarah J. Jackson, Moya Bailey, and Brooke Foucault Welles, *#hashtagactivism: Networks of Race and Gender Justice* (Cambridge, MA: The MIT Press, 2020), xix.

16   Stacey McLachlan, "Experiment: Do Long Captions Get More Engagement on Instagram?," Social Media Marketing & Management Dashboard, July 5, 2023, https://blog.hootsuite.com/long-instagram-captions-experiment/.

> The [#Me Too] movement, which sought to show the volume of sexual misconduct against women by sharing stories of harassment and assault accompanied by the hashtag, came to prominence in China after a former doctoral student named Luo Xixi shared a letter on Weibo about being sexually harassed by a former professor. The story quickly went viral, sparking a huge debate about sexual misconduct and leading Weibo to block the #MeToo hashtag. But Chinese feminists found a way around it—they began using #RiceBunny in its place along with the rice bowl and bunny face emoji. When spoken aloud the words for "rice bunny" are pronounced "mi tu," a homophone that cleverly evades detection.[17]

Finding new ways to circumvent censorship is something more users of Instagram and TikTok, specifically, are needing to do. Both platforms will flag words like "rape" and "suicide" and users have to get creative in how they write things. When scrolling through either app, the word "grape" or the grape emoji is used in place of the word "rape." Similarly, most users will write "unalived" instead of "suicide" to bypass the algorithm flagging. Even the word "sexual" can get a post taken down, so many have started to write, "seggsual." In an effort to get their posts seen more, I have witnessed users add hashtags that have nothing to do with them or their post. For example, some use "#justgirlythings" under posts about mental illness or the horrors of capitalism. In this way, people have trespassed their "content" into other spaces.

Adapting language so the mainstream community can't understand it or find it is not new, but it's newer to digital spaces. Though this coded language is a useful tool, it can feel stressful and aggravating. We shouldn't have to take the added time coding our words, our stories, so they don't get removed. Surveillance is at an all time high, and though we have mostly seen this in the form of police body cams and drones, we're also seeing it creep into our online spaces in more insidious ways. Facial recognition and social media monitoring are both more pronounced. In an April 2024 study led by associate professor of electrical and computer engineering at UW-Madison, Dr. Kassem M. Fawaz, found disturbing evidence of Instagram and TikTok's surveillance. PhD student Jack West who worked on the study said: " The

---

17   Margaret Andersen, "How Feminists in China Are Using Emoji to Avoid Censorship," *Wired*, March 30, 2018, http://www.wired.com/story/china-feminism-emoji-censorship/.

moment you select a photo on Instagram, regardless of whether you discard it, the app analyzes the photo and grows a local cache of information... The data is stored locally, on your device—and we have no evidence it was accessed or sent. But it's there."[18] Though we might be able to circumvent surveillance by interfering with hashtags, there isn't much we can do when we choose to upload a photo. Thus, if we continue storytelling and activism on social media platforms, we'll need to continue coding our language, our hashtags, and even our posts.

On a smaller, more intimate scale, the practice of digital storytelling can allow us to more efficiently read stories from members of our own communities. Even though social media is a relationship of performer and audience, and less of a "community," many of us with large followings are gifted with difficult and heartbreaking stories from those who follow us and have some level of trust in ourselves and our platforms. A few years ago I received a message on Instagram from a woman in the Philippines. As someone with a large following, receiving direct messages is not out of the ordinary for me. Some I look at, and others I don't. Sometimes I receive fifty messages in one day. I clicked on this particular woman's message to read it. She had written to say she was in an abusive marriage. She had a daughter with her abuser, and didn't know what to do, but did know that she wanted to leave her husband. In the Philippines, divorce is still illegal[19]. The woman told me she couldn't find any resources near or around her area on domestic violence. She had asked for my help. The librarian in me spent the next several days intensely researching information about domestic violence in the Philippines. I also looked at more U.S.-based sources like the National Domestic Violence Hotline. I found information and sent it to the woman. She responded with a "Thank you," and I didn't think I would hear from her again. I thought about this woman a lot in the next month or so. Then, surprisingly, I received a message from her. She had been able to take her daughter and safely

18   Jason Daley, "Popular Social Media Mobile Apps Extract Data from Photos on Your Phone, Introducing Both Bias and Errors," College of Engineering, April 2, 2024, https://engineering.wisc.edu/news/popular-social-media-mobile-apps-extract-data-from-photos-on-your-phone-introducing-both-bias-and-errors/.

19   Lauren Day, "In the Philippines, Divorce Is Banned. It Has Left Women with Few Options to Rid Themselves of Abusive Partners," ABC News, May 15, 2024, https://amp.abc.net.au/article/103828284.

leave her abusive husband. She told me the information I sent her had helped in this. This story shows just how important telling our stories, asking for help, and using digital activism can be. Having supportive and informational social media pages can be lifesaving.

Digital storytelling allows for anyone to join in on (or initiate) a conversation. The problem with this of course is that *anyone* can join in. This includes trolls or people who just generally want to be nasty online. Our own stories are sites of vulnerability, and thus, posting these vulnerabilities on Twitter, Instagram, Facebook, and TikTok open us up to harassment, conflict, and abuse. Telling our stories, and having some semblance of control over the narrative, is important and necessary in a society that already doesn't listen to people from marginalized communities. If society does listen, it seems to come from a "watching a car crash" mentality. They don't necessarily want to see or know the author—only the story of what happened to them. Dorothy Allison writes:

> We are the leavening to the salt-crusted fear of this society that only wants to read terrible stories on paperback covers at a distance. And if they're going to see that narrator, they want them carefully positioned on Oprah's couch, kind of respectful, kind of honorable, kind of animalistic, kind of gossipy sexually exciting... the place where as a culture our damage is almost universal that we are fascinated with the horrible, that we use it as a way to reassure ourselves of our own safety, our protected place.[20]

People are no doubt "fascinated with the horrible," but they're just as intoxicated by the redemption. The redemption is prettier than the trauma, but the spectacle around it feels equally grotesque. It becomes "Inspiration Porn," which seeks to tie up a person's narrative nicely with a big bow. Their resilience and survival becomes a spectacle. People will write comments under my trauma posts, saying: "And look at you now!" The butchering is complete. What if I only survived because the alternative was death? How do I post about *that*? Is telling our story and posting about it into the social media void worth the potential of being a spectacle? Is it worth the potential harassment or abuse? We each need to decide that for ourselves.

---

20   Dorothy Allison, "A Cure For Bitterness," *Critical Trauma Studies: Understanding Violence, Conflict, and Memory in Everyday Life* (New York, NY: NYU Press, 2016), 244—56.

Cis men have silenced women for centuries. Women's stories were often referred to as "gossip" by them. This gave women's stories a tone of frivolity. Storytelling and gossip are interconnected, though. Gossip was only given a bad name by those in power (specifically white cis men). People in marginalized communities, however, have utilized gossip as a form of resistance. Women talk to each other, women warn each other—much of this has been referred to as "gossip" as a way to denigrate women's words and women's activism. Canadian philosopher Ronald de Sousa, notes "Gossip has been the object of much malicious talk. But then, so have all forms of power—and gossip is power."[21]

Much has been studied and written about the reclamation of gossip. Artist, educator, advocate and librarian, Karina Hagelin writes, "Gossip is a site of resistance, productive power, and platform for sharing experiences for marginalized communities, especially survivors of sexual and interpersonal violence, who are denied access to traditional information institutions." When I think of #MeToo, I see how these stories, often referred to as "just gossip" by various media, are sites of resistance and transformation for survivors of sexual violence. Hagelin continues:

> ...gossip has been utilized as a communication practice among the most marginalized communities and peoples across society: women, people of color, queer and transgender folks, as well as survivors of sexual and interpersonal violence. Gossip is traditionally understood as spreading rumors, witch-hunting, creating drama, or otherwise attention-seeking and generally negative behaviors (with a gendered and feminized slant). Yet when we are actively and historically excluded from traditional information institutions, such as the media, our education system, and political sphere, it can become one of our only and last resorts for not only resistance—but sharing life-saving information with each other.[22]

The oppressor doesn't want the oppressed to have even an ounce of power. Women's talk is powerful and can be dangerous to men. Women's talk is lifesaving for women.

This is why the prevalence of "Are We Dating The Same Guy?"

---

21   Robert Goodman and Aharon Ben-Ze'ev, *Good Gossip* (Lawrence, KS: University Press of Kansas, 1994), 25.

22   Karina Hagelin, dissertation, *Gossip as a Site of Resistance: Information-Sharing Strategies Among Survivors of Sexual Violence* (University of Maryland, 2018), 1.

groups on Facebook and other spaces are also important. In these groups, which are based on locale, women post screenshots of men's dating app profiles and ask whether any women in the group know anything about the guy in question. Specifically, women ask about red flags, the definition of which can differ from person to person, but for the sake of the group mostly refers to abusive behavior. Women talk to each other, but men bank on women not doing so. This might be due to the fact that men see women as constantly competing with each other, especially for men, so why would they talk to each other about the same guys?

These private, locked-down information centers are the hidden, backlit rooms of storefronts. They are consciousness-raising groups where women protect women from men. It's sad that this is the world we live in, but until rape culture is dismantled, women and all marginalized folks will need our private (and public) online and offline spaces of storytelling for our own safety. We will continue to use social media to amplify our stories—including those about our survivorship and liberation. We keep each other safe, after all.

The telling of the story can be done for a variety of reasons. Whether to shed light on something, to gain more visibility on an issue, or to just vent. We tell stories to relate to one another. However, sharing stories of trauma or hardship can often revictimize the storyteller. How many women who added to the #MeToo tag felt retraumatized afterwards? Were they able to seek help if they needed it? Did they have resources? Did they know that this participation might retraumatize them? How many trolls who joined in on this hashtag further harmed survivors? Do the digital displays of solidarity outweigh the harm of revictimization?

I can't completely answer these questions, but I can say that being able to tell our own story on social media is empowering for many of us. For example, the article "Speaking 'Unspeakable Things': Documenting Digital Feminist Responses to Rape Culture," by Jessalynn Keller, Kaitlynn Mendes, and Jessica Ringrose, they write:

> Susan, a Toronto-based woman in her early thirties had been raped on three separate occasions since her teenage years and never confided her assaults to anyone. When the Ghomeshi news broke and the #BeenRapedNeverReported hashtag began trending, Susan was inspired to share her story. She

set up a simple website where she wrote about her assaults and opened a personal Twitter account so she could use the hashtag to connect her stories with the thousands of others that were being shared on Twitter. Within several days Susan had received several thousand hits on her website and countless notes of support from family, friends and strangers.[23]

The fact that Susan created a social media account *because* she wanted to participate in a viral hashtag campaign to share her story shows how important these platforms can be to survivors. Many of us fold ourselves into activist endeavors through the Twitter and Instagram cataloging technique of hashtags.

Hashtags not only catalog stories, but they also act as emotion archives, like in the case of #MeToo, #BeenRapedNeverReported, and #ShoutYourStatus (an STI+ tag that I co-created). Trauma doesn't fit into a specified number of characters; trauma rarely fits anywhere, since it's so vast and varied. As someone who has contributed to more than one viral traumatic hashtag, it feels a bit like hot coffee spilled over my heart. The burn is slow and excruciating, and I question why I did it. Yet another layer of victim-blaming.

Returning to old hashtags is like returning to a grave site. We can see an activist moment frozen in time—frozen in social media space. The hashtag becomes an archive, which can be incredibly helpful to the rich history of our collective movements. Of course the answer to *why* I added to the hashtag and *why* I decided to open myself raw on the internet is, for most of us, to be heard. Telling the story may bring about another round of trauma, but we do it to reclaim what happened to us. We do it so others who've gone through similar things know we're out there. Our stories won't get told the way they deserve to be if we aren't the ones to do it.

Digital storytelling has the potential to build community online, but more so, it has the potential to build community *offline*. If we have a modest amount of followers and we engage in digital storytelling, finding or creating online community can certainly happen. For example, I have witnessed online community-building occur amongst survivors

23   Jessalynn Keller, Kaitlynn Mendes, and Jessica Ringrose, "Speaking 'Unspeakable Things': Documenting Digital Feminist Responses to Rape Culture," *Journal of Gender Studies* 27, no. 1 (July 28, 2016): 22—36, https://doi.org/10.1080/09589236.2016.1211511.

of sexual violence. I have witnessed online micro-communities finding each other offline in their specific locales. The way in which digital storytelling can be used as solidarity, community-building, and even meet cutes is exciting. Storytelling online allows for increased visibility and support around issues affecting marginalized communities. We can then take this work offline in our own communities.

After I added to the #MeToo tag, I received vitriol in public, but also in my direct messages. I actually had a conversation with one guy who messaged me. I asked him why he was doing what he was doing. What was the point of it? He simply responded: "I dunno. I guess I'm just bored before work." When boredom is the reason for harassment, there is clearly something wrong. It's also just the standard practice of white male entitlement and white male rage. Anytime white men feel like their existence is under threat, they react by using an arsenal of antiquated patriarchal tactics: harassment, intimidation, and misogyny.

The good and bad of digital storytelling (and archiving) is that people can add to the living "document" at any given time. It's public sharing of deeply personal matters, and a survivor can be revictimized over and over and over again. What was once said in private, in-person conversations, now happens as a public-viewing spectacle on social media. While people can simply scroll on by, many unfortunately, decide not to. There is a consumptive nature to this. The storyteller (and their story) are *consumed* by an audience. Even if the storyteller did not consciously seek out to commodify their story, the relationship between storyteller and viewer can feel objectifying. Unfortunately, we can't control this. Just like in our offline worlds, our personal stories may also be questioned or attacked online. The difference with this being done online is the frequency with which trolls attack—and the potential of thousands of heinous things they might send through their keyboards. Something I often question is: do marginalized folks who add to a viral hashtag understand the potential ramifications of this? The path of social media is winding, inconsistent, and erratic.

I see the following Anne Lamott quote plastered all over social media: "You own everything that happened to you. Tell your stories. If people wanted you to write warmly about them, they should have behaved better."[24] While I, too, have loved this quote, it has also brought up feelings that can best be described as *cringe*. I'm tired of seeing people use this quote as permission to air their deepest torments, especially without much context. We see users of Instagram, Twitter, and TikTok commodify their trauma in order to get likes and visibility. In early 2024, TikTok personality Reesa Teesa went viral aftering sharing fifty, five to ten minute TikTok posts titled, "Who TF Did I Marry?" The trauma she shared about marrying a man who she referred to as a "pathological liar" and "master manipulator'" resonated with millions of people globally. Reesa Teesa had a slew of media appearances and was signed to talent agency, CAA. This wasn't the first, nor will it be the last time, that someone gets opportunities for sharing their trauma. We live in a capitalist, fascist hellscape, many people will endlessly share their trauma without a second thought, hoping that they, too, can "make it big." Trauma gets clicks and views. But how much vulnerability is too much? Is there ever a "too much?" How does this help or hinder our movements?

As a twenty-something, when I started the *Guerrilla Feminism* Facebook and Instagram pages, I shared any and everything. I wrote long-form captions on Instagram about having been raped. I posted images on Facebook of text that told the history of my anxiety and C-PTSD. I created a story highlight on Instagram about my eating disorder that wasn't about wanting to be thin, but more so just a fear of food making me feel ill. I wrote openly and honestly about the ex-boyfriend who assaulted me and gave me herpes. Even though these posts always took a lot from me emotionally and mentally, I believed in the power of speaking up. Perhaps as a twenty-something, this was initially helpful to me—to find my voice. It was also helpful in gaining likes and follows, which I didn't feel great about. I didn't want to be defined by herpes or disabilities or mental illness or any one thing. I didn't want to be known as the girl online who was always talking about sexual violence—even if my life's trajectory had been shaped by it.

A while after posting these screenshots of my past trauma, I started looking at the like count on them. I noticed how they seemed to outdo my other, more lighthearted posts, or even my posts about

---

24   Anne Lamott, *Bird by Bird: Some Instructions on Writing and Life*, (New York, NY: Vintage, 1995), 6.

broader issues of racism, sexism, ableism, and misogyny. I began to feel like I needed to always post deeply personal shit if I wanted to be seen online. My Instagram became a curated digital museum of trauma memories. I oscillated between feelings of empowerment and depletion. Every comment that told me how "brave" I was made me want to scream. Every comment of "I feel so sorry for you" made me want to hide. The likes would rise as quickly as my anxiety. The follows increased, too, and I suddenly had hundreds of thousands of eyes on me and my trauma. I knew I could lose those followers just as quickly as I gained them.

It got really bad when I realized I was only posting about my trauma. In fact, I started to have thoughts like, "Hmm, what traumatic memory can I salvage and create content around for a post today?" It wasn't coming naturally to me. Had it ever? I wasn't *selling* my trauma, as there was no exchange of money, but I felt like I was giving fragments of myself away for a chance at popularity and virality. By the time I had this realization, I had nothing left for myself. It began to scare me that my large online presence was finding its way to offline spaces. I would agree to go on dates with people who, unbeknownst to me, knew my complete trauma history before ever meeting up in person. The more I posted online about myself, the more I began to fear for my physical safety. I often had dates confront me with their knowledge of my various traumas. They'd start with, "So, I Googled you..." And in that moment, I would make sure to look for an exit just in case. After going out with one man a few times, he finally told me he had followed me online for a while. This made me queasy that he hadn't told me sooner. We fucked once (it was terrible), and immediately afterwards he made the joking comment: "Can't believe I got to fuck the creator of *Guerrilla Feminism*." I knew I wasn't a celebrity, nor did I want to be one, and though this guy was joking, his comment still grossed me out.

Is writing about my trauma right now a commodification of it? I'm not sure and I'm still struggling with figuring out where the line is. If we own all that has happened to us, then we get to decide if we want to commodify it and how we do so. However, I'm not sure we always know when we're commodifying it.

If we're going to post about trauma online, at least let it be our own. However, as I've illustrated throughout this chapter, this is a complicated task. When we identify solely with our traumas, we are shrinking ourselves and putting ourselves in boxes with no room to breathe. It's important to note here that much of this self-identification has been lumped under the term "identity politics" incorrectly. Combahee River Collective member, Barbara Smith, who coined the phrase in the 1970s, said in an article in 2020:

> By "identity politics," we meant simply this: we have a right as Black women in the nineteen-seventies to formulate our own political agendas... We don't have to leave out the fact that we are women, we do not have to leave out the fact that we are Black. We don't have to do white feminism, we don't have to do patriarchal Black nationalism—we don't have to do those things. We can obviously create a politics that is absolutely aligned with our own experiences as Black women—in other words, with our identities. That's what we meant by "identity politics," that we have a right. And, trust me, very few people agreed that we did have that right in the nineteen-seventies. So we asserted it anyway.[25]

It's important to note that this ideology was used to explain Black women's varied experiences and identities, specifically.

Not only do we seem to sell or overshare our own trauma on the internet, but, perhaps more egregiously, we seem to share others' trauma as well. The term "trauma porn," coined by writer Wayne Wax in a 2014 *Thought Catalog* article, is the idea that the media (and others) exploit tragedies and trauma for personal gain. We see this in online spaces from influencers as well. For example, anytime a white influencer shares an image showing Black people in pain or deceased, that's trauma porn. White people don't have the context or lived experience to post about this, and there's the added issue of white people *only* posting about Black pain and death, as if that's all Black people are. We've also been seeing this in how people post about Palestinians. Many Palestinians, however, have given others permission to repost these traumatic images since mainstream media has chosen to sanitize what's actually being done to them. Even during a genocide, Palestinians all over the world are posting moments of joy, too, and this is also

---

25   Barbara Smith, Demita Frazier, and Beverly Smith, "The Combahee River Collective Statement," Blackpast, August 29, 2019, https://www.blackpast.org/african-american-history/combahee-river-collective-statement-1977/.

important for the rest of us to pay attention to and repost.

As a woman online, sharing our stories or our opinions can be at best risky and at worst deadly whether we have a following or not. As a person with a large following, I often need to weigh the pros and cons before I enter a conversation with a story or comment. I receive harassment and abuse even from my own followers, depending on the topic. It's easy to think that having a following means people like you—at least to some extent—but that's not always the case. In a world where "hate-following"[26] is a thing, we can never be completely sure someone is following us because they like us. I've had various experiences of followers waiting until I fuck up just so they can then "prove" I was incorrect. I've had followers consistently message me, "Why aren't you posting about X, Y, Z? I guess you don't care." On social media, posting equals representation and endorsement. It's the difference between caring and not caring.

Most recently when posting about my pro-Palestine and anti-genocide stance, I was met with an onslaught of private messages from followers who called me names and threatened me. One follower messaged me incessantly to the point where I had to block them. Then, they messaged me from another profile. This is a common tactic used in social media spaces. It shows the person being harassed that they aren't entitled to having boundaries. Followers can think I'm great most of the time, but if I step out of line, I can be lambasted. For instance, I have had followers tell me to kill myself because I'm not vegan. The drastic swing from "Thank you so much for posting about X," turns into "Fuck you for posting about Y." We can't all agree on everything, but I find it hard to engage with people who, for example, don't agree that Israel (with the help of the U.S.) is enacting a genocide against Palestinians.

When you have a following, you have some semblance of power, but this power dynamic is rife with contention. You feel like you owe hundreds of thousands of people whatever they want. You begin to believe any and all lies told about you. As your humanity is stripped away, bit by bit, you begin to lose your identity; your self. The harass-

---

26   AUTHOR'S NOTE: Following a person on social media even though you can't stand them, but you find them captivating

ment and abuse in these moments is painful and traumatic.

The requirement to speak up about any topic at any time is that this still won't appease followers. There are sometimes claims of "virtue-signaling," defined by Cambridge Dictionary as: "an attempt to show other people that you are a good person, for example by expressing opinions that will be acceptable to them, especially on social media."[27] When I'm thinking of entering a conversation, what also goes into my pros and cons are the following questions: 1) Who will be upset if I post about it?, 2) Who will be upset if I *don't* post about it?, and 3) Is posting this virtue-signaling? This process feels a bit like what I imagine a celebrity's public relations person goes through. Nothing is ever enough and everything is too much. People have a very difficult time with nuance when they're online.

Online abuse, harassment, and cyberbullying are enormous and still have not been consistently handled, if handled at all. This becomes even more difficult when it's happening within our own circles. When we call on social media platforms to do something--anything--our calls are left unanswered; often not even acknowledged. Digital violence is specific to internet culture, though it can permeate offline as well. Even if it stays only online, we still need to be taking it seriously. Survivors of digital violence still deserve peace, understanding, and respect. I started to do conscious nervous system resets after I would face online abuse or after I would share something traumatic. This included: breathing exercises, somatic self-support exercises, shaking, and more. I noticed how much better my body felt. I noticed I was able to relax more. This, coupled with support from friends and family, has changed how I engage in online spaces.

Social media platforms are vehicles for capitalism and no amount of trauma storytelling is going to uproot or disrupt this. Our stories become capitalist propaganda. Instagram, TikTok and Twitter will all go away some day. New platforms will emerge. If we are to use and think of social media as anything other than distraction, we need to solidify our relation to each other in online spaces and offline ones. We need to say "No!" to any person or platform who attempts to use our

---

27   "Virtue Signaling Definition," Cambridge Dictionary, accessed July 27, 2024, https://dictionary.cambridge.org/us/dictionary/english/virtue-signaling.

trauma as a commodity, even if this means saying no to ourselves. We can't continue to share our stories of trauma amongst advertisements for waist trainers.

No longer am I trying to be seen by the algorithm of social media. No longer am I engaging in the spectacle of trauma porn.

HYPERVIGILANCE AS A PORTAL

Sometimes a question shoots through me: Are there people who don't have to think about their bodies? It makes me wonder what conditions, what supports, have conspired in the world to make this true for them. Why is it not true for someone like me?

—JOHANNA HEDVA

MY BODY IS A BOMB—a ticking time bomb waiting to explode. This thought moves through me daily. I hear and feel the ticking. I don't know when it will detonate. How do I live in a body that is the site of numerous crime scenes? How do I clear away the many fingerprints? How do any of us?

I clean up each mess, but there is a putrid residue that remains. I can't scrub away the smell, the feel, to what it was before. The "before" doesn't exist anymore. Did it ever? Did I dream it? Somewhere inside I know I'm not dirty; I know I don't need scrubbing. I'm just a slightly different shape than I was and this new shape needs tending and care. This new shape is ripe like a bruise. Even though a person, people, and/or events created this new shape without my consent, it is still me. I'm now a shapeshifter. I own my shapes—however many there might be (there will be many). No bombs were left at the crime scenes. There is no bomb inside me. The bomb I feel is memory—it can't hurt me. It is within me, but it is not me. I'm responding to my new shape. My heart is the same one I was born with. Its beat is limitless. I stay curious, and wonder which new shape I might become next. My heart still dances amidst the bomb threats. I make it so. Hypervigilance is a portal, but first it's a slammed door keeping me stuck.

✻

Hypervigilance is a near constant scanning and rescanning for threat in a person's environment. Those of us with hypervigilance who engage in movement work and activism are essential because we are fierce protectors with heightened senses. Our hypervigilance is enormously helpful when we're at protests or when danger might be afoot. It gives us adrenaline. We assume the position to fight, flee, freeze, or fawn. This is less helpful, however, when we're stuck in a hypervigilance loop due to past traumatic experiences. Dr. Judith Herman writes of "hyperarousal" in her highly-acclaimed book, *Trauma and Recovery: The Aftermath of Violence—From Domestic Abuse to Political Terror*, that those of us with PTSD

> ...do not have a normal "baseline" level of alert but relaxed attention. Instead, they have an elevated baseline of arousal: their bodies are always on the alert for danger. They have an extreme startle response to unexpected stimuli, as well as an intense reaction to specific stimuli associated with the traumatic event. It also appears that traumatized people cannot "tune out" repetitive stimuli that other people would find merely annoying; rather, they respond to each repetition as though it were a new, and dangerous, surprise.[1]

When I feel hypervigilant, which is often, it's as though I'm drowning in sensory overload. I'm too alert to think thoughts. My mind is blank, yet terrifying. My muscles are tense. As a neurodivergent person, I already struggle with sensory overload. I imagine the hypervigilant part of me dressed like a soldier standing guard. She can't relax. She can't do anything except scan, wait, and defend. Being in online spaces with the platform I've had for over a decade has left me paranoid and hypervigilant. I already had a lifetime's worth of hypervigilance prior to being chronically online. It started so young for me that I only vaguely remember living without it. The life I had before it doesn't feel real. Perhaps it wasn't. It seems like a fairytale.

My parents used to call me, "The Princess and The Pea," because I felt everything. "The Princess and The Pea" tells the story of a prince looking for his one true (rigtig "rightful") princess. One stormy night, a girl goes to the prince's castle to seek shelter. She declares herself

---

1   Judith Herman, *Trauma and Recovery: The Aftermath of Violence—From Domestic Abuse to Political Terror* (New York, NY: Basic Books, 1997), 36.

a princess, but the prince and the queen are doubtful. Thus, a test is prepared to see if the girl is a real princess. The queen places a single pea in her bed. The pea is covered by twenty mattresses and twenty eider-down beds. When asked how she slept the following morning, the girl proclaims:

> "Oh, miserably!" said the Princess. "I scarcely closed my eyes all night long. Goodness knows what was in my bed. I lay upon something hard, so that I am black and blue all over. It is quite dreadful!"[2]

She felt the singular pea underneath all those mattresses. She passed the test. She is a princess after all because she is so delicate to notice such a small, insignificant thing. The text reads, "No one could be so tender-hearted but a real princess."

As a child, I didn't relate to the princess. I didn't think anything of her or the story. It wasn't a particularly exciting read like some of the other stories I knew. However, when I revisited the story as an adult, I saw what my parents saw. The girl in the story clearly had Sensory Processing Disorder. The girl was me. As a child, I had many sensory issues (I still do). I remember always feeling overwhelmed and distressed by sounds, sights, and touch, specifically. There is a neurodivergent joke that goes: "Are you the type of autistic who has to wear socks all of the time or the type to never wear socks?" I am the latter. My parents would joke that they needed to have me seen by a podiatrist because I would put up such a fight when I would have to wear socks and shoes (I called them "foot prisons").

I was diagnosed with Sensory Processing Disorder, but not until I was an adult. This diagnosis explains so much about my childhood and my present day life. SPD is a neurological disorder, not a mental health one, that often involves physical symptoms and difficulty with the brain interpreting these symptoms. Anxiety and hypervigilance can often be secondary characteristics of this disorder. Mental health counselor Rachel S. Schneider writes about SPD saying, "People with sensory issues usually don't have issues with sensation, but they struggle with percep-

---

2   Hans Christian Andersen, "The Princess and The Pea/Prindsessen Paa Ærten," trans. W. A. Craigie and J. K. Craigie, Bilinguator, accessed August 10, 2024, https://bilinguator.com/en/online?book=11456.

tion and responding appropriately to what the brain perceives."[3] In a study that was done on children, those with SPD brains have white matter (a type of brain tissue that connects different areas of the brain and spinal cord, enabling them to process and exchange information) that is less well connected in areas where it should be, specifically near the back of the brain.[4] In an article for *ADDitude*, an online magazine for families and adults living with ADHD and related conditions, writer Janice Rodden explains SPD further by saying it:

> disrupts how the brain—the top of the central nervous system—takes in, organizes, and uses the messages received through our body's receptors. We take in sensory information through our eyes, ears, muscles, joints, skin and inner ears, and we use those sensations—we integrate them, modulate them, analyze them and interpret them—for immediate and appropriate everyday functioning.[5]

SPD affects all eight senses: sight, taste, touch, smell, sound, vestibular (balance), proprioception (movement), and interoception (internal). Having SPD means it's difficult to integrate everyday sensations. Just like our princess, those of us with SPD can *over* or *under* feel. That sensation is then incorrectly perceived by our brain. With SPD, people tend to crave certain sensations, avoid some, and ignore others. For me, I crave certain touch: I like to feel soft things, textured things with my fingers. I like receiving certain touch from people I love. I avoid: bright lights, lighting that changes drastically, loud noises, large groups/crowds, mixing food, haircuts, heights, head movements, feeling hungry, feeling thirsty, feeling my heartbeat pounding, feeling a full stomach, feeling a full bladder, and excessive body heat. I don't tend to ignore any of my senses, unfortunately. Most people with SPD struggle with at least one or more of their eight senses. My primary issues revolve around sight, interoception, and hearing, however, like I noted above there are some things that incorporate other senses that I struggle with.

---

3   Rachel S. Schneider, *Making Sense: A Guide to Sensory Issues* (Arlington, TX: Sensory World, 2016), 20.

4   Ibid., 59.

5   Janice Rodden, "Signs of Sensory Processing Disorder (SPD) in Adults," ADDitude, August 25, 2023, https://www.additudemag.com/sensory-processing-disorder-in-adults/#:~:text=If%20you%20are%20hypersensitive%20to,don't%20hear%20or%20feel.

Being out in the world often feels like I'm walking around with a body-sized open wound. SPD is hypervigilance as it relates to any sensory input. Rodden writes: "Many adults describe the feeling as being assaulted, attacked, or invaded by everyday experiences. They are bothered by sounds or textures that most people don't hear or feel."[6] People who don't have SPD are able to habituate to a specific stimuli, so they eventually ignore it or stop paying attention to it. However, those of us with SPD never stop noticing the stimuli. Schneider writes, "It's as if the sensory input is new each time it occurs."[7] This can make for very distressing moments. SPD, coupled with the hypervigilance I have from traumatic experiences, creates a weight so heavy, so brutally uncomfortable that it almost feels grounding. When I visualize it, it looks like The Ghost of Christmas Yet to Come from the "The Muppet Christmas Carol." I am the ghost wearing its heavy robes. SPD anchors me to the world. I feel it all, literally. When it's especially difficult, I feel afraid of my heartbeat. An octopus has three hearts. Does it notice its heartbeat in all three? How intense that must feel! Noticing and feeling my heartbeat means I'm alive. I don't always like this, because knowing I'm alive means knowing I could die at any moment. Knowing I'm alive means dealing with the possibility of immense discomfort and distress due to sensory overload at any second. Eventually, I will become so dysregulated that I have a meltdown.

The princess in "The Princess and The Pea" feels the pea because she is hypervigilant and has SPD. She feels the pea, because her perception of sensations is skewed in her brain. The princess is considered delicate, sensitive, fragile—traits only a "true" princess can possess. Nearly 100 years after its publication, fellow Danish writer and Andersen biographer, Signe Toksvig noted, "[the story] seems to the reviewer not only indelicate but indefensible, in so far as the child might absorb the false idea that great ladies must always be so terribly thin-skinned."[8] A true statement that one could say about most

---

6   Ibid.

7   Rachel S. Schneider, *Making Sense: A Guide to Sensory Issues* (Arlington, TX: Sensory World, 2016), 62.

8   Signe Toksvig, "The Life of Hans Christian Andersen: Toksvig, Signe, 1891-1983," Internet Archive, January 1, 1970, https://archive.org/details/lifeofhanschrist-t0000unse/page/n309/mode/2up, 179.

princess stories where the girls/women are more object than subject. These "objects" are consistently admired for their fragility bordering on frailty, their tentativeness, their meekness, and their desperate need for men to rescue them. Professor Maria Tatar gives a different take on our princess than Toksvig saying: "...the sensitivity of the princess can also be read on a metaphorical level as a measure of the depth of her feeling and compassion. And Andersen also gives us a feisty heroine, who defies the elements and shows up on the doorstep of a prince."[9] Unlike many princess stories, the princess in "The Princess and The Pea" doesn't wait for her prince to come to her—she seeks him out. She has a boldness, a tenacity that princesses are not supposed to have. She is also sensitive and hyper-aware.

Sensitivity is not fragility nor is it a trait put on to please the prince and taken off later. The girl is herself and this doesn't change. She is oblivious to the test that the prince and the queen created. She speaks about her inner knowing and felt-sense—that something was under all those mattresses and beds. Something as small as a pea ruined her sleep. Though sensitivity does not equal fragility, I often think I'm fragile. The world is too loud and bright for someone like me; for many of us. When I don't see others struggling in these same ways, I feel immensely alone. I feel like I could break at any time. I worry I'm a walking broken thing already. I worry I can't put myself back together. I also wonder if being fragile is really such a bad thing. It's a hard thing, for sure, but it's not bad to feel like we could shatter at any given moment. Maybe instead that means we're highly engaged in life.

Several years ago I started frequenting Reddit boards about SPD and Autism. Naturally, I thought to look to online micro-communities for belonging, solidarity, and advice. I read various posts similar to my own experiences. SPD is real. I am real. I am sensitive. I am probably fragile—at least sometimes. There have been countless times where something small, insignificant, imperceptible (to anyone else) ruined my sleep, my day, a moment. There have been too many times where I've panicked over a sensation in my body so tiny and quiet. Had I made it up? No. I *felt* it. I feel everything, and my brain process-

---

9   Maria Tartar, "The Princess and The Pea - Hans Christian Andersen," essay, in *The Annotated Classic Fairy Tales* (New York, NY: W. W. Norton & Company, 2002), 284—87, 284.

es it weirdly. It's difficult to be *so* self-aware, *so* emotionally open, *so* disoriented by sensations in a capitalist hellscape. The intensity with which I feel things, coupled with my online presence, has given way to more hypervigilance. Sometimes it feels like my Instagram is the "Town Square" and people are throwing tomatoes at me. My audience has expanded exponentially since I started *Guerrilla Feminism* on Facebook and Instagram in 2011. For the past five years, my following has slowed down, but there are still hundreds of thousands of humans there. The internet allows any and everyone to make their opinions known in real time. I have been brutally critiqued and harassed online. I'm not even famous nor am I a billionaire. I don't have the luxury of having a "team" that reads through and deletes the offending (and often abusive) comments.

The other very uncomfortable part of having an online presence, especially as someone with severe and chronic hypervigilance, is *The Lurker*. Social media lurkers don't follow people, but they like to keep tabs on them. They will watch our stories, look at our posts, and wait to attack via direct messages or by randomly commenting. They are a part of our audience, but they are hoping we fail, fall from grace. Even some followers want this to happen. I can never be sure who is following me and for what reason. I can never be sure who is gearing up to attack me at any moment. The hypervigilance I feel in the online space I started—a space I created to find and feel belonging—is burdensome.

I feel sensations every millisecond and they often disturb me. This is why I ended up on Zoloft at seventeen. These sensations were so loud that I could no longer function. Medication and Cognitive Behavioral Therapy were the only things I had access to at the time. I'm grateful for this, because it literally saved my life. However, since I've been on Zoloft now for over two decades, I question its efficacy. Because I started taking it as a teenager, I worry it blocked my natural capacity to learn how to feel and be okay with feeling sensations. Now that I'm an adult, I know that Occupational Therapy and Somatics are much more helpful than CBT. Medication helps quiet my brain's perception of what I feel, but it's not a fix. There is no fix. I'm learning how to feel sensations without being flooded.

I'm sensation stunted. I was learning how to be in my body at seventeen, even though I had experienced trauma before then. I was getting back to myself. Then more trauma happened. Then medication. Then more little deaths of what little progress I had made. This is life, I suppose. I used to think I just didn't like feeling certain things—emotions and sensations—but now I think I don't like feeling at all. Even if it's joy I'm feeling, it's uncomfortable. I feel suspicious of it. My brain can't process it as "good." Feeling anything is overwhelming to my nervous system. I used to tell my therapist when I was seventeen that I just wanted to feel like myself again. She would ask me what that meant. I couldn't articulate it. Now I can. I just wanted to go back to the lack of hypervigilance I had around my feelings and sensations. I just wanted to go back to before the trauma. I just wanted to *live* each day instead of endure.

As a woman and a rape survivor on the internet, I live in a state of what I call Chronic Digital Revictimization and Hypervigilance. It's the idea that those of us in online spaces are consistently victim-blamed, verbally abused, and disbelieved, thus, we are constantly on edge, scanning our online surroundings, fearing what horribly abusive thing we may be inundated with next. Myself and other survivors are inundated daily with cyber abuse in the form of comments and posts on social media platforms.

With Chronic Digital Revictimization and Hypervigilance, survivors doing activist work may also deal with the physiological responses to trauma. These include: *Flight, Fight, Freeze,* and *Fawn.* Regarding the first three, Peter Levine, author and psychotraumatologist, writes:

> If the situation calls for aggression, a threatened creature will fight. If the threatened animal is likely to lose the fight, it will run if it can. These choices aren't thought out; they are instinctually orchestrated by the reptilian and limbic brains. When neither fight nor flight will ensure the animal's safety, there is another line of defense: immobility (freezing), which is just as universal and basic to survival[10]

Many rape survivors, including myself, reacted to the assault(s) with the *freeze* response, and because of this, are often victim-blamed in a variety of ways including being asked, "Why didn't you *fight* back?"

---

10   Peter A. Levine and Ann Frederick. *Waking the Tiger: Healing Trauma* (New York, NY: North Atlantic Books, 1997), 95.

Even less discussed than the *freeze* response is the *fawn* response, coined by psychotherapist Pete Walker. The *fawn* response is done by attempts at pleasing or appeasing another person. There is typically a power dynamic where the person doing the *fawn* response has less power than the other person. During a *fawn* response, a person will often deny their own needs over another person's in order to "keep the peace." This is a proactive response to halt further danger. There is also another type of *fawn* response called *appease* which is a "reactive strategy to survive by self-snuffing all life force energy while conscious."[11] Many women-identifying folks exhibit these trauma responses.

How might these physiological responses show up online? *Flight* might look like a person who just decided to delete their entire social media after getting attacked by trolls in order to get out of harm's way or making all of their social media accounts private. *Fight* may show up by having an online argument with a troll or comrade that may escalate to an offline altercation. It might also look like a call-out.[12] *Freeze* may look like desensitization when reading abusive comments and shutting down internally. Finally, *Fawn* might be negotiating with a troll or doing whatever they're asking out of fear in order to keep things from escalating. A person can move through each of these or stay longer in one over another, just like offline. *Fight, Flight, Freeze,* and *Fawn* are not static and we have no conscious choice in what our body does.

In movement work, where many of us live at the intersection of multiple marginalized identities and trauma, we are constantly navigating how we each show up for and with each other. One person's *flight* response may look different from another's. One person might *freeze* while another *fights*. We have to make space for all of this. We have to make space for our differences so we can organize, mobilize, and coalition-build. Our hypervigilance can be a helpful tool in our activist work. We are hyper-aware and hyper-sensitive to global struggles. We are also the ones who can see more subtle instances of oppression and alert our comrades early on. We are excellent at protests because we constantly scan and rescan the environment for threats in order to

---

11   AUTHOR'S NOTE: from Linda Thai's training, "Befriending the Nervous System: Strategies for Trauma, Sensory Processing, and Developmental Wounds"

12   AUTHOR'S NOTE: typically one person leads the charge, and a group of people follow suit to focus on a single person who is engaging in oppressive behaviors.

keep our community safe. We're quick-thinking and fast-acting. We can burn out quickly, though.

Hypervigilance feels a lot like grief; it's a heavy, weighty, murky thing that I can't take off. It's warming, even comforting—a cocoon in a cold, unsafe world. It is both expansive and confining. I feel the way it stymies my breath. I feel it creep around my body. When I try to ignore it, it grows stronger, louder, and harsher. When I invite hypervigilance in, it does its dizzying dance, moves things around like an interior decorator, but gradually releases me from its grip. Hypervigilance knits itself in my bones—ancestral hypervigilance, communal hypervigilance, global hypervigilance, personal hypervigilance—the hypervigilance of one moment ending and being on alert for the next to begin. I worry all of the time for all of us. How do we make room for it all? How do we continue to live while chronically breaking open?

I've often felt like I wasn't made for this world. I know I'm not alone in this. Everything is too much and I don't know how to handle it. There is grief in the hypervigilance I feel every moment. I cling too much. I grasp too tight. I think I have control, but I don't. None of us do. I live in a chronic state of hypervigilance, which makes me grieve the life I could have had. I attempt to "prepare" for change. I attempt to "prepare" for loss. I've been doing this from birth, but various traumas like my parent's divorce, sexual assaults, and medical harm have increased this need for preparation. But when I "prepare," I feel the pain at least twice: during the preparation and during the actual event. I end up feeling it a third time, too: in the aftermath of the event; like an aftershock of an earthquake. In the Wikipedia definition for "Earthquake," it says: "It is the shaking of the surface of the Earth resulting from a sudden release of energy in the Earth's lithosphere that creates seismic waves."[13] My hypervigilance is a sudden release of energy, of love. I can't prepare for it. I don't need to.

I have spent so much of my life preparing for grief. I have been in a constant state of baking this pain, inhaling its bittersweetness. But when it happens; when the timer goes off and it's ready to come out of the oven, I'm never actually prepared. The preparations only hurt me.

---

13   "Earthquake," *Wikipedia*, July 2, 2024, https://en.wikipedia.org/wiki/Earthquake.

Life is always ebbing and flowing. Change is inevitable. No feeling, no experience lasts forever. This is difficult to comprehend sometimes—the loss/lack of control we feel when we truly live our lives. Grief is everywhere inside and outside of ourselves. We can't push it away. We can't prepare for it. This is a gift. We must let it come without waiting for it. We must feel it all. There is no way to avoid getting hurt in this life and I find that truth difficult. There are things I can do to lessen the risk, but there is nothing I can do to fully stop harmful things from happening to me (or the people I love).

What is so difficult for me is that it's not just experiences or events that I remain hypervigilant about; it's the sensations of my own body even when completely alone. Feeling hypervigilant and afraid of one-self is a tiresome and distressing way to live. I have fantasized about waking up one day and no longer wearing the heaviness of this hyper-vigilance; no longer feeling trapped and scared in my own body. But I know that if it were to completely disappear, that would feel like a loss. We need our hypervigilance. At a very basic level, hypervigilance keeps us safe. It also makes us aware of our own body as well as others' bodies. This is radical when living in a world where we're taught rugged individuals and to live in our heads, further disconnecting us from our bodies. Hypervigilance is a portal, it's love, and it wants us to live. I'm welcoming to my hypervigilance and hyperawareness, because it allows me to care deeply about myself and everyone else. I have a tendency to think that every bad thing will happen to me. I'm so grateful for this, because it gives me the capacity to feel into someone else's horrendous experience, realizing it could be mine someday. In activist work, we can use our hypervigilance to keep us safe, and also to tap into our well of immense compassion and empathy for what our comrades are struggling with, whether these struggles include incarceration, racism, discrimination, and more.

Hypervigilance can flood us, can overwhelm us. When this happens, I like to gently ask it to give me some space. I put up a glass wall between myself and my hypervigilance. I can still see and hear it, she can still see and hear me, and I can work with her more easily. I want to befriend this part of me; the part that is so fierce and feral and protective. I *need* to befriend this part of me. She is a portal of care. She is spell work. She is love.

The fairytale, "The Princess and The Pea," is a love letter to those of us with Sensory Processing Disorder. It's a love letter to anyone with hypervigilance. It's a love letter showing that heightened sensitivity and awareness can only aid in our collective, global struggle. We are the protectors of our movements. Our hypervigilance is both weapon and shield. It's also a portal, a gateway to collective liberation. An injury to one is an injury to all. My hypervigilance is still a seeping, glistening thing. She has not yet transformed into a portal. But I feel more openness there, I feel fluidity, I feel the portal brewing. May we all someday lean into the hypervigilance portal and feel all the love and care that lives there.

HOW DO I LOOK?

You're gonna die someday no matter how young you look.

—Jessica DeFino

MEN SCREAM AT WOMEN online for using beauty filters. These same men complain about women creating "false advertising" when they see women with and without makeup. Even some women yell at other women for these things. There is an unwritten rule that using a filter once in a while is fine, cute even, but using them repeatedly is misrepresentation. Feminists using these filters are examined more critically by non-feminists and feminists alike. They are told that they aren't "real" feminists. They are told that they are aiding in unattainable beauty standards. With these "beauty" filters, our faces create a portrait of a new being—a new us. We see ourselves with what are considered the "perfect" features for the time: symmetrical eyebrows, fake dark eyelashes, small nose, big lips, narrow jaw. We are stitched together with features from a facial detection algorithm. We are poreless, bright, and artificial. We can't stay in the beauty filter space for too long or we're interrogated, yelled at, dismissed. However, we're yelled at for showing our real, unfiltered faces as well. Comments about wrinkles, pores, and acne are constant. The loudest viewer on social media is the anonymous person sitting cozy behind their photoless account.

As girls, we do all sorts of things to fit in or stand out. I was consistently reminded that I didn't fit in. I didn't have the right clothes, the right hair, or the right kind of beauty. During story time in second grade, none of the girls wanted to play with my hair. Each girl would pair up, quietly braiding and brushing with their fingers the hair of another. Even I was paired up—with a blonde, straight-haired girl. I ran my little fingers through her glossy hair, smiling at its texture. When it came time to switch, the girl told me, "I can't play with your hair. It's too curly!" I sat, rejected and sad. I hated my hair even more than I did five minutes prior. Straight-haired girls have all the fun, I thought.

I attempted to kill my curls—death by flat iron. I read somewhere that straightening curls could damage them, so I straightened them into oblivion. I brushed them out and always wore my hair in a high pony-tail. Before we had a flat iron though, my mom would brush my hair, wrap it around, and bobby pin it in place. For countless nights, I slept, uncomfortably, with my hair like this. Each morning, I would unwrap my hair like a Christmas present, thinking that long, luxurious straight hair would magically appear. It never did. It would look a bit straighter after unleashing the massacre of bobby-pins. My hair still didn't look like the girls' hair I saw at school. I mostly kept my hair in a high ponytail—hoping no one would notice my conformity or my poor attempt at curl-killing. I felt like a fraud. I was one.

By the time I got to middle school, I had a roll-on watery glitter eyeshadow that I wore religiously. One swipe on each eyelid was all it took for me to feel like a starling. I started shaving at the first sign of peach fuzz on my legs and armpits. I received *Delia's* catalogs and circled the outfits I liked—trying to keep track of what was considered in fashion. There wasn't an emphasis on big lips or big butts at the time, but I already had a larger posterior, and white boys in middle school told me I had a "ghetto booty." I tried to shop at the stores that the popular kids shopped at, like Abercrombie & Fitch and 5, 7, 9 (which was a store that only sold clothing in those sizes), but these stores were expensive. I learned that beauty and class were reciprocal. People who had money could buy a prettier version of themselves. However, I also learned that I could wear all of the "right" stuff, but I still didn't look "right" in the eyes of the popular kids. I didn't have their specific facial features, bodies or personalities. I studied these girls like an anthropologist. I had a notebook where I would document what they wore in hopes that I could somehow replicate their outfits, their hair, their makeup, their faces. I tried on their laughter, their flirting, and their stares. This is cyborg behavior, according to poet Olivia Gatwood.

We were cyborgs, made up of the world's hand-me-downs and each other's stolen parts; girls who wanted to look like other girls while desperately attempting to look like no one and, in turn, all looking the same. We were constantly tinkering with our prized machines in the tool sheds of our bedrooms.[1]

Beauty was marketed everywhere around me. Walking the halls of middle school and highschool felt like a crash course in what beauty was and what beauty wasn't. I was hit over the head with girls who had something I didn't. Their straight hair, push-up bras, and body shimmer made a mockery of me.

In college, I bought a flat iron, and used it frequently. I singed my curls away. As the hot iron closed down on an individual curl, I would think, "Die, curl, Die!" I received more compliments with my straight hair. I was told, specifically by men, that I looked, "Pretty," "Sexy," and "Gorgeous." I took those compliments, and placed them like secrets in the corners of my mind. I tried so hard to hold what others thought was beautiful about me—even if I didn't agree. My hair isn't nearly as damaged as it could be, but I always think back to how using a straightener probably wilted my curls. Now, I want my curls fully intact, but they've had it with my shit. My curly hair, which I only started loving in my 30s, has become thinner. I fear that I am losing a sense of self. Where do I begin and where do I end? Am I still trying to look like the beautiful popular girls from highschool?

I have deep-seated "11" lines in the center of my forehead. They are almost an exact replica of my dad's. These lines carry a lineage. They have been here for a while, but I've noticed them more. They've been bothering me more. I'm not happy with how I look. I used to take so many selfies that I would then post on Instagram, and I've hardly taken any in the last few years. I try to remember that I look like my dad, my Nonno, and my grandma. I try to find solace in that, and I do, but I feel inadequate. Part of this is due to aging. I've never been this age before. I'm grateful for it, and I'm scared of it. I still recognize the person I see in the mirror, but it's clear she is older now. I'm also still getting used to my shorter hair. Many months ago, I chopped off my

---

1   Olivia Gatwood, "We Were Cyborgs: On the Construction of The Self as a Teenage Girl," *Literary Hub,* July 10, 2024, https://lithub.com/we-were-cyborgs-on-the-construction-of-the-self-as-a-teenage-girl/.

hair into a bob. I like it, but still I remember boys in middle school saying "girls are prettier with long hair."

My desire to keep my appearance from changing is not all due to vanity—it's how I know myself; how I've come to recognize myself these last several years. We get used to who we see looking back at us in the mirror. We see the micro-imperfections, but we don't see the aging—not as quickly, anyway. One day you're you, and you look like the you you've always known until, all of a sudden, mirror-you becomes unfamiliar—another person entirely. Who is this older person staring back at me? Where did these wrinkles come from? Has my lack of sleep caught up with me? Using Instagram or TikTok filters only quickens this unknowing of ourselves. Beauty filters, which are geared towards women, aren't any different than the airbrushed women we've seen on magazine covers for decades. The difference is that now us commoners have greater access to distorting and correcting our images. These filters are inherently racist as they often lighten skin color, change eye shape, and adjust facial features to meet white European beauty standards.

In her seminal essay from 1985, "A Cyborg Manifesto," professor emerita in the history of consciousness and feminist studies departments at the University of California, Santa Cruz, Donna Haraway writes:

> Communications technologies and biotechnologies are the crucial tools recrafting our bodies. These tools embody and enforce new social relations for women world-wide. Technologies and scientific discourses can be partially understood as formalizations, i.e., as frozen moments, of the fluid social interactions constituting them, but they should also be viewed as instruments for enforcing meanings.[2]

We exist as frozen moments on our curated social media pages. We delude ourselves into thinking that this is how we relate to each other. We think we're making the rules, but we don't have that power—not on these apps. The embodiment of technology is happening *to* us without our consent. How much of us is machine and how much of us is human? I'm concerned about social media platforms' biases and how they honor the continued freezing of ourselves, spe-

---

2   Donna Haraway, "A Cyborg Manifesto," *Manifestly Haraway*, April 1, 2016, 3—90, https://doi.org/10.5749/minnesota/9780816650477.003.0001.

cifically the freezing of our appearance. There is nothing subversive about a frozen face. In *Glitch Feminism*, Legacy Russel writes: "Glitched bodies—those that do not align with the canon of white cisgender heteronormativity—pose a threat to social order. Range-full and vast, they cannot be programmed." As feminists, as leftists, shouldn't we be more interested in becoming "glitched," instead of folding back into the mainstream, dominant culture?

My first experience with filters was on Snapchat. I never used it frequently, but it was fun to try on the puppy ears, the hair full of stars or butterflies, and puke a rainbow. My image was distorted, but in a darling way. Now we have filters that *yassify*[3] us. They plump our lips, darken our eyebrows, lengthen our eyelashes, lighten our skin, and make our nose smaller. These filters remove every wrinkle, every pore. We become frozen in time. Are we still human? I want to recognize myself. Filters and aging can make this difficult, though. Technology could be used in better, more important ways than creating caricatures of our faces or voices. When we think of robots, we think of women and submissiveness; women following orders from men and from capitalism a la "Alexa."[4] Our current technology has white men at the helm acting as Dr. Frankenstein.

In Haraway's view, the blending of technology with our personhood can allow for fluidity and subversion in our otherwise static socialized identities. She defines cyborgs as, "a cybernetic organism, a hybrid of machine and organism, a creature of social reality as well as a creature of fiction." We see this hybridity in online spaces where we use tools from various apps that distort and reshape our appearance. Granted, unlike the cyborg, we are using these tools to continue the status quo—to continue European beauty standards. Haraway continues: "The cyborg is a matter of fiction and lived experience that changes what counts as women's experience... the boundary between science fiction and social reality is an optical illusion."[5] In the cyborg world,

---

3   "To apply several beauty filters to (a picture or video of someone), typically making the subject look more made-up, potentially more feminine, and often unrecognizable." *Wiktionary*, https://en.m.wiktionary.org/wiki/yassify

4   AUTHOR'S NOTE: Amazon's virtual assistant technology

5   Donna Haraway, "A Cyborg Manifesto," *Manifestly Haraway*, April 1, 2016, 3—90, https://doi.org/10.5749/minnesota/9780816650477.003.0001.

there are no differences based on patriarchal gender essentialism. As cyborgs, women are not confined to specific roles or European beauty standards.

In a similar vein, Shelley Jackson's *Patchwork Girl*, a hypertext work that reimagines Mary Shelley's *Frankenstein*, also shows us the expansiveness and flexibility that cyborgs exhibit. In this work, the destroyed female monster that Dr. Frankenstein created is sewn back together with various body parts by Mary Shelley. Each body once belonged to a human woman. This is a clear commentary on the insolence of patriarchy. "Patchwork Girl" then falls in love with her creator, Mary Shelley. The reader acts as Shelley bringing the monster back to life. Patchwork Girl says: "I am buried here. You can resurrect me, but only piecemeal. If you want to see the whole, you will have to sew me together yourself." The monster "is a cyborg who is queer, disproportioned, and visibly scarred."[6] How she was created, Patchwork Girl doesn't follow orders to integrate into society. She is monstrous because her existence rejects the social order of things. Patchwork Girl refutes "womanhood." Cyborgs don't worry about how they look, nor do they buy into capitalistic beauty standards.

As an aging millennial, I think a lot about faces. I haven't had cosmetic work (yet), and I'm beginning to feel like an outlier. I'm questioning my face's imperfections each time I see someone else's taut forehead and plump lips. I'm too afraid of injections, so I buy products I'm ashamed of spending money on, like a nearly $400 red light therapy face mask or a $350 facial toning device. I've had chemical peels done and watched in excitement as flakes of my skin fell off. I feel like a bad Marxist feminist for (literally) buying into an industry that has taught me to hate myself and fix myself. I feel society's collective sense of urgency that I, as an aging woman, should hurry up and figure out what to do about my godforsaken old face. Being chronically online with so many followers/viewers hasn't helped with this.

When I started *Guerrilla Feminism* in 2011, I never posted my face. Even attaching my full name didn't happen immediately. It felt too

---

6   Heather Latimer, "Reproductive Technologies, Fetal Icons, and Genetic Freaks: Shelley Jackson's Patchwork Girl and the Limits and Possibilities of Donna Haraway's Cyborg," *MFS Modern Fiction Studies* 57, no. 2 (June 2011): 318—35, https://doi.org/10.1353/mfs.2011.0051.

scary. I craved a faceless internet existence like I had in my early teens. I didn't yet know what GF would become. I wanted some anonymity and safety for myself as I dipped my toes into the waves of social media. The lack of selfies was also because I knew I would be ridiculed for my looks. All women who post their face online are inevitably put in their place—even the women who appear to fit society's beauty standards. Nobody is too pretty to pick apart.

Eventually, I wanted people to know there was an actual human behind my Instagram and Facebook accounts. Part of this desire came about because I feared being doxxed[7]. Many people seemed to hate me and I worried that it was only a matter of time before they found out my identity. I also started to become resentful of followers who acted like I was a bot; that I was on the GF pages all day, every day. I was not at a 24-hour convenience store. I had porous boundaries during this time. I responded to private messages from followers immediately when I received them, moderated comments late into the night, and lost sleep over whether my pages would be a tangled mess when I awoke. Something needed to change, and since I didn't feel like I could take a break, I began posting selfies with captions talking about my humanity. Putting my face out there for the first time felt exciting and nerve-wracking. My followers were mostly supportive, and commented positively about my looks. This made me feel good and confident. Some followers just wanted me to shut-up and keep posting regular "content." Then came the trolls. I've read countless comments about how I have the wrong face. Trolls love to tell women they hate that they look like men. This is somehow the biggest insult, in their opinion. One troll commented to me, "You look like Jay Leno! Look at that chin!" I told my dad, who, without missing a beat, said: "At least he's Italian!"

Like most everyone, I have various insecurities about my appearance. I have a big nose made more pronounced by a delicate sparkly nose stud. I have small, thin lips, which don't currently fit the trend of big, plump ones. I have big teeth. I have curly hair, which was only

---

7   "[T]o publicly identify or publish private information about (someone) especially as a form of punishment or revenge" *Merriam-Webster,* https://www.merriam-webster.com/dictionary/doxxed?utm_campaign=sd&utm_medium=serp&utm_source=-jsonld

popular in the 1980s, but I wasn't born until 1985, so I missed out on that. I'm not skinny, not fat, but a secret third thing: average. As a former ballerina, hitting puberty was really disturbing. I wanted so badly to look strong and lithe like Suzanne Farrell or Gelsey Kirkland. My body just wasn't built that way. I'm stocky with muscular legs. I have hips that curve like parentheses. I have a big head and face (the "Greco" head as my family calls it). I have partially hooded eyes. I have more wrinkles, proving I've been here a while. None of these features are inherently unattractive, but none are considered ideal in the current aesthetic wasteland (except this big fat ass, of course).

I began to notice that after I'm on social media for too long, I start to see myself differently. I start to pick myself apart. There are things about bodies and faces that I had no idea were considered unattractive until I logged in to Instagram. At some point, I learned that my "hip dips"[8] were something that needed fixing. Never before had I given these slight indentations any thought. I also learned about how inconvenient hooded eyes are. Mainly because it means the eyes can appear "droopy." I was always fine with my eyes, but I did realize early on that I don't have much eyelid space to apply eyeshadow. Later, I learned about something called "Septum Arms," a new way to body-shame women by inferring that having larger upper arms is bad and unfeminine. "Septum Arms" has become akin to "butterface,"[9] something those of us who came of age in the 90s might remember. People on TikTok are now saying things like, "She's attractive 'cept-them arms.'" It's important to note that none of this conversation revolves around men, or very little of it does. Beauty standards *do* exist for men, but women don't tend to troll men online for not meeting those standards in the way men do women. Women will also troll each other for not meeting beauty standards or for meeting them too well via the use of a filter. Often, I have thought, "I wouldn't have survived social media as a teenager."

When I reached my mid-thirties, I noticed more "anti-aging" advertisements being shown to me every time I logged in to Instagram. I began to question where I could get some "work" done on my prob-

---

8   AUTHOR'S NOTE: An indentation where the hips meet the thighs due to a person's genetic bone structure

9   AUTHOR'S NOTE: "Everything 'but-her-face' is attractive"

lematic face. My internal monologue was rapacious: "Maybe just some Botox for these 11s? Maybe a lip lift so my top lip doesn't disappear when I smile? Maybe lip filler? Maybe I should get an eyebrow lift—especially on my left side where it's slightly lower than my right. Maybe I should get upper Blepharoplasty so I no longer have hooded eyes? Maybe I should get a nose job? Should I look into getting these hip dips removed? Is there a way I can make my head smaller? Should I just get a face lift? Fuck it, maybe I should just get a lobotomy." My mind was on the hunt for what was wrong with me; what else needed fixing, and I could always count on Instagram and TikTok to show me.

TikTok has its own shop in the app, which is essentially QVC for Gen Z. I get it, I too felt comforted watching QVC as a child when I was home alone. The difference is, I didn't have money to buy anything. Now I do have my own money and it's dangerous. On TikTok, we can watch brands discuss their products live. We can also watch paid advertisements from individual users excitedly and urgently talk about products they love. The sales are big and constant, from shapewear to sour candy to makeup. Though I wouldn't buy anything through the TikTok app, I would often search for the products on Google and buy them later. When I'm in a TikTok zone-out loop, it's easy to start rationalizing that, yes, I probably need to buy that chin lift strap. At some point, I realized that I have more money in my bank account when I delete the TikTok app from my phone.

The sense of urgency to buy things to fix things is hard to quiet. I want to look and feel my best *and* I want to resist the commodification of "anti-aging." Millions of products are marketed to women, and most have a bold "anti-aging" claim on them. We become obsessed with retinols and hyaluronic acid. We think using these products and ingredients will vanish the decades shown on our face. We all think we look a certain way, but we don't see ourselves the way others do. Watching yourself age, while an enormous privilege, can feel disorienting. I look in the mirror and I still recognize the person I see, but I linger on things I once didn't notice—if they were even there at all. I linger on my pores, new wrinkles, and hormonal acne that has been with me since I got my first period at ten-years-old.

I have a skincare routine. I wear makeup. I paint my nails. As a femme, I like these things. I *need* them to feel grounded in my gender identity. I also appreciate the ritual in them. My femme identity feels akin to the cyborg. I'm consistently creating and recreating myself in ways that subvert and feel good. Being femme is a rejection of heteronormative ideas on what a queer person is and how they look. That being said, I know that I am supporting multi-billion dollar industries that are encouraging me to attempt to look a certain way (even if I subvert this in some ways), and stay looking that way until I die. I'm not immune to this pressure. I grew up with acne and had a lot of shame around it. I started seeing a dermatologist and an aesthetician in my twenties, mostly to figure out how to care for my acne. Though my acne woes have since calmed down, I still use plenty of stuff on my face to keep the tiny bumps at bay. I also use plenty of "anti-aging" products to coax my skin into thinking it is not the age it is. I don't even want to think about how much money I've spent on these products and devices. I can't bear it.

Social media shows how easy it is for people to change their face and body. I tell myself that I could never do that. Not because of any holier-than-thou moral superiority, but because of lack of money and the fact that I'm terrified (and traumatized) by medical intervention. Even Botox scares me because of the small chance that things could go wrong. I often think: "I will be in that small percentage of people who have a horrifying reaction to it." Having Somatic Symptom Disorder and C-PTSD (which includes medical trauma) makes this more difficult. For me, I just get one face in this life. My face is my face and that's it. For better or worse.

However, I *have* changed my face and body. I have used the serums, the lotions, the peels. I do cardio and weight lifting. I'm actively aging. All of these things have changed my face and body in various ways. While some are not purposeful, they still combine to change and evolve my being in a myriad of ways. Just because I have not had injections or surgery doesn't mean I haven't been (attempting) to change my outward appearance.

Perhaps this is why I don't like posting old pictures of a younger me; a wrinkle-less, unfiltered me. I worry people will see these images and think, "What happened to her?" What happened is that I've lived, damnit. I see and hear the way we all talk about women's looks in this world, especially women's aging. Many of us are not used to seeing women age, because women are not supposed to age. Women are supposed to do everything in their power to remain young. Women are supposed to get Botox in our twenties to prevent wrinkles. We're supposed to spend copious amounts of time, money, and energy on our appearance. Makeup and skincare routines are proudly lauded as "selfcare," and "meditation." We're supposed to do whatever it takes to stay relevant, and that relevance depends on our physical beauty. If we don't fall in line, we're forgotten, spit out, crushed.

I am not anti- or pro-cosmetic procedures. I sit somewhere in the grey space. Perhaps these procedures add to our cyborg quality. It's necessary for me to note that, for many of my trans kin, makeup and cosmetic procedures are life-affirming. When I critique cosmetic procedures, I'm not critiquing the ways in which trans folks access and use them. For those of us who are cis, these procedures might also help us feel grounded in our identity. Cis queer women who identify as femme might want to look more feminine. I know countless femmes who feel intensely uncomfortable without a set of acrylics. Some of us might get laser hair removal on our face and bodies. We might get eyelash extensions. There is also a newer procedure called, "Traptox," which uses Botox in the trapezius muscle, affecting the upper back, shoulder, and neck area. While this procedure can help relieve upper back and neck pain, it is sometimes advertised as "shoulder slimming." This procedure feels less about gender affirmation and more about gender essentialism. The idea is that women shouldn't have broad shoulders simply because we are women. A cyborg would never. It's not that our bodies need to be subverting gender stereotypes all day every day. However, when we attempt to fix a "problem" that is only a "problem" because women are afraid of looking "manly," that's when I question, "What the fuck are we doing?"

I'm exhausted by the discourse on cosmetic procedures as "feminist" or "not feminist." Asking the question, "Are cosmetic procedures feminist?" is the wrong question. It makes me think about people's very basic definition of feminism: it's all about *choice*. This is the idea that whatever someone does is feminist simply because they *chose* to do it. Cosmetic procedures are neither feminist nor anti-feminist. While

I can see that it's problematic to turn oneself into a non-aging entity, I can also see how getting procedures done can make a person feel better about themselves. Who is it really hurting?

When I interviewed beauty reporter and critic, Jessica DeFino about this tension, she noted that adherence to beauty standards is about power. By engaging in these standards, we're furthering oppressive systems.[10] If beauty standards equal power, or at least access to power, then the idea that changing our faces and bodies to fit current trends, in the name of feminism, feels duplicitous. This is precisely what the cyborg rejects. Obviously, people can get cosmetic procedures and still be feminist, but to call these procedures "feminist" is harmful and alarming. DeFino says:

> Every action you take in your life does not have to be some random monument to feminism... I think there's a lot of concern in calling [cosmetic procedures] "feminist" in that it dilutes the meaning of feminism... Because then we feel like we're participating in a collectively liberating political movement by getting lip fillers.[11]

Lip fillers will not set us free, but maybe they're a fun addition to our cyborg identity.

In some ways, I wish I could get cosmetic work. I wish I could get Botox and filler. I don't want to do these things, because I don't want to deal with the upkeep. I also don't want to resist the aging process. I struggle with this, because I feel resentment towards the fact that so many people my age are getting work done, and yet, I'm supposed to just... age. We could say this is jealousy, but it feels deeper than that. It feels like grief. It feels like a loss of camaraderie or solidarity. It's hard to feel like I'm out here aging alone. In the same breath, I understand that people getting cosmetic work does not negate my own beauty, nor does it stop the aging process for anyone. It freezes people, but at some point, everyone will look old or older.

Something I often hear people say is they want to get work done so they can continue to look like themselves. While I understand the sentiment, none of us can stay looking the same forever, and why

---

10   Lachrista Greco, "'Anti-Aging' Is Anti-Living," Rage & Softness with Lachrista Greco, February 3, 2023, https://lachrista.substack.com/p/anti-aging-is-anti-living.

11   Ibid.

would we want to? We will never be able to be who we once were—before all the living we have done. Each line, each wrinkle is visual proof of life. We can't erase time. We are more our insides than we are our outsides. Both grow and change, of course, but the outside is performance. This is fun to play with, but to what extent?

Would we see wrinkles, lines, pores, acne, volume-loss, thin lips, small asses, small breasts, broad shoulders as "bad" if it wasn't shoved down our throats that we need to change these things? What would our world look like without the pressure to stay and look young forever? What would our world look like if we accepted wrinkles on ourselves and each other? What would our world look like if aging just was.. neither bad nor good? I reject the morality game we play about a process that is natural, inescapable.

The aging "gracefully" crowd is deficient. What does aging "gracefully" actually mean? "Graceful" assumes "good," but why must we place any morality on aging? People will age differently based on many factors, some we have no control over. If anything, aging is hardcore: dirty, messy, not timid and perfect. I reject the aging "gracefully" nonsense as much as I reject the "anti-aging" nonsense. Ideally, we need to divest from both.

Since I'm in my late 30s, I struggle with reconciling my desire to look "beautiful" to others while also feeling too tired to care. Everywhere I look I'm reminded that I look my age. This isn't bad, but it sometimes makes me feel a sense of urgency to find and keep a partner before I'm considered "too" old. The media does not respond to aging men in this way. Society tells us that older men are more interesting, more attractive, more desirable. Aging men have a safety that aging women don't. Men, in general, have a safety that women don't.

I don't want to play the game, but I still do. I'm not getting procedures done, but I own too many devices and products that promise youthful skin and the erasure of life. Beauty and capitalism are drenched in love for each other. I've started wearing less makeup, more out of exhaustion and lack of time than any personal beauty strike. I want to be done with caring about how I look. I want to be done caring about how to "fix" how I look. I have put in more than enough time and energy towards this. The unlearning feels like it's taking forever.

I purposely log off social media after getting too many "beauty" ads. I keep trying to show up as my authentic, wrinkled and zit-faced self.

I want to divest from anti-aging. Some days it feels too difficult to get there, though. It's brutal to feel alone in that fight. So I go about my business—do my little skincare routine, put on some makeup, look in the mirror wondering when I might not recognize the woman I see in front of me. How can we divest from anti-aging? Jessica DeFino says that the most effective thing we can do is to "reframe 'anti-aging' as living. If you replace the word 'aging'' with 'living' in any marketing materials sent your way, it really diminishes the glow and appeal. We're trying to optimize ourselves as if we are pieces of machinery and not sentient human beings."[12]

With the rise of Artificial Intelligence, human and machine will become even more blended, less discernible. We're already witnessing this on apps that create images out of our personal photos. People are also Photoshopping themselves into oblivion, so offline they are un-recognizable. Unlike the cyborg identity from Haraway's essay or Shelley's hypertext, our current AI is not being used to subvert anything, but rather, being built to continue the status quo. In a 2023 interview, Haraway noted that she isn't against AI, especially when used in interesting and helpful ways, but she doesn't approve of AI or robotization that is "a white male phallic masturbation."[13]

We are currently in the "white male phallic masturbation" portion of AI, which is concerning, useless, and, quite frankly, boring. Using AI to create filters that force our faces to fit current beauty trends is not cyborg behavior. It keeps us in a never ending loop of subjugation to mainstream, capitalist, and white supremacist culture. Maybe someday we'll utilize AI in ways that actually help, not harm, humans. As Haraway mentions, we could use AI for labor practices in ways that don't take jobs from humans, but act as partial relief, like using it to craft and send work emails. We need to break away from white Silicon Valley men and their sterile, unimaginative use of AI and technology. We need people who understand the delicate blending of nature,

---

12   Ibid.

13   "Donna Haraway on AI," *La Mapa TELEVISIÓN*, July 4, 2023, https://www.youtube.com/watch?v=4FycNIeS6GY.

machine, and human. Beauty filters are a waste of time and creation. Women are in a state of hyper-surveillance, and AI is only making this surveillance stronger. British sociologist Rosalind Gill says: "Surveillance of women's bodies constitutes perhaps the largest type of media content across all genres and media forms."[14]

Thankfully, there are activists and artists doing incredible things with makeup and hair styles to subvert AI. They are applying makeup and wearing their hair in ways that obscure the five points of facial detection: forehead, nose, each cheek and chin. CV Dazzle, a project created in 2010 by artist Adam Harvey, disrupts facial detection algorithms by concealing a person's face through asymmetry, covering parts of the face with hair, placing gems on the face, and applying makeup in bold colors and patterns[15]. Similarly, multidisciplinary artist Joselyn McDonald created a YouTube tutorial showing how to apply makeup and flowers to obscure facial detection algorithms. McDonald importantly notes: "Because surveillance harms womxn, through cyberstalking, spouseware, and facial recognition technology being used to detect identities of womxn in porn, I wanted to create femme looks to engage women (and anyone else interested in the rituals of makeup) with facial recognition topics."[16]

Perhaps we'll soon follow in the cyborg's footsteps and become ungovernable and undeterred by capitalism and beauty standards. Perhaps we'll all stop caring, or at the very least, stop focusing so much time and energy on our appearance in ways that never make us feel good. If we go the way of the cyborg, we will have more fluidity, function, and ability in shutting down normative cultural beauty standards. Haraway ends "A Cyborg Manifesto" with this:

> It is an imagination of a feminist speaking in tongues to strike fear into the circuits of the supersavers of the new right. It means both building

---

14   Rosalind Gill, "The Affective, Cultural and Psychic Life of Postfeminism: A Postfeminist Sensibility 10 Years On," *European Journal of Cultural Studies* 20, no. 6 (November 20, 2017): 606—26, https://doi.org/10.1177/1367549417733003.

15   Laura Pitcher, "How Beauty Is Being Used to Fight Back against Facial Recognition and CCTV," *Dazed*, October 3, 2023, https://www.dazeddigital.com/beauty/article/48030/1/anti-surveillance-cctv-beauty-cv-dazzle-facial-recognition-technology-joker.

16   Ibid.

and destroying machines, identities, categories, relationships, space stories. Though both are bound in the spiral dance, I would rather be a cyborg than a goddess.[17]

Let us be cyborgs. Let us short circuit and glitch from the impossible ideal of what it means to be a woman, especially an aging one.

17   Donna Haraway, "A Cyborg Manifesto," *Manifestly Haraway*, April 1, 2016, 3—90, https://doi.org/10.5749/minnesota/9780816650477.003.0001.

Chapter Eight

THE MILLENNIAL MOTHERHOOD QUESTION

When it comes to reproduction and the transition to motherhood, it is crucial to cast doubt on this rhetoric of all-embracing choice: how much room to maneuver do women actually have if we are free to choose only what society wants us to choose?

—ORNA DONATH

I FELT LIKE A VASECTOMY WHISPERER FOR A WHILE. Every man I dated was either about to get a vasectomy, had one done while we were together, or had one done before we met. I helped one partner ice his crotch right after the procedure. I made him vegan peanut butter cups to devour while he recuperated. I talked to another partner about his vasectomy consultation and he mentioned the ease of it. I responded: "Wow, sounds pretty great. Do you know how hard it is for someone with a uterus to get their tubes tied?" At least two men I dated who had gotten vasectomies when we were together ended up breaking up with me directly afterwards. I started getting superstitious. When I told my dad about these guys and their vasectomies (yes, we're that close), he responded in disgust, "They just want to have fun and try it out on everyone." He was probably right.

Long before my time as a Vasectomy Whisperer, I thought I would probably have at least one child. As a kid, I played with dolls. I played "house," where I was the mother and I cooked in my little kitchen. I had a sparkly white plastic vacuum that I loved moving across the floor. The toys that were bought for me, and the toys I showed the most interest in, were marketed towards girls—a plastic pink paradise. I got my first dollhouse when I was 4-years-old at Christmas. My dad had spent most of December building it in our basement. When I saw it on Christmas morning, I was ecstatic. It was enormous! There were so many rooms, furniture, and people. When I played with it, the tiny child dolls always had both a mom and dad, though I would rarely play with the dad. I would mostly just prop him in the living room. I was taught early on by family and media that girls are one thing and boys are another, and there isn't anything else. After my parents divorced when I was four, I believed that "four" was the magic number of people that should be in a family. I saw this structure in the families of my peers, I saw it on TV, I saw it everywhere. My OCD had me doing things four times. I looked to the right four times. I looked to the left four times. I counted things in fours. I licked my lips four times—so hungry for that "perfect" family I once had. My brain made me think the compulsion would repair the family I had for the first four years of my life. Troubled by my now "broken" family, I decided I would have a foursome of my own when I was older.

The nuclear family was ingrained in me, just like heterosexuality—another system—was ingrained in me. Even though I grew up with a feminist mother who worked outside of the home and went back to school when she had two small children, I witnessed the dynamic of my dad coming home from work and my mom making dinner or taking care of me and my brother. Though she had a job outside of the home, my mom was still expected to do the majority of housework. Scholar Patricia Hill Collins calls this "The archetypal white, middle-class nuclear family,"[1] which situates family life into two unique spaces—the men's outside space, typically working outside the home, and the women's inside space, taking care of the household and children. It's important to note that this is different for women of color. Hill Collins writes: "Since work and family have rarely functioned as dichotomous spheres for women of color, examining racial ethnic women's experiences reveals how these two spheres actually are

---

1   Patricia Hill Collins, "Shifting The Center: Race, Class, and Feminist Theorizing About Motherhood," essay, in *Mothering: Ideology, Experience, and Agency* (New York, NY: Routledge, 1994), 46.

interwoven."[2] The work that women of color perform confronts the idea that family and housework are separate. It extends beyond merely ensuring the survival of one's own biological children or those within one's family. Historically, those of us straddling a variety of marginalized identities (queer, disabled, Black, people of color, sex workers) have subverted the nuclear family by creating our own, which often don't include blood relations. Author Sophie Lewis refers to this as "feminist kinning."[3] In this way, "family" is reshaped, transformed, and abolished.

Family Abolition, the idea that the social and economic systems of "family" should be eradicated, is not new. Karl Marx and Friedrich Engels both discussed this in their early works. In 1920, Russian Marxist politician Alexandra Kollantai wrote:

> Divorce by mutual agreement now takes no more than a week or two to obtain. Women who are unhappy in their married life welcome this easy divorce. But others, particularly those who are used to looking upon their husband as "breadwinners," are frightened. They have not yet understood that a woman must accustom herself to seek and find support in the collective and in society, and not from the individual man.[4]

The practice of men being the sole earners continued to isolate and imprison women in the home. Though divorce had become legal and easier to access, many women had to contend with the fact that they had no money of their own. In an online talk from 2020, Marxist scholar Kathi Weeks noted that in the 1970s, Marxist feminists discussed family abolition as a "critique of capitalism."[5] These feminists wanted a more expansive understanding of what "family" encompassed and they wanted to be paid for their labor inside the home. Marxist feminists in the 1970s experienced and witnessed how capitalism, family and motherhood were inextricably linked. The Unit-

---

2   Ibid., 47.

3   Sophie Lewis, *Full Surrogacy Now: Feminism Against Family* (London, UK: Verso, 2021), 147.

4   Alexandra Kollontai, "Communism and The Family," Marxists.org, accessed October 6, 2024, https://www.marxists.org/archive/kollonta/1920/communism-family.htm.

5   Red May TV. "Abolish the Family! | Red May 2020." Abolish The Family! | Red May 2020—talk featuring: Kathi Weeks, Michelle O'Brien, Sarah Jaffe, and Sophie Lewis, May 30, 2020. https://www.youtube.com/watch?v=8nfeTeUgBZg.

ed States, specifically, needed its citizens to have families that would invest in and aid in the means of production.

Different from what prison abolition hopes to accomplish (the complete destruction of carceral systems and practices), family abolition looks to broaden the scope of what is considered a family unit and disconnect it from capitalism. Author M.E. O'Brien writes that family abolition "is a commitment to making nonalienated care available to all. It means unlocking care from its restriction to the private family and transforming it into something that is collectively and democratically shared... Family abolition is the communization of care."[6] Care work, which has been feminized for centuries, exists beyond rigid gender roles. Author Elissa Strauss writes: "...men flattened care into an easy and tidy fairytale. In this version, care comes easy to women."[7] Care is labor and it's not inherent in any of us. It's an evolving practice. It's not relegated to any one sex.

I would like to see an abolition of family as well as an abolition of motherhood as we currently know it. The same social and economic systems that keep us stuck in an antiquated notion of "family," also keeps us frozen in the capitalist (re)production of motherhood. In a broader approach, a "mother" is a caregiver and protector of children—*all* children, not just the ones they've birthed; not just the ones in their family of origin. In her book, *Full Surrogacy Now*, Sophie Lewis writes: "Let us build a care commune based on comradeship, a world sustained by kith and kind more than by kin. Where pregnancy is concerned, let every pregnancy be for everyone. Let us overthrow, in short, the 'family.'"[8] Liberating ourselves from the constraints of the nuclear family and motherhood would shift everything.

I didn't grow up with an inner knowing that I wanted to be a mother. I also didn't grow up with an inner knowing that I *didn't* want to be a mother. I just thought someday I would birth a child and find myself in motherhood, because that's what little girls grow up to do.

6   M.E. O'Brien, *Family Abolition: Capitalism and The Communizing of Care* (London, UK: Pluto Press, 2023), 179.

7   Anne Helen Petersen and Elissa Strauss, "I Went Into Motherhood Determined Not To Lose Myself In It.," other, *Culture Study* (Substack, August 4, 2024).

8   Sophie Lewis, *Full Surrogacy Now: Feminism Against Family* (London, UK: Verso, 2021), 26.

The idea of a "maternal instinct" in humans has been debunked by scientists.[9] Women are told they either have it or they don't, and many women base their childbearing decisions on this. If anything, what we call "maternal instinct," is more a "maternal socialization," according to Dr. Amy Blackstone, Professor of Sociology and author. Girls in the U.S. grow up being taught that motherhood should be their final destination. In her book, *Childfree By Choice*, Blackstone writes: "...the idea that any woman is innately driven toward motherhood is among the most widespread misunderstandings about why people have kids. Culturally, we hold dear the belief that women are uniquely wired to want children." Dr. Blackstone says this belief determines our roles, as well as our labor in and outside of the home. She continues: "Challenging it means questioning everything we were taught about our place in the world and even our very social structures." Choosing to challenge motherhood, in essence, means choosing to challenge womanhood. The stigma against childfree women is closely linked to the idea that being a woman is inherently tied to being a mother. Womanhood and motherhood have been forever intertwined. This construction is dangerous for many reasons. It ties women's importance to whether they do or do not birth children. It also completely ignores those who mother who are not women. It's problematic that mainstream society continues to reinforce biological essentialism and cissexism through rigid and finite definitions of what it means to be a woman. We are still, unfortunately, in a world that believes a person's genitals determine their sex and their role in society.

I don't relate to "womanhood" in the way that many cis white women seem to relate to it. I don't think of my period as "empowering" or "defining." I don't think of my womb as "magical." I don't believe specific body parts are what make a "woman." I think birth is magical and it's amazing that people can do it. However, I don't see that as being attached to womanhood. Many new age-y accounts on Instagram talk about wombs, vaginas, periods, pregnancy and birth as almost mythical things, and it makes me want to smash my head against a wall. I would argue that, yes, bringing a new life into the world is a huge, magical thing, but having a womb is not inherently magical. Hav-

---

9   Amy Blackstone, *Childfree by Choice: The Movement Redefining Family and Creating a New Age of Independence* (New York, NY: Dutton, 2019), 86.

ing a vagina is not magical. Having a period is not magical. Whenever I see these words used in conjunction with genitals, my TERF[10] radar perks up. I think about my gender queer, nonbinary and trans friends who are most often left out and excluded from this conversation.

I have never bought into the "magic" of menstruation. For a while, I wondered if it was due to some internalized misogyny and deep-seated negative feelings about having a period. I quickly realized it wasn't, because getting a period is not a woman-only experience. I feel uncomfortable about any rhetoric that presumes menstruation is a "woman-only" experience. This is trans-exclusive. People of various genders have a period. The idea that menstrual blood is the key to womanhood is an exclusion of those who don't fit in with this pre-scribed version of womanhood. It's also just very odd framing. I am not someone who hates my period, but I also see it as just a thing I deal with once a month that reminds me I'm not pregnant. I generally enjoy getting my period. I have PCOS[11] and cramps, but nothing as bad as what I know other women struggle with. I'm all for witchy and woo-woo things, but I will never support the idea that my monthly bleed is a symbol of my womanhood. Having a vagina or a uterus does not make a person a woman. Becoming pregnant does not make someone a woman. Birthing a child does not make someone a woman, but society's enmeshment of womanhood and motherhood is reinforced and potent.

For a long time, I think I told myself I didn't want a kid because I didn't want something that I didn't know I could have. Most people who have uteruses—particularly those with less access to healthcare—don't know much about our fertility or the health of our eggs. The testing to find this out is inaccessible to most of us due to cost. Many of us also don't have the ability to freeze our eggs. I would have liked to do this in my twenties had it been available to me. I was afraid of wanting something that might never happen. I always loved children. A common myth about childfree people is that we hate children. Perhaps some do (which is distressing), but the majority of us love and re-spect children. Many of us have children in our lives by way of family,

---

10   AUTHOR'S NOTE: Trans-Exclusionary Radical Feminist.

11   AUTHOR'S NOTE: Polycystic Ovary Syndrome.

friends and even our jobs. As a teenager and early twenty-something I babysat kids of various ages. Even if the job itself was difficult, I always liked the children. I have two nephews whom I love dearly. When they were both born, I felt my heart grow bigger and softer. It is precisely my love for children that makes me question bringing my own into the world. Possibly it's this deep love and respect that makes all of childfree women question whether we could or should have one of our own.

Because I was never adamant about having children, I wasn't interested in going at it alone (on purpose). I never wanted it badly enough. Also, I was (and am) afraid of childbirth and motherhood. My feelings about it now lie somewhere in the middle. People fear ambivalence. Cultural theorist and author Lauren Berlant writes: "When we think about ambivalence, it's tilted negatively, as an alienation toward."[12] Berlant argues to return ambivalence to its "dynamic etymology, as being strongly mixed, drawn in many directions, positively and negatively charged."[13] Some of us who are swimming in this ambivalence prefer to just let it happen. I've known plenty of women who didn't think they could get pregnant because they never had a pregnancy scare only to then "fall into" motherhood after not using birth control. This is the whole "if it happens, it happens" crowd, who seem devoid of any intentionality. They don't want to have to make a choice. I get it. Making that choice, if there is the option to do so, can be profoundly difficult. Making the choice to be childfree is laughing in the face of cisheteropatriarchy.

Most of the men I've dated (Millennials and Gen Xers) quickly and easily knew they didn't want children. Many never even gave it a second thought. When I had conversations with them about this, they didn't have the same societal or interpersonal pressure that women have about having children. Dr. Blackstone writes that this pressure is unique to women "because it is tied up with their very identities *as women*."[14] When I've fantasized about having children, I've felt immense

---

12   Lauren Berlant, *On the Inconvenience of Other People* (Durham, NC: Duke University Press, 2023), 27.

13   Ibid.

14   Amy Blackstone, *Childfree by Choice: The Movement Redefining Family and Creating a New Age of Independence* (New York, NY: Dutton, 2019), 106.

fear over losing myself—losing my identity pre-motherhood. This fear is a common one. In an interview with author, Elissa Straus, she writes about this contention:

> A woman frames motherhood as an assault to her identity, or runs away from motherhood to find herself: bestselling, buzzy book... Meanwhile, stories about finding the experience challenging in a meaningful way, not to mention sometimes pleasurable, seemed relegated to conservative mom blogs.[15]

Motherhood is, indeed, an "assault" to a woman's identity. After Straus had tried to separate her "mother" self from her "woman" self, she realized the cost and stopped. Instead, she integrated "motherhood as a form of identity expansion rather than colonization." Women fear losing our identity to motherhood precisely because of how the ideal of motherhood has been constructed by white cis hetero patriarchal society. Attempting to undo this fabricated identity by separating ourselves from "mother" and "woman" only invites more fragmentation.

Generally, our culture accepts men who decide not to be parents. Men are not interrogated by other men for not having children, whereas women are often confronted by other women about this. In online spaces, I see many mothers who seem to resent women who don't have children. If I post about enjoying being childfree on social media, I'm immediately met with parents (mostly mothers) telling me how selfish I am. They will say various things like, "Enjoy being lonely!" and "Who will take care of you in your old age?" The attitude of these wounded women tells me they are angry at the fact that they didn't know they had a choice (depending on their circumstances, maybe they didn't). They hold a deep resentment around motherhood. There are many articles out there titled some variation of, "I love my kid, but I hate being a parent," which puts into perspective the extreme labor demands that (mostly) mothers face. I don't blame mothers for their resentment, especially if they live in the U.S. where mothers and children are treated deplorably. Thus, how much better would we all be if parenthood was a communal experience? Feminist scholar Donna Haraway writes: "The point for me is parenting, not reproducing. Parenting is about caring for generations, one's own or not; reproducing is

---

15   Anne Helen Petersen and Elissa Strauss, "I Went Into Motherhood Determined Not To Lose Myself In It.," other, *Culture Study* (Substack, August 4, 2024).

about making more of oneself to populate the future, quite a different matter."[16] Every one of us has the ability to provide support and care for generations.

Though the pressure to have one's own biological child is primarily on women, some men also feel this stress. One guy I dated faced pressure about not wanting kids—from his parents, specifically from his mother. Luke, a thirty-something who was my partner for two and a half years, got a vasectomy in his mid-twenties. He told me this on our third date at a cat cafe. There was a tiny part of me that was saddened by his choice. Knowing kids would never be an option in this relationship made me think deeply and intentionally about choosing to stay with him—choosing to continue to follow my feelings for him. At one point during the relationship, his mom pulled me aside to ask, "Are you sure you don't want kids? I mean, really? You should go out and find someone who does since Luke doesn't." Deeply uncomfortable with this woman giving me permission to break up with her son over a baby I didn't know I wanted, I told her: "No, I don't want kids. I'm good. Don't worry." Then I excused myself. I told Luke about the conversation later and he was unsurprisingly upset with his mom. He told me his mom had hassled him for years about having kids, so when he told her he had gotten a vasectomy, she was shocked and saddened. In his retelling of his mother's grief over this, he seemed delighted, which only made me realize the intensity of his "mommy issues." Luke's vasectomy was a fuck-you to his mother and her incessant pressure. His body, his choice.

Millennials have a distinct relationship to parenthood. We were the generation that was promised everything, only to be sideswiped repeatedly. Unlike Gen X who were able to have careers, own homes, and have a savings, (most) millennials never got any of those things. People often refer to Gen Z as the "nihilist" generation, only because Gen Z saw what happened to millennials. They heard about the broken promises. They're smarter and haven't once trusted the government. They were promised nothing. When I'm on TikTok, a primarily Gen Z space, I rarely see anyone talk about wanting kids. Millennials, on the other hand, are still feeling the push and pull. To reject motherhood is

16   Sophie Lewis, *Full Surrogacy Now: Feminism Against Family* (London, UK: Verso, 2021), 158.

to reject an entire identity of societal standards placed on women. It's the death of a socialization that started when we were in the womb. This can be immensely difficult to face.

If women deny motherhood, they deny womanhood. We're subverting something that we're told we're destined for, and if we don't follow this destiny then we're refusing white cis womanhood. This is why conservatives and anyone on the political right are attempting to enforce archaic abortion laws. There are too many recent stories of women, many already mothers, who have been in legal battles due to miscarrying or the need to terminate their pregnancy for health reasons. In Ohio, Brittany Watts, a Black woman, miscarried at 22 weeks in the toilet and was charged with a felony. In Texas, Kate Cox fought in court to end her pregnancy after her fetus was diagnosed with Trisomy 18, which results in miscarriage or stillbirth. In both cases, the fetus was shown more care and respect than the women carrying them.[17]

Conservatives want to go back to women in the kitchen, barefoot and pregnant. This is evident in the influx of "trad wife" content on social media. A "trad wife," or "traditional wife" is a cishet woman, usually white, upper class, who fits perfectly into society's gender roles. She is a stay-at-home-mom, bakes everything from scratch, and manages the household. A trad wife's videos are almost always created in the home, which gives the viewer a feeling of claustrophobia. I begin to wonder, "Is she allowed to leave?" The trad wife holds up a mirror to the violence of a capitalist system and illuminates some of the harshest truths. In their article, "The Agoraphobic Fantasy of Tradlife," writer Zoe Hu says: "The twist that makes tradlife a phenomenon of our times is that it also includes earnest criticisms of life under capitalism." In most tradwife content, their labor is never referred to as work; it's considered "easier" and "better" than work outside of the home. Through tradwife content, we are witness to the coziness of staying home and loving on our people—both of which capitalism takes from us. As a tradwife, there is no worry about money, as that is the husband's role. The tradwife, though also doing important and difficult labor, believes her existence to be simple and pristine.

---

17   Lyz Lenz, "America Is Killing Its Mothers," Men Yell At Me, December 13, 2023, https://lyz.substack.com/p/america-is-killing-its-mothers?utm_source=publication-search.

She seems simultaneously distant from feminism, and, yet up close and personal with intrigue by how she might use it for herself. For example, in summer of 2024, *Vanity Fair* ran a profile of Hannah Neeleman, or "Ballerina Farm" as she is known to her ten million Instagram followers. Neeleman, the ultimate trad wife, started to say she was a feminist, but then stopped, instead saying, "There's so many different ways you could take that word. I don't even know what feminism means any more."[18] Did she ever know what feminism means? She can't possibly understand the desires of childfree women. She spits in the face of Boomer women's "we can have it all" mentality, which includes a job outside of the home. If Neeleman truly understood feminism, she might realize that her ability to live the life she is living is, at least in part, due to feminism.

Childfree women are told they are not *real* women because they don't have children. They are told they are career-hungry, selfish, un-nurturing individualists. Women who are childfree can get a pass for not having children, if they are career-centered capitalist monsters. In *Revolution at Point Zero: Housework, Reproduction, and Feminist Struggle*, Marxist feminist theorist Silvia Federici writes: "Only from a capitalist viewpoint being productive is a moral virtue, if not a moral imperative. From the viewpoint of the working class, being productive simply means being exploited."[19] Pregnant women and mothers are exploited workers. There is rarely any consideration that conception, pregnancy, birth and motherhood are labor. Sophie Lewis writes:

"Full surrogacy now," as I see it, is an expression of solidarity with the evolving desires of gestational workers, from the point of view of a struggle against work. It names a struggle that, by redistributing the burden of that labor, dissolves the distinction between reproducers and nonreproducers, mothers and nonmothers, altogether.[20]

---

18   Erin Vanderhoof, "Ballerina Farm Influencer Hannah Neeleman Says She Doesn't 'Identify' as a Trad Wife," Vanity Fair, July 25, 2024, https://www.vanityfair.com/style/story/ballerina-farm-interview.

19   Silvia Federici, *Revolution At Point Zero: Housework, Reproduction, and Feminist Struggle* (Oakland, CA: PM Press, 2020), 32

20   Sophie Lewis, *Full Surrogacy Now: Feminism Against Family* (London, UK: Verso, 2021), 28.

If a woman's life doesn't revolve around a job, including the job of pregnancy, and if they don't have children, then what kind of woman is she?

The thought of bringing a child into the mess that is climate change, pandemics, genocides, school shootings, and every other terrible thing feels unbearably heavy. Also, the fact that I live in the U.S., which has one of the highest rates of maternal mortality for a high-income country feels deeply unsettling. Some have said that motherhood has a "marketing" problem. The truth about it is too real, too scary. But we deserve to know the truth of how difficult it is, even if it is equally joyous. Motherhood has a problem of labor equity. The cost of motherhood seems more than the reward—if one even lives through the birth to see it. Motherhood is precarious, especially for women living in the U.S. Frankly, being a parent has never looked less appealing or daunting. I love children, but motherhood seems like a horrific joke. There is not nearly enough help, support, or community, and most of the care falls on the woman/mother. If a government wants its people to have babies, then the government needs to support these people. This isn't happening in the U.S. When people can't afford housing or food, why would they choose to have children?

Historically, religion was one of, if not the, primary reason for having children. This can still be seen today in various denominations. Blackstone writes: "Religion is among the strongest forces driving us to believe in both our purpose and our duty to reproduce."[21] Unfortunately, even if we weren't raised religious, this has seeped into mainstream culture so deeply that having a child quickly became a societal expectation of anyone with a uterus. There were also reasons to have children (a whole brood of them) related to manual labor. Blackstone continues: "Children were at one time essential to the economic survival of their families."[22] My Danish ancestors had twelve children, and I'm sure much of that was so they had enough people to work on the family farm. Not to mention, many babies died shortly after birth during this time, so having several gave a family a greater chance at continuing their economic livelihood and legacy. Children were forced

21   Amy Blackstone, *Childfree By Choice: The Movement Redefining Family and Creating a New Age of Independence* (New York, NY: Dutton, 2019), 4.

22   Ibid., 6.

workers.

Another major reason for having children was capitalism. Like in the case of my Danish ancestors, having many children who could work, whether on the family farm, or factories, meant money, which meant survival for the family unit. Since women weren't allowed to work in many spaces outside of the home, having boy children was preferred. Women and their children were property while their husbands and fathers owned them. Then, in the U.S., Pronatalism boomed in the 1980s, a "direct response to the feminist movement of the preceding two decades, with the goal of keeping women 'in their place'—at home, with their children."[23]

During my twenties and early thirties, I thought I would probably have a kid someday. I thought I would have a husband and two kids, to be precise. I didn't reflect on why. This is a common experience for women. Even though I was raised by parents who never bullied me to procreate, I still feel the immense pull to do so by society. I thought I would have a kid because that's just what women do. I never confronted this until my relationship with Luke. Did I actually want a kid or was I just conditioned into thinking I wanted one because I'm a woman? I found it to be the latter. I didn't want to end that relationship for a baby I had never met. I didn't have that "I *have* to be a mother" urgency that I know some people have. Though that relationship ended, it changed my perspective and I'm thankful the experience helped me to excavate my feelings and thoughts.

Millennials were the first generation to fully and deeply question compulsory motherhood en masse without much guilt.[24] On a broader level, queer folks have also consistently questioned social constructed ideas of motherhood. Boomers and Gen Xers also have questioned this, of course. Many Boomer women, however, were not given much choice in their reproductive lives. Those who made the conscious choice to be childfree were often ostracized, singled out, and shunned by society. Boomer mothers were fed the capitalist lie of "having it all"—meaning motherhood and a job outside of the home. Author

---

23   Ibid., 101-102.

24   AUTHOR'S NOTE: Much generational analysis also disregards issues of race and class.

and former editor-in-chief of *Cosmopolitan* magazine, Helen Gurley Brown, is often credited with coining "having it all."[25] She wrote a book of the same name in 1982. Her "feminism" was that women should be allowed to have sex without marriage, a career, children, and a lot of money. Though having sex without the need for marriage was certainly an exciting idea to mainstream culture at the time, the rest of her commandments left much to be desired. Gurley Brown believed that women's equality rested on being able to do the same things as men, with the addition of childrearing. Gurley Brown's *Cosmopolitan* version of feminism bled into the mainstream.

It wasn't all on Gurley Brown. Once more women had entered the workforce, the U.S. realized the potential for exploitation. This was how women began working even harder for a life that wasn't their own. These women were now in the labor force and still managing everything at home with no help from their husbands. Many Gen X women have upheld compulsory motherhood that Boomer women passed down. Millennial women, with our student loan debts, low-paying jobs, economic crises, and living through multiple wars and pandemics realized quickly that having a child would be difficult, if not impossible.

Many people predicted that the Covid-19 pandemic would disproportionately affect women in a variety of ways. In a tweet from March 2020, author and family abolitionist, Madeline Lane-McKinley wrote: "Households are capitalism's pressure cookers. This crisis will see a surge in housework—cleaning, cooking, caretaking, but also child abuse, molestation, intimate partner rape, psychological torture, and more. Not a time to forget to abolish the family."[26] Women who were forced to stay home and quarantine with their family unit were at heightened risk for abuse. Not to mention, since women's labor in the home is not accounted for, more women lost their jobs outside of the home. According to Pew Research Center, Hispanic women had the biggest job loss at the start of Covid-19 at twenty-one percent, Asian women at nineteen percent, Black women at seventeen percent, and

---

25   Sali Hughes, "Helen Gurley Brown: How to Have It All," The Guardian, August 14, 2012, https://www.theguardian.com/lifeandstyle/2012/aug/14/helen-gurley-brown-cosmopolitan-sex.

26   Madeline Lane-McKinley, "Tweet on X.Com," X (formerly Twitter), March 17, 2020, https://x.com/la_louve_rouge_/status/1239997457456443392.

white women at thirteen percent. McKinsey and Company's *Women in the Workplace 2023* report found that one third of working mothers have had to consider reducing their work outside of the home.

The pandemic highlighted, yet again, how the division of labor between working mothers and fathers does not exist. Women tend to do more for and with their children, because of the societal expectation placed on them. Thus, many mothers had to quit their out-of-home jobs in the first two years of the pandemic to assist with childcare, especially while schools were closed. Fathers were not expected to do this, and many did not. Society consistently decides that mothers and their labor (inside and outside of the home) are unimportant and frivolous. The myth of innate "soft" qualities that make a mother/wife was something marketed and sold to us. Federici writes:

> Housework had to be transformed into a natural attribute rather than be recognized as a social contract because from the beginning of capital's scheme for women this work was destined to be unwaged. Capital had to convince us that it is a natural, unavoidable and even fulfilling activity to make us accept our unwaged work. In its turn, the unwaged condition of housework has been the most powerful weapon in reinforcing the common assumption that housework is not work, thus preventing women from struggling against it, except in the privatized kitchen—bedroom quarrel that all society agrees to ridicule, thereby further reducing the protagonist of a struggle. We are seen as nagging bitches, not workers in struggle.[27]

Witnessing this treatment over and over again has made it difficult, if not impossible, for me to feel like I would (or even *could*) want to be a mother.

In an Instagram post, writer Aja Barber says: "How many of us cannot separate whether we didn't want kids in our youth because we simply don't want them from the feeling of knowing that society offers you no support or safety net currently? Because I could never separate the two. Did I not want them or did I not feel I was allowed to have them?"[28] I think I want/wanted at least one child, but from early on knew it would not be possible for me, whether due to fertility reasons or cost. I'm currently making the most money I've ever made, but it's

---

27   Federici, Silvia. *Revolution At Point Zero: Housework, Reproduction, and Feminist Struggle.* Oakland, CA: PM Press, 2020, 77.

28   Aja Barber, "Aja Barber on Instagram," Instagram, June 13, 2024, https://www.instagram.com/p/C8KAQuEoFGp/.

still not enough to live in the medium-sized midwestern city I live in. I still don't make nearly enough money to live on my own. There is no way I could financially support a child."

Sometimes I lurk on the "Child Free," "Regretful Parents" and "Motherhood" subreddit communities. A wide assortment of opinions from a variety of people: women who want children, women who have children, women who regret having children, women who regret *not* having children. There seems to be one underlying theme: motherhood is fucking hard and there isn't appreciation for the labor it entails. There is little help unless a person has money or family nearby. Motherhood is a choice, and yet, not everyone has the same exact variation of this choice. I'm glad that these online communities exist for those seeking belonging in their ambivalence to motherhood, those still deciding to mother, and those who regret either choice. With so many terrifying anti-abortion and anti-birth control laws attempting to be passed in the U.S., how much longer will many of us have the choice to either get pregnant and birth children or not? The labor imbued in motherhood is overlooked, disregarded. Women's bodies are overlooked, disregarded. Federici writes:

> To say that we want wages for housework is to expose the fact that housework is already money for capital, that capital has made and makes money out of our cooking, smiling, fucking. At the same time, it shows that we have cooked, smiled, fucked throughout the years not because it was easier for us than for anybody else, but because we did not have any other choice. Our faces have become distorted from so much smiling, our feelings have got lost from so much loving, our oversexualization has left us completely desexualized.[29]

Women are overly sexualized until we become mothers and then we are desexualized. A mother's labor is not considered work. This labor became inherent. Perhaps if this labor was recognized, if it was paid, I would have been more interested in motherhood. Perhaps if I lived in a country that had services and communities that helped parents, I would have had a child by now. Perhaps many of us would.

I find it interesting that the question is always, "Why didn't you have kids?" versus "Why *did* you have kids?" Many people don't have

---

29   Silvia Federici, *Revolution At Point Zero: Housework, Reproduction, and Feminist Struggle* (Oakland, CA: PM Press, 2020), 19.

very good reasons for having kids. Most of them have never done a thought exercise about it. The responses range from: "I just knew I always wanted them" to "I wanted someone to love me unconditionally" to "I want to carry on the family lineage." My question back is always, "But *why* did you want them?" Did it come from you or society? Do you even know? Most don't respond with anything other than "I don't know, I just did." This compulsory parenthood is problematic. I wish the norm was inviting ourselves to really sit with our intentions and reasons for both wanting a kid or not wanting a kid. I think too many people are afraid to go there, though.

Though I have consistently dated people who don't want kids, I sometimes wish they were open to the idea. If I'm deeply in love with someone, I want to make this decision *with* them. I have a hard time with absolutes. I like options. I like choices. I like to keep the doors (and windows) open. I recognize that much of this is due to my trauma history—my lack of choice. On the other side of this, I'm grateful that the people I date don't aggressively want kids, because then there is no pressure on my end. I don't have to worry about whether I can get pregnant. I don't have to think about the status of my fertility. I don't have to worry that the relationship will end because of this. I have dated exactly two men with whom I felt compelled to have a child. I felt a desire, an urge that was overwhelming. I felt so in love with them that I wanted to make a child with them. I wanted the family I didn't get to have growing up. The first man was the man who assaulted me, cheated on me and gave me herpes. I was 27 when we met. My hormones were raging. This man is now divorced with two kids and is still in active addiction. The second man was eleven years older than me and already had a kid from a previous relationship. He would not have been a supportive co-parent. Looking back, I'm glad no babies were made with these men.

I have forever felt unsettled by the way others make the big decision of having a child by way of, essentially, not deciding. Obviously, this has nothing to do with me, but I do feel a pang of frustration, annoyance, resentment at people who decide without really deciding. The people who are mostly in their 30s, in heterosexual relationships, and who decide not to use birth control one day to see what happens. The folks for whom "falling pregnant" really does seem to be a fitting phrase as they seem to have no fertility issues or concerns. This non-decision ends up deciding for them. I have been immensely intentional in most areas of my life—to the point of it feeling nauseating. I have sometimes wished that I could leave various things up to "fate," but I also know I don't actually want it that way.

If I decide to have a kid, I want to be as intentional about it as I possibly can. Though I lean towards not having one, the decision becomes more fluid when I meet people who I feel like I could co-parent with in beautiful ways. It is more about the partner for me—especially since the U.S. generally treats parents (and children) like shit, so a good partner seems important. Unfortunately, partners can come and go, so at the very least, one would need a good community around to help. This isn't always reachable, though. I know that I can live a fulfilling life if I have a kid or if I don't have one. I know that I haven't felt any regret (thus far). Part of the sadness that comes up around choosing to not have a kid is really just fear of missing out (fomo) on an experience that billions of women have had. I have often wondered what pregnancy, birth, and motherhood would look like on me. At times, I have envisioned a tiny curly-haired child who looks and acts like me, but is their own person. It's only natural to speculate about these things.

I often think about and re-read a specific letter from Cheryl Strayed's "Dear Sugar" column from online magazine, *The Rumpus*. In it, she writes: "Every life...'has a sister ship,' one that follows 'quite another route' than the one we ended up taking. We want it to be otherwise, but it cannot be: the people we might have been live a different, phantom life than the people we are."[30] We each have a "sister ship" path in life that we can't take. What would my life have been like if I stayed in Italy in 2006? What would my life have been like if I stayed in Chicago in 2012? What would my life have been like if I hadn't been assaulted various times? Who would I be if I didn't go to grad school and incur thousands of dollars of debt? Some of these were choiceless. I didn't have an option. Some I did have options. Options feel good. They're expansive, and in my experience, especially important

---

30   Cheryl Strayed, "Dear Sugar, The Rumpus Advice Column #71: The Ghost Ship That Didn't Carry Us," The Rumpus, October 12, 2022, https://therumpus. net/2011/04/21/dear-sugar-the-rumpus-advice-column-71-the-ghost-ship-that-didnt-carry-us/.

for those of us who are survivors of sexual violence.

When I think about the "kid" question, it's about choosing the path that has the least amount of grief attached to it. However, as someone who is ambivalent, how do I determine which path that is? I don't believe in regrets so I know I wouldn't regret whichever choice I make, but the fomo around this is strong. Either way, I will miss out on something: whether I have a kid or whether I don't. There is stuff to be lost and gained in both scenarios.

Strayed continues:

If I could go back in time I'd make the same choice in a snap. And yet, there remains my sister life. All the other things I could have done instead. I wouldn't know what I couldn't know until I became a mom, and so I'm certain there are things I don't know because I can't know because I did. Who would I have nurtured had I not been nurturing my two children over these past seven years? In what creative and practical forces would my love have been gathered up? What didn't I write because I was catching my children at the bottoms of slides and spotting them as they balanced along the tops of low brick walls and pushing them endlessly in swings? What did I write because I did?[31]

There are so many things that terrify me about pregnancy, birth, and motherhood (especially since I live in a state that cares more about the fetus than the person carrying the fetus). I am someone who feels terrified living in my body every day, so the fear around "All Things Baby" doesn't necessarily help me rule it out. I do know that I can be happy in either scenario. I do know that my worth is not tied to cis-hetero-patriarchal norms and expectations. I am, perhaps, lucky that my ambivalence shows up in this way. It feels subversive to not be completely steeped in societal capitalist norms. I know that I have *mothered* various children—those I'm related to and those I'm not. I feel a deep sense of *mothering* when I look after my nephews. They know I'm another safe adult in their lives that cares for and loves them. I feel a sense of urgency to care for and support all children. Sophie Lewis writes:

Everywhere about me, I can see beautiful militants hell-bent on regeneration, not self-replication. Recognizing our inextricably surrogate contamination with and by everybody else (and everybody else's babies) will not so much "smash" the nuclear family as make it unthinkable. And that's what

---

31   Ibid.

needs to happen if we are serious about reproductive justice, which is to say, serious about revolution.[32]

If we can truly abolish the archaic versions of family and motherhood, all children will flourish because all adults will be happier. When I reimagine family and motherhood outside of the social and economical constructs that white cis heteropatriarchy has created, I have no more fear of making the "wrong" choice. If I think about the ways I can mother and be an "othermother"[33] to various children, I feel at ease. I don't need a child to "belong" to me.

At the end of Strayed's advice column, she writes:

> I'll never know and neither will you of the life you don't choose. We'll only know that whatever that sister life was, it was important and beautiful and not ours. It was the ghost ship that didn't carry us. There's nothing to do but salute it from the shore.[34]

What if we didn't need to choose, though? Where if there were more than the two options of having a child or not having one? If we abolish the family, any of us can be mothers and do the work of mothering. We have more than two choices. We can love and care for all of the children in our community. Our love is endless.

My ambivalence is the ship that carries me. Maybe if we lean into ambivalence, we will have reproductive liberation. What really is ambivalence but the ability to be flexible, open, and bursting with options?

---

32   Sophie Lewis, *Full Surrogacy Now: Feminism Against Family* (London, UK: Verso, 2021), 167.

33   Patricia Hill Collins, "Shifting The Center: Race, Class, and Feminist Theorizing About Motherhood," essay, in *Mothering: Ideology, Experience, and Agency* (New York, NY: Routledge, 1994), 45—65, 55.

34   Cheryl Strayed, "Dear Sugar, The Rumpus Advice Column #71: The Ghost Ship That Didn't Carry Us," The Rumpus, October 12, 2022, https://therumpus.net/2011/04/21/dear-sugar-the-rumpus-advice-column-71-the-ghost-ship-that-didnt-carry-us/.

Chapter Nine

FRIENDSHIP IN THE TIME OF COVID AND GENOCIDE

Big Friendship is a bond of great strength, force, and significance that transcends life phases, geography, and emotional shifts. It is large in dimension, affecting most aspects of each person's life. It is full of meaning and resonance. A Big Friendship is reciprocal, with both parties feeling worthy of each other and willing to give of themselves in generous ways. A Big Friendship is active. Hearty. And almost always, a Big Friendship is mature. Its advanced age commands respect and predicts its ability to last far into the future.

—AMINATOU SOW & ANN FRIEDMAN

I INVITED ONE OF THE FOUR MOST POPULAR GIRLS in my grade to my eighth birthday party. Our mothers had us days apart in the same hospital and knew each other. I invited Caitlin the year prior, too. I didn't understand at the time that she probably only showed up the first time out of some weird sense of obligation. The day of my eighth birthday party, Caitlin's mom called my dad letting him know that Caitlin wouldn't be able to attend because she had something else she needed to do, but would drop off a gift. I was bummed, but I had other friends coming. Before my party was to start around 5pm, I was looking out the front window of my dad's house to watch as my guests arrived. I saw Caitlin's mom's car pull into the driveway. Then I saw Caitlin and one of the other four most popular girls sitting together in the backseat. I was crushed. I realized she didn't want to be with me at my party. She wanted to stick to her class. I stopped inviting her to my birthday parties after that.

As a neurospicy[1] femme, I've had more friendship difficulties

---

1   AUTHOR'S NOTE: Used in various online spaces to mean neurodivergent.

than the average neurotypical. As a kid, I preferred one-on-one friend time when everyone else seemed to want group hangs. In group settings, I was fighting for attention, which felt a lot like fighting for my life. Being liked and noticed was too important to me; it was rarely something I felt and I really wanted to feel it. I also couldn't understand how people even had a *group* of friends—actual *friends*, not just acquaintances. I craved friendships like the ones I saw on tv: Lucy and Ethel, Kimmy Gibbler and D.J. Tanner, Buffy and Willow. Early on, I made a conscious distinction between friends and acquaintances. Friends were people I had a deep connection with; people who I could be completely myself with and them with me. Acquaintances were people I would see once in a while or hang out with in a group setting. I didn't feel as comfortable with them. There was a distance between us that I created. There was a wall I put up, but they didn't seem interested enough to attempt to breach it.

When I would talk about the difference I felt between friends and acquaintances to my neurotypical friends, it was clear that they didn't feel the same way. I remember getting upset with friends in the past with how easy going they were about friendship. I still have trouble if friends of mine refer to everyone they have ever talked to as a "friend." It cuts me deeply, even though it's not about me. I question whether my friendship with them is as deep as I think it is. I see this a lot in online spaces, too, where someone will refer to many people as their "friend," and it bothers me (even if I'm not in that person's life). It's something I don't understand. Friendship is sacred to me, and I can't envision that sacredness being supported or sustained with more than a handful of people. And yet, I also try to broaden my perspective and see what others might see that I'm missing.

I have always prioritized my one-on-one friendships, maybe because of the trauma I faced after being bullied by a former group of friends at seventeen. I never wanted to be a part of a group of friends ever again. At the time, I thought: "I can only depend on my family. Nobody else." Granted, I was (and still am) lucky to have amazing parents and a great older brother to depend on. When I talk about friendship, I include my parents and my brother. However, as a kid, I felt isolated and lonely since everyone else my age had friends who seemed to love and care about them. That's all I ever wanted. After those bullies licked me clean, I eventually found what has been my longest friendship—my longest relationship—with my friend Anju who I met in dance class. She went to a different high school, but had been in the same ballet and jazz dance classes for years. I had remembered Anju from ballet class when we were kids. She stood out amongst the sea of pale blue leotards and pink tights because she wore white socks over her tights. Once we were teenagers, we would often dance next to each other in class. We finally started hanging outside of dance and this friendship began to heal the wound my bullies created. Since Anju, I have gained more close friends. Audrey, my concert-loving bestie who I met during my first grad program in Chicago. Kelly, the tiny but mighty yoga instructor who reached out to me via email after she had been following me on Instagram, who I met when I moved back to Madison. I don't see any of my friends much since two of them live out of state. Any romantic partner I have either starts as a friend or becomes one along the way, which is a lovely addition to my friendship roster. As we age, we tend to have less groups of friends and more individual friendships with people. We don't always live near our friends; sometimes oceans apart.

In September of 2019, I was dumped. I then went and officiated my brother's wedding in New Orleans. By late October, I was in a new relationship that felt so exciting I could barely hold it in my body. My life was getting good, I thought. Then, right before my 34th birthday, I passed out from overheating in front of one hundred people at work. They called an ambulance. It was all very dramatic. For most of my life, my biggest fear was exactly that: fainting in front of a large crowd of people and an ambulance being called. This fear was so bad that it became obsessive, and it was part of the reason I was put on Zoloft at seventeen. At the time, I couldn't stop thinking about fainting. I had intrusive thoughts about it daily, sometimes hourly. I became mildly agoraphobic. When it happened at work, I was on my period and had taken some Valtrex because I thought I was getting a herpes outbreak. I was seated as we all listened to the speakers. I had no fear that I would faint. It just happened: one moment awake and in the world, the next blissfully unaware that I had left it.

My boyfriend at the time and my parents came to the hospital immediately upon hearing. After I was admitted to the ER, my vitals and an EKG were done. Everything was perfect. I cried during the EKG—not out of fear, but out of relief. The bad thing had happened and I had survived. I felt immense gratitude that my parents were in the waiting room, along with my boyfriend. I momentarily wondered what it would feel like to have no one. This made me cry more. I was then referred to the Faint & Fall Clinic for a follow-up. I was the youngest person in the waiting room there. First rule of Faint Club is that we all faint, regardless of age. My doctor was great. She told me how, when one of her other patients fainted, someone immediately started doing CPR, which then broke the patient's ribs.[2] My doctor told me I exhibited classic symptoms of Vasovagal Syncope (now called Neurocardiogenic Syncope), which is the most common fainting condition there is. It has specific triggers (heat, pain, alcohol, needles, blood). I felt relief having this diagnosis. I felt taken cared of by friends who checked in on me from afar via text and by my parents and boyfriend. Everyone should have this, I thought.

Beyond whatever our own definitions of friendship might be, many of us find ourselves with fewer and fewer friends, close or otherwise. In her popular newsletter, writer and culture critic Anne Helen Petersen notes that 38 percent of Americans reported having five or more close friends, 55 percent reported having between one and four close friends, and 8 percent reported having no close friends.[3] Petersen discusses a general trajectory of friendships from stemming from young adulthood to old age. For most young adults up to the mid-twenties, a person will have a decent number of close friends. However, late-twenties to early thirties shows a gradual decrease due to people getting married, having children, and generally prioritizing friendship less. In a person's mid to late 30s, these friendships dwindle even more. Petersen argues this is often due to things beyond our control: more care responsibilities for aging parents, children, divorces, jobs, and illnesses. People hardly have the time to keep up with the friends they have, let alone try to make new ones.

Our society in the U.S. also doesn't help us with this. Petersen

---

2   AUTHOR'S NOTE: Please make sure the person is not breathing before attempting CPR.

3   Anne Helen Petersen, "The Friendship Dip," *Culture Study*, November 5, 2023, https://annehelen.substack.com/p/the-friendship-dip.

writes: "...we have a prolonged stretch of adulthood that is not conducive to forging or sustaining friendship or community. In many cases, I'd say it's actually hostile to it."[4] In an individualist, capitalist nation like the U.S., it's no wonder we don't have the time or energy to water our friendships. Work and making money are prioritized for survival. Then there's the commodified version of "self-care," which is labor in a different way, and also zaps our time. Whether it's a 12-step skincare routine or exercising into oblivion, there is little time or energy for our friendships. This lack of time seemed to get worse when the Covid-19 pandemic hit in early 2020. The care that it takes to sustain and even grow relationships can be a lot. The care this takes was tested for many of us when Covid hit.

I was still reeling from experiencing my biggest fear (fainting) when the pandemic bloomed. I left work one day and was told not to come back. I was scared, but relieved to stay home, indoors, where I feel the most safe. The first two years of the pandemic were enjoyable for me. I was allowed to work fully remote. I had more time and energy to care for myself and others, because I didn't have to endure onsite work culture. I prioritized my relationships, including the one I have with myself. I went outside more. I explored more hobbies like fiber arts and diamond painting. I didn't have many local friends, but I FaceTimed and texted with friends from afar. I mostly only hung out with my parents and my boyfriend during this time. My mental health improved. I was moving my body daily. I felt so capable. Initially I was concerned that my agoraphobia from years' prior might return. Instead, I had more energy and more confidence to go out into the world. I was so incredibly in love with my partner. This love propped me up. It felt miraculous that we had found each other right before the world shut down.

When we broke up in the spring of 2022, I felt disoriented. It was like the pandemic had been suspended during my relationship, and it only hit me two years later. I had more time to think about it—to feel it. I felt alone and lost. I tried to re-prioritize my friendships. We would text or call each other often, but I felt like I initiated the majority of contact. I never stopped wearing a mask in public spaces, and though

---

4   Ibid.

people around me seemed to support this, they themselves didn't necessarily wear masks. I started to feel like an outsider in every space yet again. This hurt the most when it was a purported "feminist" or "leftist." How does our politic not include caring for immunocompromised and disabled comrades (and ourselves)?

We are inconvenienced by each other, but this isn't a bad thing. We owe this to each other. Some of us are more *inconveniencing*, perhaps. Cultural theorist and author Lauren Berlant writes of this in their book, *On the Inconvenience of Other People*:

> We know that, just by existing, historically subordinated populations are deemed inconvenient to the privileged who made them so; the subordinated who are cast as a problem experience themselves as both necessary for and inconvenient to the general supremacist happiness.[5]

Those of us who are disabled demand a level of care in our friendships that non-disabled people don't, but they should. The care I've witnessed and received from disabled comrades is monumental. Disabled friendships not only have emotional and physical intimacies, but also "access" intimacy. We all have access needs, including ableds and neurotypicals. Writer, educator and trainer for transformative justice and disability justice, Mia Mingus writes:

> Access intimacy is that elusive, hard to describe feeling when someone else "gets" your access needs... Access intimacy is also the intimacy I feel with many other disabled and sick people who have an automatic understanding of access needs out of our shared similar lived experience of the many different ways ableism manifests in our lives... Instantly, we can hold the weight, emotion, logistics, isolation, trauma, fear, anxiety and pain of access. I don't have to justify and we are able to start from a place of steel vulnerability.[6]

For me, access intimacy looks like my friends recognizing and celebrating my neurodiversity. It's the friend who knows to tell me how many people might be at an event they invite me to. It's the friend who validates that I don't need "fixing." Asking each other what we need instead of assuming we know what's best is something we all should be

---

5   Lauren Berlant, *On the Inconvenience of Other People* (Durham, NC: Duke University Press, 2023), 4.

6   Mia Mingus, "Access Intimacy, Interdependence and Disability Justice," Leaving Evidence, April 27, 2018, https://leavingevidence.wordpress.com/2017/04/12/access-intimacy-interdependence-and-disability-justice/.

doing. These needs may change over time, so a consistent checking-in around access is imperative to our loving and caring of each other.

Those of us who live in the United States don't know how to depend on each other. We grow up depending on caregivers and adults, but it's quickly squashed out of us in favor of rugged individualism and independence. In *How to Tell When We Will Die: On Pain, Disability, and Doom*, Johanna Hedva writes:

> Becoming disabled, for me, was an education in many things, but sometimes I think it was elementally about relearning how to understand dependency, and how disability makes it impossible to ignore that we are ontologically dependent, knotted into each other and everything.[7]

Those of us who become disabled later on in life must relearn how to depend on others. Even as a third grader, I had already learned that I needed to be independent. When I was then diagnosed with learning disabilities, I felt like I slipped backwards. As a child, I needed to depend on the adults in my life, however, adults were my first bullies so this was problematic. My desire to be fiercely independent led me to bottle up emotions and only share half of my feelings with partners and friends. I didn't want to depend on anyone—even those who loved me.

Many of us are afraid of people leaving our lives when things get hard. We're afraid our loved ones can't handle things, and we don't want to be a bother or a burden. Being human is being a burden—at times. Being human and having needs is natural. The resistance to dependence, to asking for help, to leaning on others is what keeps us stuck in the loop of hyper-individualism and capitalism. We all have a right to dependency. We all have a right to need others' help. We have a right to know that having a body and living in this world means we are inherently dependent on each other. Our personal need for dependence might wax and wane, but if we don't lean into it when we need it—if we don't *relearn* it, as Hedva says—then we will continue to struggle isolated and alone. Capitalism wants us this way, but we can resist. Often, those of us who are disabled don't have a choice in this. Dependency is needed for liberation.

---

7   Johanna Hedva, *How to Tell When We Will Die: On Pain, Disability, and Doom* (New York, NY: Hillman Grad Books, 2024), 6.

Those of us who are disabled demand this level of care and vulnerability because we need it to survive in a world that doesn't want us alive. Disabled love and friendship is radical in an individualist, capitalist society. Being a part of a society means living with and around others. We are all inconvenient to each other at various times. But we also all owe each other this disruption. Non-disabled and neurotypical people's friendships are often surface-level, because they've never had to dream up other ways of doing and being in relationship to others. They are often stuck in a white settler colonial individualist frame of mind. Writer, organizer, performance artist, and educator, Leah Lakshmi Piepzna-Samarasinha asks the question:

> What does it mean to shift our ideas of access and care (whether it's disability, childcare, economic access, or many more) from an individual chore, an unfortunate cost of having an unfortunate body, to a collective responsibility that's maybe even deeply joyful?[8]

Later, Piepzna-Samarasinha asks, "If collective access is revolutionary love without charity, how do we learn to love each other?" Care is a part of the human condition. This is why many disabled people were rightfully enraged by abled people's lack of response to Covid-19. This is why so many had to end friendships.

Many people's friendships have changed or ended in the last few years of the pandemic. Some have ended because of friendship differences with Covid precautions. Others have ended due to friends showing their unbridled and unchecked support for Israel, while the Israeli government and the U.S. government work in tandem to slaughter Palestinians. I learned a great deal about Palestine from a Lebanese professor I had in my first grad program (Women's & Gender Studies at DePaul University). During one of my two years in the program, I was in an elective course for the degree: Women & Religion. It had students from my cohort and those studying other subjects. A friend of mine from my cohort and her boyfriend were both in this course. The boyfriend and I butted heads one day when he was espousing Zionism and I vocally critiqued this. I left class pissed off, but shrugged it off. He left class pissed off, but he wouldn't let it go.

This grown man began harassing me via text message. He wanted

---

8   Leah Lakshmi Piepzna-Samarasinha, *Care Work: Dreaming Disability Justice* (Vancouver, BC: Arsenal Pulp Press, 2021), 33.

to force a conversation with me. No matter how many times I texted back telling him I wasn't available for discussion, he wouldn't stop. He called me antisemitic due to my support of Palestine and my anti-Zionist stance. I asked my friend (his girlfriend) to please tell/ask him to stop. She said, "Well, this is between you two." I silently wondered, was she in an abusive relationship, was she just a shitty friend, or maybe both? The incessant texts continued for a week. He wouldn't stop until I finally agreed to meet up with him at a Dunkin' Donuts in Logan Square. We sat in a booth. I was far too anxious to drink my coffee. He was animated, confrontational, sitting across from me ready to pounce. He was talking so quickly and I couldn't hear anything. Because I couldn't take it anymore, I agreed with whatever bullshit point he made. I had to acquiesce/fawn/appease so he would finally leave me alone. My "friend," (his girlfriend) was happy that we "worked it out."

My friendship with this woman was never the same after that.

Though I have not had to end any recent friendships due to Palestine or pandemic denial, there are people I used to hang out with that I don't anymore, solely because of their risky behaviors during a global pandemic. There are acquaintances that I no longer speak to because they don't seem to care about the genocides in Gaza and Sudan. Though this chapter is about friendship, there are other relationships in other spaces where I have lost a considerable amount of respect for people once finding out their pro-Israel stance. Some have lost respect for me when finding out about my pro-Palestine stance. In the fall of 2023, a student of mine who was graduating that semester went to the chair of my department and accused me of antisemitism. The student, a Zionist, had found my Instagram account and didn't agree with or appreciate my support of Palestinians. She told the Chair of the department that she wanted "nothing to do" with me and that she didn't feel "safe" with me. I had only interacted with the student once. I wasn't in trouble because of free speech, but I certainly felt like I was. University support for those of us who are against genocides does not currently exist. This support also doesn't exist for those of us wanting more Covid precautions. I can't relate to people who can continue on with life as normal when our current times are anything but normal. I refuse to be gaslit. I refuse to comply.

The pandemic created more shifts and fractures in friendships/relationships for everyone. I felt I needed to work harder at maintaining my relationships, and some did not survive (eg. my romantic relationship). My friendships have mostly remained intact—and some are even stronger—but the time and effort it has taken me and others to attend to "friendship maintenance" has been intense. I continue on because the people in my life are worth it. In pre-pandemic times, I ate at the occasional restaurant. I went to the occasional bar. I saw a movie at the theater. I haven't done any of these things since fall of 2019 and I don't miss them. I don't miss the cost, the time, the distraction. This is why it's difficult for me to understand peoples' overwhelming desire to do these things now, when we're still very much in a pandemic. Friends have always meant so much to me—probably more than what is healthy. I am a very caring and loyal friend and expect the same in return. I have a difficult time getting close to people since I've been burned in ways I never knew possible. I have a few very close friends in my life. Some who live in town, and some who don't. I know them all from different places/spaces in my life: dance school, college, grad school, yoga, etc. I am fortunate to know and love these people and for them to know and love me.

I polled my Instagram followers about this and so many people sent me private messages. The responses ranged from, "I want to support service workers" to "I'm a parent and being able to sit at a restaurant without my child and with other adults is amazing." The messages people sent me about why they choose to eat at restaurants made sense to me, even if my newly socially anxious self thinks it sounds exhausting. Many also said it was about the convenience and being taken care of: having someone cook for you, clean up for you, wait on you. I can understand wanting those things. But doing them even during a pandemic? That's harder for me to understand.

There is so much I wish and hope and dream for this world. I'm incredibly distressed and saddened by the lack of pandemic response from the U.S. People should have been paid to stay home (this still could be done). We can't respond to a global pandemic individually—it doesn't work—and yet, that's what we're all tasked with doing. I don't like it, but I wish more people—especially so-called "leftists"—would commit to it. Wear a mask in public spaces. Go out to eat slightly less or go to places with outdoor seating. We need to find ourselves and each other outside of capitalism. I think there are ways we can have community—safely—without spending money; without capitalist distractions. Though life is never completely free of risk, there are ways we can all lessen the harm we might create or encounter.

I keep thinking about disabled and immunocompromised folks. I keep thinking about home-bound folks. I keep thinking about how many people we are leaving behind (have left behind), and outright excluding because of our own search for momentary joy (or connection?) at restaurants or other establishments. Before I think about doing anything that I deem "risky," I ask myself: "Is this worth getting Covid (or any illness)?" Most of the time it's not. Eating food right when it comes out of the oven is nice, but I'm not willing to risk getting sick (or worse) for it. Takeout exists.

Obviously we have limited control around getting sick, but if we can make things slightly less risky for ourselves and each other, then why wouldn't we do it? When we're assessing risk, why wouldn't we take into account those who are most in harm's way; most affected by risky decisions. Why, at the very least, would we not wear a mask in public spaces? Why, at the very least, would we go out to an establishment a bit less? Life is inherently risky and we each need to assess these risks for ourselves on a continual basis. In an article about risk and safety, social psychologist and author, Dr. Devon Price discusses the difference between risk admission and risk tolerance/acceptance emphasizing that we can never fully avoid risk. We can only choose *which* risks we're willing to take on. Sometimes we don't have a choice and this choice is made for us, like those who are unwilling to wear a mask anywhere. Most of us are assessing and taking risks every day. The "spectrum" of *safe* to *dangerous* doesn't exist like many of us think it does. Price discusses this as it applies to sexual health, but it's also applicable to Covid:

> ...all choices are treated as if they exist on a single spectrum that runs from "safe" to "dangerous," with the same relative risk levels for all people. But the reality is that every person experiences risks differently, and weighs certain harms over others when they decide how to behave.[9]

9   Devon Price, "There is no safe sex. There is no safe life", August 15, 2024, https://drdevonprice.substack.com/p/there-is-no-safe-sex-there-is-no.

Most of us have a kaleidoscope of health issues, and due to this, our risk assessment is going to differ and change based on our current level of ability, disability, and health. We also have to be aware and thoughtful of our loved ones' health issues. Even if two friends have the same autoimmune disease, their bodies might deal with this disease very differently. None of us can expect to feel the same or have the same level of risk. Friendship in the time of Covid means openly discussing our comfort and discomfort around risk-taking with our friends. Wearing a mask in public spaces or with friends who we know need this of us is the bare minimum. It is a choice made from a place of love and care. With mask bans in various counties, this makes choice nonexistent, but those of us who can still wear a mask without the threat of fines should continue doing so. In a post about the importance of mask-wearing, Mia Mingus writes:

> We should all continue masking because masking is a concrete practice of love for each other. Masking is an in-real-time practice of interdependence, collective care and abolition. Plus, there are many who can't mask such as some of our disabled kin and infants, as well as millions more who are forced to work in high risk environments such as restaurants, large offices or stores. Masking supports safety for everyone.[10]

The fact that many people abandoned wearing a mask as soon as the government deemed it okay is infuriating. Seeing leftists not walking the talk, but continuing to wax poetic about community and coalition-building is replete with cognitive dissonance. People want to "go back to normal," when our "normal" was also killing us and our disabled comrades.

I think back to the beginning of the pandemic when so many things moved to the digital world. There was a Zoom link for any and everything. I know many people are "Zoom'd" out. I also know that the many online opportunities that have since been dropped are sorely missed by those who are immunocompromised and/or disabled, as well as their loved ones and allies. When we denigrate online spaces and say they can't be opportunities for community-building, we are actively excluding some of the most marginalized people in our society. It's no wonder that disabled people continue to be forgotten about or

---

10   Mia Mingus, "Mia Mingus on Instagram," Instagram, May 23, 2023, https://www.instagram.com/p/CsmIQBPuh6e/?igsh=MWlrYjJyeXphd3o5NQ.

pushed aside throughout the pandemic. People who are home-bound, bed-bound, or just can't make it to in-person meetings/hangouts need and deserve community. Who is anyone to say that online spaces cannot exist as community building? Many of us Millennials who grew up with childhoods pre- and post-internet access know that community building can happen in online spaces, because we've experienced it. Many of us have "online friends" who we've known for a decade or more. How could that happen if online spaces didn't exist as sites of friendship and community building? Have we forgotten how to sit with ourselves (and each other) away from bustling capitalist distractions?

When I see the push to return to in-person everything, I question whether people learned anything from this pandemic. So much was moved to virtual initially, only for it to be taken away the second abled people were "done" caring (if they ever cared to begin with). If we are truly committed to inclusion, then why aren't we listening to those who ask us, at the very least, to consider people who can't or don't want to return to in-person everything? Why are we saying that friendship and community-building can *only* happen in-person? Why do we act as though the internet is not IRL?[11]

I don't separate my online life from my offline life. I am the same person online as I am offline. I know some people need this separation for safety reasons. However, what I need people to understand is that *IRL* is both online and off. Online life is not fake or less than. When we talk like it is, we do an incredible disservice to those whose lives might look vastly different from ours. We do an incredible disservice to online communities that include very real people. This isn't the internet of the 90s—so much can (and *is*) happening online. There isn't much of a separation anymore, and that's a good thing in a lot of ways. We have already lost so many people, specifically disabled people, Black people, and People of Color, to Covid. Let's not continue to lose any more valuable perspectives just because abled folks think friendship and community-building can only happen in-person.

If you are someone who doesn't have a disability, you might someday. Now might be a good time to start thinking about how you will respond when told there is only an in-person option for something you

---

11   Author's Note: In real life.

would like to do. I wrestle with my own internalized ableism. I wrestle with the fear of becoming more disabled than I already am, precisely because I see how badly people are treated. We don't all start out in this world on a level playing field. We don't all end up that way either.

I also know that the disabilities I have gained in adulthood have allowed me to be more expansive in both mind and body; in vulnerability; in compassion; in empathy. These disabilities and illnesses that have come to me have, in some way, helped me in subverting the status quo. Disabled folks know the most about care—we have to since it's so infrequently offered in our mainstream, ableist culture. In their essay, "Sick Woman," Johanna Hedva says about care and protest:

> The most anti-capitalist protest is to care for another and to care for yourself. To take on the historically feminized and therefore invisible practice of nursing, nurturing, caring. To take seriously each other's vulnerability and fragility and precarity, and to support it, honor it, empower it. To protect each other, to enact and practice a community of support. A radical kinship, an interdependent sociality, a politics of care.[12]

I dream of this "radical kinship," where people give a shit about each other even if they don't know each other. I dream of a world distant from hyper individuality. I dream of feeling comforted by the fact that the world I live in and its people will help me when and if I need it. We all will need it at some point. Disability justice allows us the understanding that nothing has to be the way it is[13]. This idea benefits everyone, even those who aren't disabled yet.

It sounds so simplistic, and yet, we continue to see during the Covid pandemic and the genocide of Palestinians that most people can't even muster an ounce of empathy. It doesn't help that here in the U.S. we have a collapsing healthcare system that doesn't care whether we're in pain or not; whether we're ill or not; whether we'll live or die, especially if we're disabled. In her book, *The Future is Disabled*, Leah Lakshmi Piepzna-Samarasinha asks the question:

> What would a future look like where the vast majority of people were disabled, neurodivergent, Deaf, Mad? What would a world radically shaped by

---

12   Johanna Hedva, "Sick Woman Theory," *Topical Cream*, March 12, 2022, https://topicalcream.org/features/sick-woman-theory/.

13   Leah Lakshmi Piepzna-Samarasinha, *The Future is Disabled: Prophecies, Love Notes, and Mourning Songs*, (Vancouver, CA: Arsenal Pulp Press, 2022), 144.

disabled knowledge, culture, love, and connection be like? Have we ever imagined this, not just as a cautionary tale or a scary story, but as a dream?[14]

People are terrified of disability, because they see how disabled people are treated. Some of these people are the ones who treat disabled people as disposable. It's revolutionary to imagine what our world could look like if we prioritized disabled and neurodivergent comrades.

As so many disability activists have reminded us: we are all moments away from becoming disabled (or further disabled) ourselves. Ableism lets us think this will never happen to us, thus, we don't need to care. In her essay from 2022 titled, "You Are Not Entitled To Our Deaths: COVID, Abled Supremacy & Interdependence," Mia Mingus writes:

> Abled supremacy means that many of you mistakenly think that if you do get COVID and if you end up with long COVID, that the state will take care of you or that your community will. You believe this because you do not know about the lived reality of disability in this country... Our government does not care about the disabled people that already exist. So, if you think it will care for you if you become disabled from COVID, as millions more will, then that is a function of your ableist ignorance.[15]

The state doesn't care about us now. They certainly won't care about us when we become disabled. Isn't that infuriating? Isn't it terrifying? We need to care for each other. The U.S. does not have nearly enough services for the folks already disabled, nor do they seem to care about this. We all should want better for those who have had to put up with the state's violence for decades with no change. As disabled people, we are used to this, which is why disabled community care has been a forever collective action and has often superseded waiting around for the state's response. I want people to reflect on *why* they do the things they're doing. Do people go out all the time because they can't be alone? Do people only see loved ones at establishments because it's too difficult to sit with them alone on a park bench or at home? I think most of us have at least one thing we're running from.

---

14   Ibid., 22.

15   Mia Mingus, "You Are Not Entitled to Our Deaths: Covid, Abled Supremacy & Interdependence," *Leaving Evidence*, August 1, 2022, https://leavingevidence.wordpress.com/2022/01/16/you-are-not-entitled-to-our-deaths-covid-abled-supremacy-interdependence/.

What is it we can't sit with? Reflection brings connection and I think we all could use both right now.

I think many people take their friendships for granted. I think many people assume that friendships don't need water and sunlight to grow and expand. Many don't seem to understand that we have to till the soil; we have to get our hands dirty. Friendship is not a "set-it-and-forget-it" thing, at least not in my world. It takes energy, and unfortunately, due to the pandemic, genocides and many other horrific things, many of us are lacking energy. It's hard to care for others when we can barely manage caring for ourselves, especially during such an untenable time. Questions I have been asking myself around friendship during Covid are:

1.   How can I best care for myself so I can then have the capacity to check in on others?
2.   What does checking-in look like? (This can/might be different from friend-to-friend).
3.   What is our friendship agreement? How can we feel supported and cared for by each other?
4.   What are my expectations around this friendship and what does communication look like? What are theirs?
5.   While granting my friends the utmost grace and best intentions during a (hopefully) once-in-a-lifetime pandemic, does this friendship feel reciprocal and nourishing?

I am thinking about these questions a lot more as of late. I am, again, realizing how important and necessary my friendships are to me. Most of us desire human relationships with each other. Most of us crave loving, trusting, and supportive people to be in our lives; to help walk us through life. We can't have this if we're unwilling to commit to friendship maintenance. And we can't commit to friendship maintenance without committing to maintenance of ourselves.

With the deluge of genocide, mass shootings, Covid deniers (and people who just stopped caring and the loneliness I've felt with that), and capitalism in general, we all have many reasons to be depressed. Watching a genocide in real time that our government is aiding in feels surreal. I remind myself that I have seen it before as it happened (and continues to happen) to Indigenous people in the U.S. The genocide of Palestinians is the first to be broadcasted on social media. It is necessary to see the images across our feeds. It is necessary for us to not look away. One way I am trying to be there for Palestinians is to listen and bear witness to their stories. I am reposting their cries, their bodies, their voices and urging my friends to do the same. It doesn't mean it's easy, and I find myself resentful and angry at the fact that we are supposed to continue going to work like nothing is happening. This is the American way. I have lost opportunities and relationships due to my support of Palestine and its people, I could easily decide to back down, to shut up. However, my integrity and conscience doesn't allow this of me. I can't sit by while we're all watching the same genocides through our phones. As a white person in the U.S., I am physically safe in the current moment—many of us are—and owe it to those who don't have this safety to speak up.

I have been thinking about, and trying to grieve, the last few years, especially since I live in a country that makes it so difficult to tend to one's grief. It's radical to bring in *pacing* to this moment. I have lost a great deal due to the pandemic. I am not the same person I was. I don't have friends locally. I don't have much of a social life. I have mostly become a shut-in, which doesn't feel all bad, but it can get isolating, especially knowing and seeing people who are just out doing any and everything. I don't trust non-Covid-cautious people with my body. I don't trust people who stopped wearing a mask with my body. There aren't many left to trust and feel safe with—including supposed "leftists." I want to be with people, but I don't want to be with people.

I have developed a social anxiety that I have never had before. My illness phobia has gotten darker, deeper, other worldly. I have had to face trauma from my childhood as I endure uncomfortable medical issues that are not life-threatening, but still overwhelming to a body that has been traumatized by the Medical Industrial Complex.

I don't like going out much due to the pandemic, but also because of the potential for a mass shooting. I work on a university campus in the Gender & Women's Studies department, and I worry often about some man coming in with a gun. I don't think it's paranoia, when this is sadly a very real possibility in the country that I live in. Being forced to be onsite a few days a week is incongruent to my nervous system and what it needs. I don't like overriding my nervous system, but a girl's gotta get paid. Some might say I'm "living in fear," but I'm actually living in survival mode—and have been since I was a child. That's all I know. The current state of the world is unsustainable, especially without friendship and care networks. I'm trying to remember the words of Mariame Kaba, "Hope is a discipline." I am trying to go down avenues of hope instead of despair.

I'm at a point in my life where I do wish I had more friends—actual friends, not acquaintances—but making new friends in our late 30s is tough, especially if neurodivergent. It's difficult finding people who have the same level of Covid cautiousness as I do. It's difficult finding friends who are fervently against genocide. I try to put feelers out there with people I'm interested in for friendship, but I have a very difficult time trusting people, so this is often difficult and draining. I have three close friends at the moment, but only one lives in my city. I would love to have a close friend that lives close, is Covid-cautious, against genocide, and can hang more regularly. I miss friend dates. I hope to return to them someday. I want more friendship intimacy and care. I think of the gorgeous quote by Lora Mathis:

> Kiss your friends' face more / Destroy the belief that intimacy must be reserved for monogamous relationships / Be more loving / Embrace platonic intimacy / Embrace vulnerability / Use emotionality as a radical tactic against a society which teaches you that emotions are a sign of weakness / Tell more people you care about them / Hold their hands / Tell others you are proud of them / Offer support readily / Take care of the people around you[16]

I want to live in a world like that. I want my friendships to be deep, fluid, and spacious. I want care webs, access intimacy, and love that stays.

Think of the world we could have if we care deeply for each other; where our friendships are prioritized, whether they're romantic or platonic; where everyone gets what they need (and then some). A world that doesn't throw people away. A world where nobody has to worry about going to work (ever) especially when they are sick or having a flare. I want to live in a world that loves people over profits and invests in its bright kaleidoscopic communities. Maybe we'll get there when more people become disabled by Covid, when more people have a

---

16   Lora Mathis, "Lora Mathis on Instagram," *Kiss your friends' faces more*, February 14, 2022, https://www.instagram.com/p/CZ-m2Axv58J/.

better understanding of the necessity for mutual aid and care amongst our friends and those we're in community with. Hedva writes:

> ...once we are all ill and confined to the bed, sharing our stories of therapies and comforts, forming support groups, bearing witness to each other's tales of trauma, prioritizing the care and love of our sick, pained, expensive, sensitive, fantastic bodies, and there is no one left to go to work, perhaps then, finally, capitalism will screech to its much needed, long-overdue, and motherfucking glorious halt.[17]

Our sick, disabled, and "fantastic bodies" might break capitalism, redefine our friendships, and create a societal landscape of care and trust.

---

17   Johanna Hedva, "Sick Woman Theory," *Topical Cream*, March 12, 2022, https://topicalcream.org/features/sick-woman-theory/.

Chapter Ten

GET OFF THE INTERNET

We cannot know each other without being inconvenient to each other. We cannot be in any relation without being inconvenient to each other. This is to say: to know and be known requires experiencing and exerting pressure to be acknowledged and taken in. Acknowledgment requires a disturbance of attention and boundaries. Sustained acknowledgment requires self-reorganization.

—LAUREN BERLANT

PEOPLE KEEP PUNCHING ME IN THE FACE on the internet. Everything I post is problematic. Everything I am is vexing. When I post about my personal experiences within my varied marginalized identities on my *personal* Instagram account, I'm told I'm taking up space. I am not the "right" kind of disabled. I am not the "right" kind of former sex worker. I am not the "right" kind of queer. I am not the "right" kind of feminist. I have spent years apologizing for who and what I am. I have spent years trying to erase myself. I wrote a Tweet once that said: "Some of you have never had to change and grow in front of hundreds of thousands of people and it shows." Even those who follow me expect me to be infallible. I'm in the panopticon[1] and my followers are in the guard tower. I can't live inside this pressure-cooker. I have always tried to be open and honest when I have fucked up, and yet, that's not good enough. In the online world, you are either good or bad—there is no nuance, no in between, no shapeshifting. I want to disappear. I want to be a bog witch nestled somewhere off grid where

---

1   AUTHOR'S NOTE: First introduced by English philosopher Jeremy Bentham. Critiqued by philosopher, Michel Foucault. A prison design that has the incarcerated person surveilled at all times by a guard.

no one knows me and those who do can't find me. Baba Yaga[2] was misunderstood.

At its core, social media is meant as a distraction. It doesn't like nuance, and it's set up to add to our already hypervigilant and fragmented selves. Author Aurora Levins Morales writes, "We are a society of people living in a state of post-traumatic shock: amnesiac, dissociated, continually distracting ourselves from the repetitive injuries of widespread collective violence.[3]" I understand the protective reasoning for people to continuously distract themselves, but it doesn't help any of us. For example, pretending we aren't all witnessing the Palestinian genocide at the hands of Israel and the U.S. on Instagram doesn't disappear this pain and trauma. We owe it to humanity to look, to watch, to cry. Using social media in this way is subverting its intended use of distraction. We are instead practicing hyper awareness and attention.

When I think of the internet these days, I immediately feel paranoid and unsettled in my body. My stomach swirls, my jaw clenches, my fingers freeze. Opening up Instagram stokes my ever-present hypervigilance. I don't feel like I belong in these spaces any more. Maybe I never did. I don't know if I want to belong in the current digital climate. With call-outs, misinformation, and feminist infighting, I'm feeling more ambivalent about my presence in online worlds. But if I can't find belonging where I once used to, what does that mean? What does that say about me?

Despite having a large following on social media, I am planning my exit, or at least planning to divest from Instagram. I'm at the point where I don't want to build community online unless it's private and small. I question how community can be built on social media when there is typically a "follower" and a "leader." I gag at users with large followings who talk about what a great *community* they have. It's not a community—it's a performer with an audience. It's a parasocial relationship. It's not reciprocal on either end and there's a clear hierarchy and power dynamic. We simply cannot use social media platforms as our only method of mobilizing and organizing. We can barely use it to

---

2   AUTHOR'S NOTE: A character from Slavic folklore.

3   Aurora Levins Morales, *Medicine Stories: History, Culture and The Politics of Integrity* (Cambridge, MA: South End Press, 1999), 13.

disperse factual information, and these platforms are always changing. We can't trust the algorithms. We can't trust these systems that keep us in a holding pattern of staying on social media. The platforms will eventually die out. It's far too dangerous to depend on Instagram, Tik-Tok, or Twitter for our ideas and our communication. Many of us use these apps to knowingly or unknowingly engage in distractive call-outs, "cancellation," and disinformation.

The fragmentation that occurs online spreads like frost. There are still entire groups of people committed to call-outs as their brand of "activism." A call-out is attention-grabbing, both for the person being called-out and any witnesses. It's meant to be this way. It needs to be. Call-outs aren't all negative, though they're often talked about like they are. They can be quite helpful in curtailing and/or ending harm caused by an individual. Call-outs, when sincere and respectful of all parties, can be beautiful messy moments of learning and growth in real time. The issue with call-outs on social media, however, is that the entire experience becomes a spectacle. Any audience, even a "feminist" or "social justice" one, loves a good spectacle. Hundreds, thousands, potentially millions of people are watching. It's free entertainment that never ends, because social media apps don't have open and close hours. I'm concerned that the internet has made us all so detached and desensitized, we forget, or choose not to see, someone's humanity.

When I started *Guerrilla Feminism*, I gravitated towards a call-out and mob mentality online. I'm not proud of this. I felt a rush whenever I participated in a call-out. I felt like I was doing something. I thought I was helping. I began to mistake this feeling of power for passion. As a white person, I felt like I was doing "the work." I believed I was *right* (because, of course, there is a "wrong"). As feminists, many of us have managed to disrupt the gender binary, but not the binary of "right" vs "wrong" or "bad" vs "good." Participating in a call-out by dogpiling, cross-platform stalking, and shunning is powerful, invigorating even. In *Conflict Is Not Abuse*, Sarah Schulman writes:

> Shunning, interestingly, often accompanies the trigger reaction. Rather than talk openly to the other person, exchanging reasoned, self-critical ideas or feelings, the triggered person eliminates the other, hiding from them while lashing out. The new technologies like email and social media make this very easy. You can attack while hiding. You can articulate threats, misperceptions,

and false accusations, and make sure that you never, ever hear information that could alter those perceptions.[4]

Schulman continues by saying that some people might then send emails stating, "'I consider this matter closed' or 'Do not respond.'" Sure, this can be looked at as a boundary, but it's also a way to wield power by shutting down communication. On the other side of this is something I often see on platforms like Twitter and Instagram: incessant and repetitive tagging of an individual. In essence, *forcing* the person into dialogue. I have witnessed people have full-blown arguments this way. The idea is to overwhelm the person you're calling out to the point where they must respond. It's a tactic that works because it pressures the person to respond immediately. However, since the person being called-out is being forced to act out of reaction and not reflection, they most likely haven't learned anything. They might not even know fully what they're being accused of. Then, this person either acquiesces or attempts to deny the accusations with an explanation. The latter can often come across to outsiders as fake and phony. There isn't *justice* for anyone in this scenario. It doesn't help the broader community.

It's important for me to note that through all of the call-outs I've experienced (and witnessed), it has been mostly white women who exhibited excitement of a potential downfall; a potential for collective, lateral harm. Call-outs can be positive tools for change, but the intention of those initiating or participating in the call-outs matters. It also matters if the person (or people) doing the call-out is operating from a gaping wound. Many white women seem to lean towards the idea of call-out campaigns and "cancellation." We seem to enjoy engaging in mob mentality. White women find solidarity with other white women through shared hatred disguised as passion for a cause. Author and activist, Mikki Kendall created the #SolidarityIsForWhiteWomen hashtag on Twitter to show how time and again white women dismiss women of color. Many white women don't have solidarity with each other, because we have no camaraderie. This is consistently demonstrated by how we (mis)treat and maim each other online. White women with large online followings (like myself) can haphaz-

---

4   Sarah Schulman, *Conflict Is Not Abuse: Overstating Harm, Community Responsibility, and The Duty of Repair* (Vancouver, BC: Arsenal Pulp Press, 2021), 143.

ardly choose a target and command their followers to "attack!" Too many white women don't think about or care about the dynamics of race, sexual orientation, gender identity, or disability when initiating a call-out. I'm not saying that people with varied marginalized identities can't inflict harm, of course they can. I'm saying that white women don't take these identities into account when directing their following to "call out" another person. It's reminiscent of the many stories I've read about white women "telling on" People of Color, specifically Black people. It reminds me of Emmett Till, a Black teenager who was lynched in Mississippi in 1955 after Carolyn Bryant, a white woman, accused him of offending her in some way.[5] In online spaces, I've seen white women Democrats go after Black women and Palestinian women who have posted about not voting in elections due to systemic racism. White women go after each other to score brownie points with People of Color and consider this "doing the work." Though we're not killing each other, we might as well be. Using these tactics in online spaces further divides our movements.

I've talked to many white people online about why they participated in call-outs the way they did, and more often than not, I'm met with some variation of: "It felt good to be a part of something." As white women, we seem to struggle to understand the fundamental truth that we don't know how to collectivise without alienation, isolation, and ostracization. This inability doesn't excuse anything, but it's why we have a deep longing to feel a part of something. I'm reminded of white women suffragists who explicitly chose their race over their sex[6]. During the first U.S. women's rights convention in Seneca Falls, New York in 1848, suffragists advocated for the right of white women to vote. No Black women were even invited to the convention. Specifically, Elizabeth Cady Stanton and Susan B. Anthony were less concerned about getting the vote for Black women. Stanton and Anthony failed to take into account the intersectionality of marginalized

---

5   AUTHOR'S NOTE: The story is that Till whistled at Bryant, but that has never been corroborated or substantiated. Whatever Till did or didn't do was no reason to kill him.

6   Tammy L. Brown, "Celebrate Women's Suffrage, but Don't Whitewash the Movement's Racism: ACLU," *Celebrate Women's Suffrage, but Don't Whitewash the Movement's Racism*, February 27, 2023, https://www.aclu.org/news/womens-rights/celebrate-womens-suffrage-dont-whitewash-movements-racism.

identities that Black women exhibit.[7] Since then, white women have sided with our race over our sex. We've been consistently renewing this agreement. Every time a white woman is at the helm of a call-out, a "cancellation" campaign gets its wings.

Call-outs can, at the very least, be neutral tools for stating harm caused, but white women don't know how to use them without resulting in punitive measures that, as an abolitionist, I am fervently against. To be an abolitionist feminist means to be move "beyond binary either/or logic and the shallowness of reforms... these collective practices of creativity and reflection shape new visions of safety."[8] Many feminists still have difficulty thinking of expansive and imaginative ways to address harm without vengeance or punishment.

In 2020, comedian, TV host, actress, and writer, Ellen DeGeneres was "canceled" after many workers on her show called her out for creating and taking part in a toxic work environment. There were numerous news articles and Twitter threads calling attention to DeGeneres's seemingly two-faced behavior. She eventually put out a statement accepting some responsibility and promising to do better. She was considered "canceled," and yet, she didn't actually lose anything or disappear. Forbes reported that she had a net worth of $414 million in 2020. So, how was she canceled? Regarding cancel culture, podcaster Dylan Marron tweeted: "Cancel culture is an imprecise term that falsely groups together three real but separate things: justified criticism, unnecessary pile-ons, and mob mentality."[9] Most humans have difficulty being critiqued, and thanks to the internet and social media, we can critique each other all the time if we want to (and many people do just that). We have a disposability culture. We have an ostracization culture. We have a culture of people who enjoy alienating others for various reasons, some completely benign.

I don't believe we have a "Cancel Culture"—at least, not for white,

---

7   Author's Note: Or just didn't care.

8   Angela Y. Davis et al., *Abolition. Feminism. Now.* (Chicago, IL: Haymarket Books, 2022), 3.

9   Dylan Marron, "Tweet on X.Com," X (formerly Twitter), September 17, 2019, https://x.com/dylanmarron/status/1174184328730959873?lang=en.

big-name celebrities.[10] They seem to do just fine anytime the public calls them out and "cancels" them. I do think the idea of Cancel Culture works a bit differently with ordinary people. While people are negatively affected by online call-outs in ways that are often punitive and disconcerting, the term "canceled" posits an ending, a finality. For most people who are "canceled," they're not gone—not forever, anyways. Cancellation is about loss, but not the forever kind. A cancellation campaign may result in someone losing their job, their social status, their online platform(s), or any future opportunities for a time. However, everyone loves a good comeback story. Celebrities and their publicists do this quite well. There's always an "apology tour," which is just another way for celebrities and their managers to continue making money while also profiting off of the harm they've caused. In 2017, various women came forward accusing comedian Louis C.K. of sexual misconduct. C.K. issued a half-assed apology and said he would be taking some time off. He was back on stage a mere nine months later. In 2020, he self-released a comedy special, "Sincerely Louis C.K." This special won him the Grammy Award for Best Comedy Album in 2022. He continued to make money (and still does). He was never "canceled."

When this happens to ordinary people, most of us don't have publicists or a team of people helping us behind-the-scenes. Most of us aren't use to fucking up in front of hundreds, thousands, or millions of people. Most of us aren't rich, and can't run off and hide in our piles of Scrooge McDuck money. When a celebrity is effectively "canceled," they usually take a break and are right back at it. When an ordinary person is disposed of, real, tangible loss can and does happen. Writer Sarah Hagi says, "...cancel culture isn't real, at least not in the way people believe it is. Instead, it's turned into a catch-all for when people in power face consequences for their actions or receive any type of criticism, something that they're not used to."[11] This is the difference: celebrities/rich people have power-over; the rest of us don't—at least,

---

10   AUTHOR'S NOTE: For example, the famous singer and actress, Ariana Grande, has never lost opportunities due to her *Blackfishing* (when white people specifically appropriate Black cultures)

11   Sarah Hagi, "Cancel Culture Is Not Real-at Least Not in the Way You Think," *Time*, November 21, 2019, https://time.com/5735403/cancel-culture-is-not-real/.

not in the same way. So, what do we call it when we incessantly organize punishment online (and sometimes offline) against people not in power or people who don't have power over others? It's carceral ostracization.

We live in a society that gets off on ostracizing each other. It's a big part of living in a capitalist, punishment-driven culture. Our culture thrives on surveilling each other, and social media has made this only more efficient. We're poised to react, respond, and attack at any time—and we often do. This hyper surveillance can lead to call-outs and then ostracization. Most of us have been ostracized offline, and know how isolating and painful this can be. Clearly, we don't know how to be in conflict with each other offline, so how can we be expected to know how to do this online? While calling-out a celebrity online might be our only recourse for harm caused by the celebrity, certainly we can choose a different path for each other—those we're in community with and those we're not. But also, should we be calling out people we're not in community with? How can we expect people we don't know who don't know us to take accountability? We can't demand accountability. We can't "hold" people accountable. The accused person needs to want this as well. It's a reciprocal, consensual relationship.

I don't remember the first time I was ostracized online. It has happened too many times to recall. I also don't remember the first time (or last time) I ostracized someone. In the past five years, I've worked hard at changing this behavior. It's still difficult and frustrating sometimes, but I'm doing better. Because of all of my experiences (and witnessing) of ostracization, I especially don't believe white people should ostracize other white people. It's not helpful nor conducive to correcting our behavior. When white people do this to each other, instead of taking the time to actually talk to the person about what they did and how it was harmful, it doesn't change the behavior. There is a high likelihood that this white person will then further harm People of Color. We can't actually get rid of people—we try this consistently with our creation and use of prisons. If we throw away other white people, those white people will inevitably continue their harm and a person of color will end up having to deal with them when it should be us (white people) dealing with them.

After Trump was elected, white people everywhere said they would end relationships with racist family and friends. While this frustration is reasonable, it only continues the harm that People of Color face and doesn't actually do anything to dismantle white supremacy. When I see other white people in comment threads dogpiling on each other, dragging each other, shunning each other, I wonder whether they actually care about activism. I wonder if the desire to make things better is even there. I worry they might not want to end white supremacy. Dogpiling is a punishment tactic, and to use it in the name of "accountability" is disturbing. We can call-out each other without resorting to dehumanization. We can be firm, civil, and non-coddling. White people obviously don't listen to People of Color, so it's up to us as white people to talk to and educate each other.

One of the major problems with call-outs and demands for accountability online, especially within social justice spaces, is that there is incentive to act this way. The more volatile you are when initiating a call-out, the more "likes" and social currency you receive. I've seen it time and again. It's actually quite impressive how some Twitter and Instagram users have been able to grow their following exponentially because they initiated a call-out. Even when the person deserves to be called-out, it's gross how many "likes" or "hearts" you can get. I once called-out a white woman for being racist and treating a Black woman terribly. She had a fairly large following. Though this woman deserved some type of call-out, my way of doing it afforded me over 11,000 "likes" on an Instagram post, and probably hundreds of new followers. Our egos are in overdrive, especially when we've created a tweet or post that goes viral. I did reach out to this white woman privately and ask if she wanted to talk about the situation. However, at this point, why would she take me up on talking when I essentially ordered my nearly 250,000 followers at the time to attack her? She eventually blocked me anyway. In an era where people have receipts on everyone in the form of screenshots, why would anyone want to privately chat with a stranger online? The Black woman received fame-level status almost overnight because of this entire incident. Did anyone win, though? Now there's just more white people following a Black woman thinking that's enough and that's "the work," and the Black woman is faced with being even more inundated by white people's feelings and their thinking that they are all "above" the silly white woman who got called-out. Who would even want to take accountability in this type of environment?

A couple of years ago, I witnessed a "community accountability process" on Instagram. It was done by using the livestream function where you can instantly be seen and heard by whomever is on Instagram at the time. It is not private. It is not for a few people. The person leading the process "went live" with the person who had caused harm to a community member. These two people and the survivor were all in community together offline. The thousands of people who watched were not. Only the two people on video are seen and heard, but others can type comments. Hundreds of people watched. I remember feeling like I was somewhere I shouldn't be. It felt like we were throwing tomatoes at the person accused of harm-doing. As you watch a livestream, you can tap the heart button which sends a cascade of colorful hearts for all to see. It made me uneasy to watch people send their flurry of hearts during this extremely vulnerable and important conversation. I eventually left the livestream, because I felt so bad participating as an audience member. This process was all done in the name of "Accountability," and for the demand that as a "community," we *hold* this person accountable. It didn't feel good (or helpful) as I watched, and it felt triggering as a survivor. The person who caused harm seemed completely disconnected, and potentially dissociating, from what was happening. The entire thing seemed more like a punishment than anything else.

As someone who has studied abolition and considers herself an abolitionist, I am committed to finding and using non-punitive measures to address harm. I'm invested in each person taking accountability for their actions, but they have to *want* to do this. We can't attempt to use the idea of accountability or accountability processes as punishment. Scholar Ann Russo writes in her book, *Feminist Accountability: Disrupting Violence and Transforming Power*: "...often accountability is conflated with punishment. When we say we want someone to be held accountable, we often mean that we want them to be punished, penalized, excluded, abandoned, or hurt in some way."[12] We confuse

12   Ann Russo, *Feminist Accountability: Disrupting Violence and Transforming Power* (New York, NY: New York University Press, 2019), 97.

punishment with justice and justice with punishment. I appreciate what performance poet and author, Kai Cheng Thom says about accountability in her essay, *What To Do When You've Been Abusive*, "When we think of accountability in terms of listening and love, instead of accusation and punishment, everything changes."[13] But how do we do this online? How do we do this with people we don't know intimately? How do we do this with strangers who happen to be a part of our internet communities? These are questions I still wrestle with. If accountability and call-outs are essentially loving endeavors, how do we do this with people we barely know, yet, share space with? To do this would mean we have to believe in every single person's humanity. And I'm not sure we're there yet. Accountability is a step towards healing for the victim, the harm-doer, and the community, but each entity needs to be committed to the process. As Mariame Kaba writes, "Healing requires parties who actually want to heal."[14] Is it possible to know if a person online wants to heal? I'm not sure.

Doing an "accountability process" on a social media app that is tracking our every move, and essentially acts as the "town hall," isn't a good idea. The space isn't appropriate nor adequate for addressing interpersonal and intra-communal harm. I question whether anyone can effectively, sufficiently, and caringly lead or participate in an accountability process on platforms that rely heavily on disconnection and power differences. Social media platforms often refer to themselves as micro-communities. In reality, these spaces function as theater: there are performers and there are audiences. The "show" never really ends. As author Jia Tolentino writes in her book, *Trick Mirror: Reflections on Self-Delusion*: "In physical spaces, there's a limited audience and time span for every performance. Online, your audience can hypothetically keep expanding forever, and the performance never has to end."[15]

---

13   Cheng Thom, Kai. "What to Do When You Have Been Abusive." *Truthout*, January 26, 2020. https://truthout.org/articles/what-to-do-when-you-have-been-abusive/.

14   Janaé E. Bonsu, "Black Queer Feminism as Praxis: Building an Organization and a Movement," *Black Women's Liberatory Pedagogies*, November 29, 2017, 211—24, https://doi.org/10.1007/978-3-319-65789-9_12, 218.

15   Jia Tolentino, *Trick Mirror: Reflections on Self-Delusion* (New York, NY: Random House, 2020), 15.

If we now understand social media to *not* be a community, then we can glean that any potential for an accountability process on these platforms would not work. If we are hoping to create an accountability process online, perhaps there doesn't need to be an audience. Perhaps we shouldn't use social media. Maybe by using audio and/or video applications like Skype or Zoom, to make things accessible (and, because, afterall, we're still in a pandemic), but on social media platforms? No way. On applications like Twitter and Instagram, where we are constantly commodifying ourselves and being sold to, even *attempting* a community accountability process seems laughable and completely antithetical to the cause. If we want to heal and repair our communities, we need to heal ourselves, and we can't do this with capitalist structures. Sarah Schulman writes about this saying:

> ...when groups bond over shunning or hurting or blaming another person, it is the state's power that is enhanced. Because the state doesn't want to understand causes, because the state doesn't want things to get better, it doesn't want people to understand each other. State apparatuses are there to maintain the power of those in control and punish those who contest that power...[16]

The state wants us to dispose of each other. The state wants us to rip each other apart. We are strong in numbers, and the state knows this. If we stop eating our own, and start working through lateral conflict and harm, maybe then we will dismantle the oppressions in this world.

Throughout my years in social media spaces, I've reconsidered whether these platforms are helpful to social justice issues and movements. Though social justice issues have received much more visibility through the use of Twitter, Facebook, Instagram, and TikTok, I believe these platforms are now harming our movements. I would know, because I thought I could educate, inform, and amplify—and maybe this was possible for a time, but that time feels like it has passed. Social media is dying and my biggest regret is ever having relied on it in the first place. I wish I didn't care that famous people follow me. I wish I didn't squeal when the most popular girl from my highschool found my account. I wish I didn't worry that if/when I leave, nobody will

---

16   Sarah Schulman, *Conflict Is Not Abuse: Overstating Harm, Community Responsibility, and The Duty of Repair* (Vancouver, BC: Arsenal Pulp Press, 2021), 255.

care or be interested in what I'm doing or what I have to say. Did they ever, anyways? I know some do, but it feels very skewed since my follow count is so high and the engagement is so low. Again, I'm not an influencer. I'm not a model. I'm a writer.

Social media is on life support. Each platform has changed for the worse. Each algorithm is less forgiving than the next and cares little about what its users actually want. Meta has been dying a slow death for at least a decade. Facebook is where Boomers, Gen X, and elder Millennials are put out to pasture. Most Millennials who have a profile don't actually use it anymore though; our profiles exist as ghosts of what once was. Twitter began a rapid descent the second that guy bought it[17]. Instagram, owned by Meta, began its own downfall because, let's be honest, it's no TikTok. Instagram has tried to compete with the video creation giant with its "Reels," but Gen Z is not having it (good for them!) The primary downside of Instagram for Gen Z (and everyone) is its lack of reach and ability for a post or reel to go viral. TikTok's algorithm identifies a user's preferences and shows videos within those preferences whereas Instagram attempts to push through content to users that they might not like or be interested in. Also, many Gen Z seem to feel that Instagram is more buttoned-up and "serious" than TikTok.[18] There is more pressure on Instagram to show a pristine and vibrant life. On TikTok, anything goes and everything has the potential to go viral.

Alongside call-outs and cancellations, we see an influx of mis- and disinformation on social media apps. We may think we're digitally literate, because we can navigate our way around the internet and "Google" things, but are we really? Do we understand privacy online? Do we know when we're seeing and reposting mis- and disinformation? The National Forum for the Prevention of Cyber Sexual Abuse, of which I was a collaborator, says of digital literacy:

> While information literacy focuses on finding and understanding educational resources, digital literacy focuses on the tools and techniques used to find and understand such resources online. Digital literacy goes beyond, for instance, knowing how to search a library database. To be 'digitally literate'

---

17   Elon Musk bought Twitter (now "X") in 2022.

18   Hibaq Farrah, "Why Instagram Gives Gen Z the Ick," *Nylon*, March 29, 2022, https://www.nylon.com/life/gen-z-instagram-cringe-tiktok.

means that a person has the skill set to navigate the complexities of online life. This necessitates not only a fluency in how to use technologies, but also a fluency in how technologies impact intellectual freedom and personal agency.[19]

The terms "disinformation" and "misinformation" are frequently used interchangeably online, but they are, in fact, different. Dr. Nicole A. Cooke, an assistant professor at the School of Information Sciences of the University of Illinois, Urbana-Champaign, writes: "Misinformation is simply information that is incomplete, but it can also be defined as information that is uncertain, vague, or ambiguous."[20] Misinformation is often misleading. Whereas disinformation is "false information which is intended to mislead, especially propaganda issued by a government organization to a rival power or the media."[21]

Unlike misinformation, disinformation is always incorrect. Both are troubling, problematic, and rampant online. We have seen this play out in various instances, though most recent (and most egregious) throughout the Covid-19 pandemic. In an interview, Tara Kirk Sell, PhD, a senior scholar at the Johns Hopkins Center for Health Security, says there are four types of false information that come about during major health crises. These include: 1) "mischaracterization of the disease or protective measures that are needed; 2) false treatments or medical interventions; 3) scapegoating of groups of people; and 4) conspiracy theories."[22] Back in February of 2020, when the pandemic was just starting here in the United States, Surgeon General Dr. Jerome Adams tweeted:[23]

Seriously people—STOP BUYING MASKS! They are NOT effective in

---

19   Paige Walker, Adam Jazairi, and Chelcie Rowell, "Handbook · National Forum on The Prevention of Cyber Sexual Abuse," National Forum on the Prevention of Cyber Sexual Abuse, 2022, https://nfpcsa.pubpub.org/handbook.

20   Nicole A. Cooke, rep., *Fake News and Alternative Facts: Information Literacy in a Post-Truth Era (ALA Special Report)* (Chicago, IL: ALA Editions, 2018), 6.

21   See: https://www.dictionary.com/browse/disinformation.

22   Tara Kirk Sell, "Meeting Covid-19 Misinformation and Disinformation Head-On," Johns Hopkins Bloomberg School of Public Health, July 8, 2024, https://publichealth.jhu.edu/meeting-covid-19-misinformation-and-disinformation-head-on.

23   Leah Asmelash, "The Surgeon General Wants Americans to Stop Buying Face Masks," CNN, March 2, 2020, https://www.cnn.com/2020/02/29/health/face-masks-coronavirus-surgeon-general-trnd/index.html.

preventing general public from catching #Coronavirus, but if healthcare providers can't get them to care for sick patients, it puts them and our communities at risk!

This tweet has since been deleted. In April of 2020, federal government health officials changed this guidance. Later, in July of 2020, The Centers for Disease Control and Prevention published a study showing how mask-wearing may have prevented two Covid-positive employees at a hair salon from spreading the infection to their 139 clients. Had The Centers for Disease Control and Prevention made the recommendation to wear masks from the beginning, perhaps we wouldn't continue to see such vitriol and confusion amongst citizens. The misinformation around masks from our own government is terrifying.

In running a large social media account, I have felt pressure to post any and everything—and be the first to do so. It's almost as if you are a newspaper fighting for the first story. I see this with other social justice accounts as well. The sense of urgency is palpable and spreads like wildfire. This then leads to posting mis- or dis-information. People are too quick to post false or skewed information, which then gets shared hundreds or thousands of times. There have been many times, especially early on with *Guerrilla Feminist*, that I shared stories without fully vetting them. My now librarian self cringes at this. However, according to a recent research study, social media platforms are more to blame for the spread of misinformation than individual people. This particular study found that misinformation is a "function of the structure of the social media sites themselves." Gizem Ceylan who led the study says:

> The habits of social media users are a bigger driver of misinformation spread than individual attributes. We know from prior research that some people don't process information critically, and others form opinions based on political biases, which also affects their ability to recognize false stories online... However, we show that the reward structure of social media platforms plays a bigger role when it comes to misinformation spread.[24]

Part of how this happens, on an individual level, is pressure from

---

24   Susie Allen, "How Social Media Rewards Misinformation," Yale Insights, March 31, 2023, https://insights.som.yale.edu/insights/how-social-media-rewards-misinformation.

followers to post any and everything about an issue. I knew that I couldn't post about every injustice, but if I didn't post about everything, I would get inundated with messages from people. My DMs would be full of questions like: "Why haven't you posted about X yet? You clearly don't care." I didn't set out to be a feminist news space, but that's what I became—and I didn't like it. I have mostly stopped posting anything other than funny Tweets and my own writing on "the grid" of Instagram these days. Part of this is for my own sanity, but part of it is also because I'm tired of putting so much labor into educational posts (researching, vetting, writing) only for them to not be seen. The algorithm is fully responsible for this since most of the time Instagram doesn't even know my posts to my followers (unless my posts go viral).

As a librarian, I want to educate people about mis/dis-information, but I also don't have the time to do unpaid labor. Librarianship is already demeaned by many people, and I don't want to add to this by creating toolkits, educational posts, or anything else if it's not given the attention it's deserved. If we don't have people, like librarians or other educators, creating resources, how will we ever combat fake news? With the rise of AI and deep fakes, mis- and dis-information are only going to become more common and more insidious.

I don't think there is a way to continue with social justice work on social media platforms mostly because of the rampant mis- and dis-information. Especially since Meta, Twitter, and TikTok are not doing anything to prevent it. I realize that this will continue to negatively impact disabled folks, specifically homebound folks who rely on social media spaces to engage with activism. On-the-ground activism is still unfortunately inaccessible for many people. I've read far too much about organizers not enforcing mask-wearing during a global pandemic, and thus, making their events and protests harmful to disabled and immunocompromised folks. We simply have to do a better job of making outdoor activism accessible as well as creating more authentic and purposeful spaces for online activism—away from social media platforms.

I don't think we can utilize public social media spaces to educate and inform. Perhaps we'll start seeing a resurgence of private message boards or private social media accounts that vet folks who join. Either way, things will need to shift and change. Continuing to rely on social media platforms for our collective organizing and education is going to lead to scary, untenable situations.

In the early days of Facebook, Instagram, and Twitter, the majority of the content a person would see would be from friends or other people they follow. These days, users see content that an algorithm thinks they'll like and they see less from those they follow. There are also more advertisements from brands. We see these ads in your Instagram stories and in our feeds. In 2016, Instagram changed their algorithm to no longer show things chronologically. Since then, we see what they want us to see. Reels are pushed in our faces (even as Meta has now announced the end of Reels bonus plays which is one way creators made money). Ads are pushed in our faces. We barely see the people we want to see.

The current algorithms across all social media platforms are biased. How can an algorithm be biased? In her book, *Algorithms of Oppression: How Search Engines Reinforce Racism*, Dr. Safiya Noble writes:

> Part of the challenge of understanding algorithmic oppression is to understand that mathematical formulations to drive automated decisions are made by human beings... The people who make these decisions hold all types of values, many of which openly promote racism, sexism, and false notions of meritocracy, which is well documented in studies of Silicon Valley and other tech corridors... we are supposed to believe that these same employees are developing 'neutral' or 'objective' decision-making tools.[25]

Though Dr. Noble's research is specific to search engines, this framework can be applied to social media platforms and their algorithms.

When we hear talk of "the algorithm," it's often in a way that is distanced, sterile, and ghost-like. The way we discuss it only benefits social media platforms. They want us to think it's "computer error" if anything should go awry. They want us to think it's not on them. The problem though, like Dr. Noble said, is that real humans are behind these algorithms; real humans with bigoted views get to decide what is seen by a majority of users.

25   Safiya Umoja Noble, *Algorithms of Oppression: How Search Engines Reinforce Racism* (New York, NY: NYU Press, 2018), 1.

In 2020, Vox reported on a study that found that "by teaching an artificial intelligence to crawl through the internet—and just reading what humans have already written—the system would produce prejudices against black people and women."[26] We saw this during the height of #BlackLivesMatter. Many posts and tweets were pushed down. Some weren't even shown in people's feeds. TikTok actually apologized to Black users for what they called a "glitch" during this time. Dr. Noble writes: "Many people say to me, 'But tech companies don't mean to be racist; that's not their intent.' Intent is not particularly important. Outcomes and results are important."[27]

We've also seen how the biased and unfair algorithm has hurt sex workers. In 2020, Instagram announced updated censorship rules. According to Dazed, these included: explicit sexual solicitation, sexually suggestive emojis, and sexually explicit language. The article quotes London-based sex worker, Rebecca Crow, saying: "(Instagram's censorship) leaves already precarious sex workers without any platform for online content promotion, which is the safest way to work during the global pandemic."[28] All social media platforms have only ever been hateful to sex workers, so this continued censorship is not surprising. There is also the issue of "shadowbanning" in which a user's posts are consistently not shown in their followers' feeds resulting in little to no engagement. Instagram's CEO has consistently said that shadowbanning "is not a thing." Perhaps it's the terminology that is "not a thing," and what we should actually call it is "algorithmic bias." That is, indeed, a thing.

During my time on these platforms and doing my own "content creation," I know firsthand how frustrating it is to spend your time, energy, and love on a post just for it to have zero engagement. I often wonder if my current following count is even correct, because I

---

26   Rebecca Heilweil, "Why Algorithms Can Be Racist and Sexist," *Vox*, February 18, 2020, https://www.vox.com/recode/2020/2/18/21121286/algorithms-bias-discrimination-facial-recognition-transparency.

27   Safiya Umoja Noble, *Algorithms of Oppression: How Search Engines Reinforce Racism* (New York, NY: NYU Press, 2018), 90

28   Brit Dawson, "Instagram's Problem with Sex Workers Is Nothing New," *Dazed*, December 24, 2020, https://www.dazeddigital.com/science-tech/article/51515/1/instagram-problem-with-sex-workers-is-nothing-new-censorship.

will get maybe a hundred likes on some posts. Even as someone who struggles with dyscalculia, I know that the math ain't math-ing. Do I have bots following me? What's even happening? I don't often post anything that I consider "inappropriate," but part of the problem with algorithms is that they will flag what they deem "inappropriate." This is how certain hashtags get hidden as well. For example, Instagram has been known to hide hashtags like "#sexualhealth" but not racial slurs. The humans who created the algorithm clearly need to do better.

There is a continuous lack of reciprocity I have felt in having my large Instagram account, especially as I see little to no engagement on each post. This is why I have mostly stopped creating information image carousels for the 'gram. We can all joke about the Canva-ication of social justice posts, but it *is* labor. It takes time and energy to research, vet information, double-check it, write it in a way that is digestible (accessible language), and also make it visually appealing. I see the work that so many accounts put in just for their posts to barely get seen. It's diminishing to those of us who have been on these platforms for over a decade. I don't blame my following (although I do wonder sometimes why people don't double-tap that damn heart button), I primarily blame Instagram.

The algorithm (and the people behind it) are continuing to harm our social justice movements. Information is either scarce (and not being shown) or it's incorrect. Transphobia, whorephobia, racism, ableism, and sexism run rampant and appear louder than anything else. In the current dangerous political climate, social media algorithms are only going to make things worse for real people. These platforms have to change and we have to stop relying on them as our primary online spaces. Posting about current events on social media is a fast and easy way to gain visibility for these events. However, because of the quickness with which we all post, fact-checking becomes non-existent. This has been an ever-increasing issue in social media spaces. As a librarian, I am committed to ending dis/mis-information (even if I also sometimes get swept up in it). As I have been consistently reading and reposting things to my Instagram stories about the genocide of Palestinians, I have seen so much misinformation, and it leads me to wonder how helpful is social media to our collective movements?

The idea of "Digital Sandcastles" is that our online landscapes, specifically on social media, are precarious. Many of us have spent time, effort, energy, blood, sweat, and tears crafting our online worlds. This is obviously near and dear to me since I created *Guerrilla Feminism* on Facebook in 2011 and then the Instagram page in 2013. The issue with digital sandcastles is that they were never meant to last forever. They were never meant to be used as "archives." [Side note: people really love using that term when they don't know what it means!] They have no permanent infrastructure. Besides the impermanence and precarity, these spaces repeatedly hide anything that the company doesn't want to show its users. Currently, we are seeing this with how Meta is purposely suppressing any sort of "pro" Palestine post.

Posting through a genocide feels incredibly bleak and dystopian, and yet, what else can we do in the current moment? Organizing and attending in-person protests is great, but what about those who are homebound or have other disabilities that inhibit them from attending these protests? Clearly, a digital component is needed and necessary. I have personally learned so much from Palestinians who have been able to record video and take pictures of what is happening on the ground in Gaza. All I feel I can do (aside from give money and attend local protests) is to repost all of the injustices I see from the people living through them. Digital sandcastles, like a regular sandcastle, will eventually get washed away and destroyed.

I am tired of fighting with social media platforms who are tits-deep in corporate greed. I am tired of asking for crumbs. I am tired of seeing celebrity nonsense get the most visibility. Everything is an ad and I don't want to see our movements become further fractured by commodification. What is the point in having a following if no one even sees my posts? What is the point in feeling beholden to a platform who has not done anything for its users? What is the point of creating an informational carousel on Instagram when it just seems to go into a void? I have more questions than answers related to the future of posting through horrific times. Questions I'm thinking about and asking myself:

1.   How can we ensure that voices from marginalized communities or those posting about issues that affect marginalized communities, will be listened to and seen?

2.   Where should we be archiving digital resistance efforts?
3.   How should we be communicating these things with others committed to the same causes as us?
4.   Are there other digital spaces or structures that we could collectively inhabit that have less precarity?
5.   Are there ways to circumvent suppressive digital tactics? If so, how can we share information about this?

Sometimes the internet is good, sometimes it's terrible. Either way, we can't depend on it for our mobilizing, organizing, and activism. We have to meet elsewhere online and off. If we truly want to get free, if we truly want liberation for all people, we have to be willing to build community offline. We have to talk to each other in person. We have to divest from corporations. We can't rely or depend on Meta, Twitter, and TikTok to amplify our needs. We have to create options for how people can get involved. Relegating our activism to one sphere minimizes our collective power.

I am still toying with the idea of deleting my Instagram. I am still trying to figure out what to do or where to go next. I don't want to be an influencer or a social media creator. Although, I still long for community and belonging in any way I can get it, and there is a lot of it on online spaces. This chaotic internet playground is vastly different from the one I first played on. The rules and people are different. I don't want us to be lost to each other when social media apps eventually disappear. My desire for belonging has shifted over time, and I'm sure it will shift again. The belonging I've spent my entire life searching for has always brought me back to myself. Maybe the internet is bringing us back to ourselves. Perhaps it's our innate humanness that continues hunting and prowling for each other.

Acknowledgements

THIS BOOK WAS WRITTEN ON HO-CHUNK LAND. While land acknowledgments are not the same as land back, it's important I use them as a way to pay respect to those whose land I occupy. I encourage readers to check out: "From Land Acknowledgement to Action" by Dr. Karla J. Strand, the Gender & Women's Studies Librarian at University of Wisconsin-Madison. This resource is always evolving: https://bit.ly/3UCXEcs.

Because music is important to my writing process, this book was written while listening to the albums "Centrifics" by Marina Allen and "Alligator Never Bites" by Doechii on repeat.

Enormous thanks to Iskra Books, specifically Ben Stahnke and my editor Talia Lú. Thanks also to Jenna Blazevich for the gorgeous book cover and for designing many incredible logos for me over the past decade.

My ideas in this book were greatly informed by everyone I've cited, but I'd like to all attention to these specific people: Kimberlé Williams Crenshaw, Johanna Hedva, Donna Haraway, Leah Lakshmi Piepzna-Samarasinha, Patricia Hill Collins, Audre Lorde, Céline Semaan, Angela Davis, Mia Mingus, and Mariame Kaba. My feminism is also informed by my Italian and Italian-American ancestors, those I'm related to by blood and those I'm not. Thank you to the following: Maria Roda, Silvia Federici, Leopoldina Fortunati, Antonio Gramsci, Rosa Ursula Fumo Greco, and Giuseppina Cairo Fumo.

Big thanks to the people who helped with *Guerrilla Feminism* while it was briefly a nonprofit (and for a time before that, too): Cortney Alexander-Doyle and Audrey Leon (thank you also for helping me flier way back when!), Tasia Wagner, Sloane Cornelius, Olivia Dixon, and Xeph Kalma (rest in peace). At one point in time, there were over fifty GF branches, from Australia to Iran. I have a deep sense of gratitude towards those who asked to create these branches. Thank you for all that you did for GF!

I have also appreciated the kindness, friendship and expertise from the following people: Raechel Anne Jolie, Molly Boeder Harris, Mary Purdie, Melissa Fabello, Kate Phelps, and Nisha Mody.

Thank you to my family: Mom, Dad, Kael, Veronica, and the two sweetest nephews a zia could ever want. Your love and support means everything.

Thank you to my nearest and dearest: Audrey Leon, Anjulie Palta, Kelly Fox, Karla J. Strand for your love and support over many moons.

Thank you to Nick Propheter. Your love and support is capacious, effervescent, and extraordinary.

From the river to the sea, PALESTINE WILL BE FREE!

Bibliography

Allen, Susie. "How Social Media Rewards Misinformation." Yale Insights, March 31, 2023. https://insights.som.yale.edu/insights/how-social-media-rewards-misinformation.

Allison, Dorothy. "A Cure For Bitterness." Essay. In Critical Trauma Studies: Understanding Violence, Conflict, and Memory in Everyday Life, 244—56. New York, NY: NYU Press, 2016.

Andersen, Margaret. "How Feminists in China Are Using Emoji to Avoid Censorship." Wired, March 30, 2018. http://www.wired.com/story/china-feminism-emoji-censorship/.

Anzaldúa, Gloria, and Cherríe Moraga. *This Bridge Called My Back: Writings by Radical Women of Color.* New York, NY: State University of New York Press, 2015.

Asmelash, Leah. "The Surgeon General Wants Americans to Stop Buying Face Masks." CNN, March 2, 2020. https://www.cnn.com/2020/02/29/health/face-masks-coronavirus-surgeon-general-trnd/index.html.

Barber, Aja. "Aja Barber on Instagram." Instagram, June 13, 2024. https://www.instagram.com/p/C8KAQuEoFGp/.

Berlant, Lauren. *On the Inconvenience of Other People.* Durham, NC: Duke University Press, 2023.

Bitch Media, interview with Caitlin Wood, podcast audio, https://soundcloud.com/bitch-media/lets-talk-about-crip-culture, 2015.

Blackstone, Amy. *Childfree by Choice: The Movement Redefining Family and Creating a New Age of Independence.* New York, NY: Dutton, 2019.

Bono, Paola, and Sandra Kemp. *Italian Feminist Thought: A Reader.* Oxford: UK. Basil Blackwell, 1991.

Bonsu, Janaé E. "Black Queer Feminism as Praxis: Building an Organization and a Movement." *Black Women's Liberatory Pedagogies*, November 29, 2017, 211—24. https://doi.org/10.1007/978-3-319-65789-9_12.

Brown, Brené. *The Gifts of Imperfection: Let Go of Who You Think You're Supposed to Be and Embrace Who You Are*. Center City, MN: Hazelden Publishing, 2022.

Brown, Tammy L. "Celebrate Women's Suffrage, but Don't Whitewash the Movement's Racism: ACLU." Celebrate Women's Suffrage, but Don't Whitewash the Movement's Racism, February 27, 2023. https://www.aclu.org/news/womens-rights/celebrate-womens-suffrage-dont-whitewash-movements-racism.

Cavarero, Adriana. *Relating Narratives: Storytelling and Selfhood*. Hoboken, NJ: Taylor and Francis, 2014.

Cheng Thom, Kai. "What to Do When You Have Been Abusive." Truthout, January 26, 2020. https://truthout.org/articles/what-to-do-when-you-have-been-abusive/.

Christian Andersen, Hans. "The Princess and The Pea/Prindsessen Paa Ærten." Translated by W. A. Craigie and J. K. Craigie. Bilinguator. Accessed August 10, 2024. https://bilinguator.com/en/online?book=11456.

Clouser, Lauren. "What Is Dyscalculia?" Learning Disabilities Association of America. Accessed August 10, 2024. https://ldaamerica.org/what-is-dyscalculia/.

Cooke, Nicole A. Rep. *Fake News and Alternative Facts: Information Literacy in a Post-Truth Era (ALA Special Report)*. Chicago, IL: ALA Editions, 2018.

Crenshaw, Kimberlé, Neil Gotanda, Gary Peller, and Kendall Thomas, eds. *Critical Race Theory: The Key Writings That Formed the Movement*. New York, NY: The New Press, 2010.

Daley, Jason. "Popular Social Media Mobile Apps Extract Data from Photos on Your Phone, Introducing Both Bias and Errors." College of Engineering, April 2, 2024. https://engineering.wisc.edu/

news/popular-social-media-mobile-apps-extract-data-from-photos-on-your-phone-introducing-both-bias-and-errors/.

Davis, Angela Y., Gina Dent, Erica R. Meiners, and Beth E. Richie. *Abolition. Feminism. Now.* Chicago, IL: Haymarket Books, 2022.

Dawson, Brit. "Instagram's Problem with Sex Workers Is Nothing New." Dazed, December 24, 2020. https://www.dazeddigital.com/science-tech/article/51515/1/instagram-problem-with-sex-workers-is-nothing-new-censorship.

Day, Lauren. "In the Philippines, Divorce Is Banned. It Has Left Women with Few Options to Rid Themselves of Abusive Partners." ABC News, May 15, 2024. https://amp.abc.net.au/article/103828284.

Debord, Guy. *Society of The Spectacle.* Translated by Fredy Perlman. Detroit, MI: Black & Red, 2000.

Donath, Orna. *Regretting Motherhood: A Study.* Berkeley, CA: North Atlantic Books, 2017.

"Donna Haraway on AI." La Mapa TELEVISIÓN, July 4, 2023. https://www.youtube.com/watch?v=4FycNIeS6GY.

"Earthquake." Wikipedia, July 2, 2024. https://en.wikipedia.org/wiki/Earthquake.

Emerson, Ralph Waldo. *Essays - First Series.* Independently published, 2024.

Estés, Clarissa Pinkola. *Women Who Run With The Wolves: Myths and Stories of the Wild Woman Archetype.* London, UK: Rider, 2022.

The Ethics Centre. "Ethics Explainer: The Panopticon - What Is the Panopticon Effect?" The Ethics Centre, December 14, 2021. https://ethics.org.au/ethics-explainer-panopticon-what-is-the-panopticon-effect/.

Farrah, Hibaq. "Why Instagram Gives Gen Z the Ick." Nylon, March 29, 2022. https://www.nylon.com/life/gen-z-instagram-cringe-tiktok.

Federici, Silvia. *Revolution At Point Zero: Housework, Reproduction, and Feminist Struggle.* Oakland, CA: PM Press, 2020.

Felix, Camonghne. "Two Poems." Boston Review, June 4, 2024. http://www.bostonreview.net/articles/two-poems-camonghne-felix/.

Fiorenza, Elisabeth Schüssler. "Between Movement and Academy: Feminist Biblical Studies in the Twentieth Century." Essay. In *Feminist Biblical Studies in the Twentieth Century: Scholarship and Movement* 9, 1st ed., 9:1—18. Atlanta, GA: Society of Biblical Literature, 2014. https://ebookcentral.proquest.com/lib/wisc/detail.action?docID=3118320.

Field, Emily, Alexis Krivkovich, Sandra Kügele, Nicole Robinson, and Lareina Yee. "Women in The Workplace 2023." McKinsey & Company, October 5, 2023. https://www.mckinsey.com/featured-insights/diversity-and-inclusion/women-in-the-workplace.

Gatwood, Olivia. "We Were Cyborgs: On the Construction of The Self as a Teenage Girl." Literary Hub, July 10, 2024. https://lithub.com/we-were-cyborgs-on-the-construction-of-the-self-as-a-teenage-girl/.

Gingold, Naomi. "People with 'invisible Disabilities' Fight for Understanding." NPR, March 8, 2015. http://www.npr.org/2015/03/08/391517412/people-with-invisible-disabilities-fight-for-understanding.

Gill, Rosalind. "The Affective, Cultural and Psychic Life of Postfeminism: A Postfeminist Sensibility 10 Years On." *European Journal of Cultural Studies* 20, no. 6 (November 20, 2017): 606—26. https://doi.org/10.1177/1367549417733003.

Giovannitti, Sophia. *Working Girl: On Selling Art and Selling Sex.* New York, NY: Verso Books, 2024.

Goodman, Robert, and Aharon Ben-Ze'ev. *Good Gossip.* Lawrence, KS: University Press of Kansas, 1994.

Gramsci, Antonio. *The Gramsci Reader: Selected Writings, 1916-1935.* Edited by David Forgacs. New York, NY: New York University Press, 2014.

Greco, Lachrista, and Jessica DeFino. "'Anti-Aging' Is Anti-Living." Other. *Rage & Softness.* Substack, February 3, 2023.

Greco, Lachrista. "When, Where, and Why: Telling Your Partner You Have an STI." Scarleteen, 14AD. https://www.scarleteen.com/read/sexual-health/when-where-and-why-telling-your-partner-you-have-sti.

Griffin, Penny. "In Popular Form (Feminism and Antifeminism in Popular Culture)." Essay. In *Popular Culture, Political Economy and the Death of Feminism: Why Women Are in Refrigerators and Other Stories (Popular Culture and World Politics)*, 1st ed., 119—75. London, UK: Routledge, 2015.

Guerrilla Girls. "Our Story." Guerrilla Girls. Accessed August 10, 2024. https://www.guerrillagirls.com/about.

Guglielmo, Jennifer. *Living the Revolution: Italian Women's Resistance and Radicalism in New York City, 1880-1945*. Chapel Hill, NC: University Of North Carolina Press, 2012.

Hagelin, Karina. Dissertation. *Gossip as a Site of Resistance: Information-Sharing Strategies Among Survivors of Sexual Violence*. Dissertation, University of Maryland, 2018.

Hagi, Sarah. "Cancel Culture Is Not Real-at Least Not in the Way You Think." Time, November 21, 2019. https://time.com/5735403/cancel-culture-is-not-real/.

Hanna, Kathleen. *Rebel Girl: My Life as a Feminist Punk*. New York, NY: HarperCollins, 2024.

Hanna, Kathleen, and Tobi Vail. *Bikini Kill Zine*. Vol. 2. New York, NY: Kathleen Hanna, 1991.

Haraway, Donna. "A Cyborg Manifesto." Manifestly Haraway, April 1, 2016, 3—90. https://doi.org/10.5749/minnesota/9780816650477.003.0001.

Hassler, Chelsea. "XoJane Actually Just Published a Personal Essay Called 'It Happened to Me: My Friend Joined ISIS.'" Slate Magazine, August 23, 2016. https://slate.com/human-interest/2016/08/xojane-actually-just-published-a-personal-essay-called-it-happened-to-me-my-friend-joined-isis.html.

Hedva, Johanna. *How to Tell When We Will Die: On Pain, Disability, and Doom*. New York, NY: Hillman Grad Books, 2024.

Hedva, Johanna. "Sick Woman Theory." Topical Cream, March 12, 2022. https://topicalcream.org/features/sick-woman-theory/.

Heilweil, Rebecca. "Why Algorithms Can Be Racist and Sexist." Vox, February 18, 2020. https://www.vox.com/recode/2020/2/18/21121286/algorithms-bias-discrimination-facial-recognition-transparency.

Herman, Judith. *Trauma and Recovery: The Aftermath of Violence—From Domestic Abuse to Political Terror*. New York, NY: Basic Books, 1997.

Hill Collins, Patricia. *Black Feminist Thought: Knowledge, Consciousness, and The Politics of Empowerment*. 2nd ed. New York, NY: Routledge, 1999.

Hill Collins, Patricia. "Shifting The Center: Race, Class, and Feminist Theorizing About Motherhood." Essay. In *Mothering: Ideology, Experience, and Agency*, 45—65. New York, NY: Routledge, 1994.

hooks, bell. *Ain't I A Woman: Black women and Feminism*. 2nd ed. New York: Routledge, 2014.

Hu, Zoe. "The Agoraphobic Fantasy of Tradlife." Dissent Magazine, December 22, 2023. https://www.dissentmagazine.org/article/the-agoraphobic-fantasy-of-tradlife/.

Hughes, Sali. "Helen Gurley Brown: How to Have It All." The Guardian, August 14, 2012. https://www.theguardian.com/lifeandstyle/2012/aug/14/helen-gurley-brown-cosmopolitan-sex.

Invisible Illness Awareness Week, October 12, 2023. http://www.invisibleillnessweek.com/.

Jackson, Sarah J., Moya Bailey, and Brooke Foucault Welles. *#hashtagactivism: Networks of Race and Gender Justice*. Cambridge, MA: The MIT Press, 2020.

Jackson, Shelley. *Patchwork Girl*. Watertown, MA: Eastgate Systems, 2001.

Jaffe, Sarah. "This Valentine's Day, Let's Look to Marxists to Reimagine Love, Romance and Sex." In These Times, February 13, 2023. https://inthesetimes.com/article/this-valentines-day-lets-look-to-marxists-to-reimagine-love-romance-and-sex.

Johnson, Olivia. Women, Work, & Covid-19. Accessed July 26, 2024. http://covid.womens-work.info/.

Johnson. "Why Words Die." The Economist, March 4, 2017. http://www.economist.com/books-and-arts/2017/03/04/why-words-die.

Kalanik, Julia. "How Instagram Keeps Users Scrolling for More." Digital Innovation and Transformation, March 22, 2021. https://d3.harvard.edu/platform-digit/submission/how-instagram-keeps-users-scrolling-for-more/.

Keller, Jessalynn, Kaitlynn Mendes, and Jessica Ringrose. "Speaking 'Unspeakable Things': Documenting Digital Feminist Responses to Rape Culture." *Journal of Gender Studies* 27, no. 1 (July 28, 2016): 22—36. https://doi.org/10.1080/09589236.2016.1211511.

Kendall, Mikki. *Hood Feminism: Notes From the Women that a Movement Forgot.* New York, NY: Penguin Books, 2021.

Kirk Sell, Tara. "Meeting Covid-19 Misinformation and Disinformation Head-On." Johns Hopkins Bloomberg School of Public Health, July 8, 2024. https://publichealth.jhu.edu/meeting-covid-19-misinformation-and-disinformation-head-on.

Kochhar, Rakesh. "Hispanic Women, Immigrants, Young Adults, Those with Less Education Hit Hardest by Covid-19 Job Losses." Pew Research Center, June 9, 2020. http://www.pewresearch.org/short-reads/2020/06/09/hispanic-women-immigrants-young-adults-those-with-less-education-hit-hardest-by-covid-19-job-losses/.

Lakshmi Piepzna-Samarasinha, Leah. *Care Work: Dreaming Disability Justice.* Vancouver, BC: Arsenal Pulp Press, 2021.

Lakshmi Piepzna-Samarasinha, Leah. *The Future is Disabled: Prophecies, Love Notes, and Mourning Songs.* Vancouver, CA: Arsenal Pulp Press, 2022.

Lamott, Anne. *Bird by Bird: Some Instructions on Writing and Life.* New York, NY: Vintage, 1995.

Lane-McKinley, Madeline. "Tweet on X.Com." X (formerly Twitter), March 17, 2020. https://x.com/la_louve_rouge_/status/1239997457456443392.

Latimer, Heather. "Reproductive Technologies, Fetal Icons, and Genetic Freaks: Shelley Jackson's Patchwork Girl and the Limits and Possibilities of Donna Haraway's Cyborg." *MFS Modern Fiction Studies* 57, no. 2 (June 2011): 318—35. https://doi.org/10.1353/mfs.2011.0051.

LDRFA. "What Is Language Processing Disorder?" LD Resources Foundation, Inc, March 18, 2023. https://www.ldrfa.org/what-is-language-processing-disorder/.

Lenz, Lyz. "America Is Killing Its Mothers." Men Yell At Me, December 13, 2023. https://lyz.substack.com/p/america-is-killing-its-mothers?utm_source=publication-search.

Levine, Peter A., and Ann Frederick. *Waking the Tiger: Healing Trauma.* New York, NY: North Atlantic Books, 1997.

Levins Morales, Aurora. *Medicine Stories: History, Culture and The Politics of Integrity.* Cambridge, MA: South End Press, 1999.

Lewis, Sophie. *Full Surrogacy Now: Feminism Against Family.* London, UK: Verso, 2021.

Marron, Dylan. "Tweet on X.Com." X (formerly Twitter), September 17, 2019. https://x.com/dylanmarron/status/1174184328730959873?lang=en.

Mathis, Lora. "Lora Mathis on Instagram." Kiss your friends' faces more, February 14, 2022. https://www.instagram.com/p/CZ-m2Axv58J/.

May, Katherine. *Wintering: The Power of Rest and Retreat in Difficult Times.* Waterville, UK: Thorndike Press, 2021.

McAlpin, Heller. "In 'wintering,' Katherine May Encourages 'the Active Acceptance of Sadness.'" NPR, November 10, 2020. https://www.npr.org/2020/11/10/933008027/in-wintering-katherine-may-encourages-the-active-acceptance-of-sadness.

McConnell, Marty. *Wine for a Shotgun.* Channahon, IL: EM Press, 2012.

McLachlan, Stacey. "Experiment: Do Long Captions Get More Engagement on Instagram?" Social Media Marketing & Management

Dashboard, July 5, 2023. https://blog.hootsuite.com/long-instagram-captions-experiment/.

Mingus, Mia. "Access Intimacy, Interdependence and Disability Justice." Leaving Evidence, April 27, 2018. https://leavingevidence.wordpress.com/2017/04/12/access-intimacy-interdependence-and-disability-justice/.

Mingus, Mia. "Mia Mingus on Instagram." Instagram, May 23, 2023. https://www.instagram.com/p/CsmIQBPuh6e/?igsh=MWl-rYjJyeXphd3o5NQ.

Mingus, Mia. "You Are Not Entitled to Our Deaths: Covid, Abled Supremacy & Interdependence." Leaving Evidence, August 1, 2022. https://leavingevidence.wordpress.com/2022/01/16/you-are-not-entitled-to-our-deaths-covid-abled-supremacy-interdependence/.

Noble, Safiya Umoja. *Algorithms of Oppression: How Search Engines Reinforce Racism*. New York, NY: NYU Press, 2018.

O'Brien, M.E. *Family Abolition: Capitalism and The Communizing of Care*. London, UK: Pluto Press, 2023.

Odell, Jenny. *How to do nothing: Resisting the attention economy*. New York, NY: Melville House, 2021.

Palahniuk, Chuck. *Fight Club*. London: Vintage Books, 2007.

Pelto, Aliza. "Is Dior Just Capitalizing on Femini$m?" BUST, February 26, 2020. https://bust.com/dior-capitalizing-feminism/.

Petersen, Anne Helen. "The Friendship Dip." Culture Study, November 5, 2023. https://annehelen.substack.com/p/the-friendship-dip.

Petersen, Anne Helen, and Elissa Strauss. "I Went Into Motherhood Determined Not To Lose Myself In It." Other. *Culture Study*. Substack, August 4, 2024.

Pitcher, Laura. "How Beauty Is Being Used to Fight Back against Facial Recognition and CCTV." Dazed, October 3, 2023. https://www.dazeddigital.com/beauty/article/48030/1/anti-surveillance-cctv-beauty-cv-dazzle-facial-recognition-technology-joker.

Plant, Sadie. *The Most Radical Gesture: The Situationist International in a Postmodern Age*. London, UK: Routledge, 1992.

Price, Devon. There is no safe sex. There is no safe life., August 15, 2024. https://drdevonprice.substack.com/p/there-is-no-safe-sex-there-is-no.

Radics, Clementine von. *A Whore's Manifesto: An Anthology of Writing and Artwork By Sex Workers*. Edited by Kay Kassirer. Portland, OR: Thorntree Press, 2019.

Red May TV. "Abolish the Family! | Red May 2020." Abolish The Family! | Red May 2020 - talk featuring: Kathi Weeks, Michelle O'Brien, Sarah Jaffe, and Sophie Lewis, May 30, 2020. https://www.youtube.com/watch?v=8nfeTeUgBZg.

Rodden, Janice. "Signs of Sensory Processing Disorder (SPD) in Adults." *ADDitude*, August 25, 2023. https://www.additudemag.com/sensory-processing-disorder-in-adults/#:~:text=If%20you%20are%20hypersensitive%20to,don't%20hear%20or%20feel.

Rubin, Gayle. "Thinking Sex: Notes for a Radical Theory of the Politics of Sexuality." Essay. In *Deviations: A Gayle Rubin Reader*, 137—81. Durham, NC: Duke University Press, 2011.

Russell, Legacy. *Glitch Feminism: A Manifesto*. London: Verso, 2020.

Russo, Ann. *Feminist Accountability: Disrupting Violence and Transforming Power*. New York, NY: New York University Press, 2019.

Samuels, Ellen J. "My Body, My Closet: Invisible Disability and the Limits of Coming Out." The Disability Studies Reader, May 2, 2013, 321—37. https://doi.org/10.4324/9780203077887-34.

Santuzzi, Alecia M. "Invisible Disabilities." Psychology Today, June 26, 2013. http://www.psychologytoday.com/intl/blog/the-wide-wide-world-of-psychology/201306/invisible-disabilities.

Schneider, Rachel S. *Making Sense: A Guide to Sensory Issues*. Arlington, TX: Sensory World, 2016.

Schulman, Sarah. *Conflict is Not Abuse: Overstating Harm, Community Responsibility, and The Duty of Repair*. Vancouver, BC: Arsenal Pulp Press, 2021.

Shane, Charlotte. "Men Consume, Women Are Consumed: 15 Thoughts on the Stigma of Sex Work." Jezebel, September 1, 2015. https://jezebel.com/men-consume-women-are-consumed-15-thoughts-on-the-sti-1727924956.

Shire, Warsan. *Teaching My Mother How to Give Birth*. United Kingdom: Mouthmark, 2011.

Slice, Jessica, and Caroline Cupp. *Dateable: Swiping Right, Hooking Up, and Settling Down While Chronically Ill and Disabled*. New York, NY: Hachette Go, 2024.

Smith, Barbara, Demita Frazier, and Beverly Smith. "The Combahee River Collective Statement." Blackpast, August 29, 2019. https://www.blackpast.org/african-american-history/combahee-river-collective-statement-1977/.

Sow, Aminatou, and Ann Friedman. *Big Friendship: How We Keep Each Other Close*. New York, NY: Simon & Schuster, 2021.

Strand, Sophie. "Chronic Pain Is Psychedelic." Make Me Good Soil, June 12, 2024. https://sophiestrand.substack.com/p/chronic-pain-is-psychedelic.

Strayed, Cheryl. "Dear Sugar, The Rumpus Advice Column #71: The Ghost Ship That Didn't Carry Us." *The Rumpus*, October 12, 2022. https://therumpus.net/2011/04/21/dear-sugar-the-rumpus-advice-column-71-the-ghost-ship-that-didnt-carry-us/.

Tartar, Maria. "The Princess and The Pea - Hans Christian Andersen." Essay. In *The Annotated Classic Fairy Tales*, 284—87. New York, NY: W. W. Norton & Company, 2002.

"The Spice Girls Visit The Oprah Winfrey Show." Episode. *The Oprah Winfrey Show* 12, no. 1. Chicago, IL: Harpo Productions, January 13, 1998.

Toksvig, Signe. "The Life of Hans Christian Andersen: Toksvig, Signe, 1891-1983." Internet Archive, January 1, 1970. https://archive.org/details/lifeofhanschrist0000unse/page/n309/mode/2up.

Tolentino, Jia. *Trick Mirror: Reflections on Self-Delusion*. New York, NY: Random House, 2020.

Tolentino, Jia. "The Personal-Essay Boom Is Over." The New Yorker, May 18, 2017. https://www.newyorker.com/culture/jia-tolentino/the-personal-essay-boom-is-over#:~:text=These%20essays%20began%20to%20proliferate,she%20gained%20and%20 lost%20from.

Vanderhoof, Erin. "Ballerina Farm Influencer Hannah Neeleman Says She Doesn't 'Identify' as a Trad Wife." *Vanity Fair*, July 25, 2024. https://www.vanityfair.com/style/story/ballerina-farm-interview.

"Virtue Signaling Definition." *Cambridge Dictionary*. Accessed July 27, 2024. https://dictionary.cambridge.org/us/dictionary/english/ virtue-signaling.

Wacera, Charity. "Griots: Living Historians and Musicians of West Africa." Our Ancestories, October 6, 2023. https://our-ancestories.com/blogs/news/griots-living-historians-and-musicians-of-west-africa.

Waheed, Nayyirah. *Salt*. CreateSpace Independent Publishing Platform, 2013.

Walker, Paige, Adam Jazairi, and Chelcie Rowell. "Handbook · National Forum on The Prevention of Cyber Sexual Abuse." National Forum on the Prevention of Cyber Sexual Abuse, 2022. https:// nfpcsa.pubpub.org/handbook.

Wendell, Susan. *The Rejected Body: Feminist Philosophical Reflections on Disability*. Hoboken, NJ: Taylor and Francis, 2013.

Wertheimer, Eric, and Monica Casper. "Within Trauma: An Introduction." Essay. In *Critical Trauma Studies: Understanding Violence, Conflict, and Memory in Everyday Life*, 1—16. New York, NY: NYU Press, 2016.

Whaley, Kayla. "Nobody Catcalls The Woman in the Wheelchair." *The Establishment*, August 10, 2018. https://theestablishment.co/nobody-catcalls-the-woman-in-the-wheelchair-82a6e4517f79/index. html.

Williams, Mary Elizabeth. "Worst Personal Essay Ever? Xojane Scrapes the Bottom of the Hate-Read Barrel." *Salon*, May 23, 2016. https://www.salon.com/2016/05/20/worst_personal_essay_ever_xojane_scrapes_the_bottom_of_the_hate_read_barrel/.

Wilkinson, Peter. "Thatcher: Revered and Reviled, in Death as in Life." *CNN*, April 15, 2013. https://www.cnn.com/2013/04/12/world/europe/thatcher-divisive-force/index.html.

"Yassify." *Wiktionary*, December 23, 2023. https://en.wiktionary.org/wiki/yassify.